Dr Blain

Prsonl Property

NEUROPSYCHOLOGY ACROSS THE LIFE-SPAN: Assessment and Treatment

Neuropsychology Across the Life-Span: Assessment and Treatment

Arthur MacNeill Horton Jr.,
Ed.D., ABPP (CL), ABPN, ABBP
Editor

SPRINGER PUBLISHING COMPANY
New York

To my wife, Mary,
my lifespan love.

Springer Publishing Company, Inc.
536 Broadway
New York, NY 10012

90 91 92 93 94 / 5 4 3 2 1

Library of Congress Cataloging-in-Publication Data

Neuropsychology across the life–span : assessment and treatment /
edited by Arthur MacNeill Horton, Jr.
p. cm.
Includes bibliographical references.
Includes index.
ISBN 0-8261-6800-0
1. Clinical neuropsychology. 2. Brain Damage--Diagnosis.
3. Geriatric neurology. 4. Pediatric neurology. I. Horton, Arthur
MacNeill, 1947- .
[DNLM: 1. Behavior Therapy. 2. Neuropsychology.
3. Neuropsychological Tests. WL 103 N4934]
RC386.6.N48N493 1990
616.8--dc20
DNLM/DLC
for Library of Congress. 90-9757
CIP

ISBN 0-8261-6800-0

Printed in the United States of America

Contents

Preface

Currently, surveys of neuropsychologists suggest the topic area of highest interest is child neuropsychology. On the other hand, demographic data indicate that the elderly population will continue to increase in the coming years. As the number of elderly persons grows, so grows the need for greater attention to neuropsychology of the aging. This book is unique in the range of its coverage. Including the full spectrum of development, from childhood to old age, the book includes age-appropriate problems, assessment procedures, and interventions. Its developmental focus is intended to promote an integrative and comprehensive neuropsychological approach.

The objective of this book is to provide clinicians with an introduction to life-span neuropsychological assessment and its implications for designing behavioral interventions. The book includes (1) a review of neuropsychological disorders, (2) an overview of screening techniques for brain damage, (3) discussion of neuropsychological assessment of children, adolescents, adults and the elderly, (4) review of behavioral and cognitive retraining intervention, and (5) overview of single subject research design. Readers are expected to be experts in neuropsychology, but need not be familiar with basic principles of behavioral psychology. The book is clinically oriented, making use of case examples and suggestions for further reading.

The book is intended for professionals as well as graduate students enrolled in clinical psychology, clinical neuropsychology, and geropsychology training programs. Other audiences include clinical psychologists and clinical neuropsychologists in private practice or institution-based clinical work. It is also hoped that geriatric and child psychiatrists and pediatric neurologists and rehabilitation medicine specialists may find it of interest.

Contributors

DuAnn Beck, M.S., received her masters degree from Northwestern State University in 1987. She is currently a Research Assistant and Psychometrist for the Neuropsychology Service at the University of MS Medical Center in Jackson, MS.

Richard A. Berg, Ph.D., received his doctorate from the University of Houston in 1980. He is currently Director of Neuropsychology at Cardinal Hill Hospital in Lexington, Kentucky and is an adjunct faculty member in the Department of Psychiatry at the University of Kentucky Medical Center. He spent a postdoctoral year continuing his studies in neuropsychology at the Nebraska Psychiatric Institute at the University of Nebraska Medical Center in Omaha. He spent four years at the St. Jude's Children's Research Department of Behavioral Medicine and Psychiatry at the West Virginia University Health Sciences Center—Charleston Division. Dr. Berg has published over 50 scientific papers and authored several book chapters. He has co-authored a number of books including *Screening for Brain Impairment: A Manual for Mental Health Practice* (1987), and *Screening Children for Brain Impairment* (1989).

Fredda Blanchard-Fields, Ph.D., received her doctorate from Wayne State University in 1983. She is Associate Professor of Psychology at Louisiana State University. She has published articles in the areas of cognitive reorganization in adulthood and aging, and adaptive coping from an adult developmental perspective. She was recently awarded a NIA grant on attributional processes in adulthood and aging.

Linda M. Brown, M.S., will receive her doctorate from Louisiana State University in 1990. She is currently completing her clinical internship with a specialization in neuropsychology at the Veterans Administration Medical Center in New Orleans, Louisiana. She will serve, upon graduation, as Staff Neuropsychologist for the Drug Dependent Treatment Unit at the VAMC New Orleans. Ms. Brown has participated in the publication and presentation of several scientific papers in the area of neuropsychology.

Steven Cody, Ph.D., received his doctorate from the University of Connecticut in 1983. After teaching in the psychology programs at Marshall and Morehead State University, he joined the Department of Psychiatry at Marshall University in 1988, where he is currently Director of the Neuropsychology Service for the School of Medicine.

Michael D. Franzen, Ph.D., received his doctorate from Southern Illinois University in 1983. Currently, he is Director of Neuropsychology at West Virginia University Health Sciences Center where he is an Associate Professor of Behavioral Medicine and Psychiatry. He is also an Associate Professor of Psychology at West Virginia University. His research interests include the application of psychometric evaluation methods to clinical neuropsychology, and the application of behavioral methodology and assessment strategies to neuropsychological assessment.

Wm. Drew Gouvier, Ph.D., received his doctorate from Memphis State University in 1983. He currently holds a position of Associate Professor of Psychology at Louisiana State University. He completed his residency training at the University of Mississippi Medical Center and held a faculty position in the department of Rehabilitation Medicine at the University of Alabama at Birmingham for two years prior to joining the faculty at Louisiana State University. He remains active in rehabilitation and neuropsychological practice and research, and has published over 50 scientific papers and chapters in these areas.

Lawrence C. Hartlage, Ph.D., received his doctorate from the University of Louisville in 1968. Currently, he serves as president of the National Brain Injury Research Foundation medical advisory council. He served as Assistant Professor of Neurology (pediatric neurology) at Indiana University Medical Center, 1970–1972; as Professor of Neurology, Professor of Pediatrics and Head of Neuropsychology at the Medical College of Georgia, 1972–1985; and as Marie Wilson Hassell Professor at the University of Arkansas, 1985–1986. He has been president of the National Academy of Neuropsychology and of the American Psychological Association, division of clinical neuropsychology. He has written or edited nine books, thirty invited chapters, and more than one hundred articles in the field of child neuropsychology, and has been named in a national survey of the individuals most influencing child clinical neuropsychology in the United States.

Arthur MacNeill Horton, Jr., Ed.D., received his doctorate from the University of Virginia and has earned a Diplomate in Clinical Psychology from the American Board of Professional Psychology. He also has earned Diplomates in Neuropsychology (from the American Board of Professional Neuropsychology), and Behavior Therapy (from the American Board of Behavioral Psychology). He was for a number of years Director of the Neuropsychology Clinic, Psychology Service, Veterans Administration Center, Baltimore, MD and recently accepted a position with the National Institute of Drug Abuse in Rockville, MD. Dr. Horton is also a Clinical Assistant Professor of Psychiatry at the University of Maryland, Medical School. The founder of the Behavioral Neuropsychology Special Interest Group of the Association for the Advancement of Behavior Therapy, Dr. Horton has published over ninety scientific papers and edited *Mental Health Interventions for the Aging* and co-authored *Clinical and Behavioral Neuropsychology* (with D. Wedding). He also co-edited *The Neuropsychology Handbook* (with D. Wedding and S. Webster).

Grant Iverson, B.A., received his bachelors degree in 1987 from the University of Northern Iowa, and is currently in doctoral studies at West Virginia University. He intends to specialize in Neuropsychology. His primary research interest involves developing and evaluating objective assessment procedures for the detection of dissimulated memory deficits.

Kathryn Lawson-Kerr, Ph.D., received her doctorate from Louisiana State University in 1986. She is currently an Assistant Professor in the Department of Psychiatry and Director of the Neuropsychology Service at the University of Mississippi Medical Center. She worked as a Health Science Specialist at the Geriatrics and Education Clinical Center in the Minneapolis Veterans Administration Medical Center. Dr. Karr is actively involved in teaching, research, and consultation services. Her clinical and research interests include the evaluation of affective neuropsychological problems associated with traumatic brain injury and dementia.

Antonio E. Puente, Ph.D., received his doctorate from the University of Georgia. He is currently Professor of Psychology at the University of North Carolina at Wilmington and in private practice in Wilmington, North Carolina. He is president–elect of the National Academy of Neuropsychology. His interests focus on the assessment and rehabilitation of disordered nervous system behavior.

Paul R. Rasmussen, M.A., is currently a candidate for the Ph.D. degree at the University of Georgia. His area of specialization is Behavioral Medicine, particularly as it relates to cardiovascular reactivity and disease, neuropsychological assessment and rehabilitation, and eating disorders. Areas of interest include: identification of individual differences in cardiovascular disease, and development of computerized programs for neuropsychological rehabilitation.

Stanley S. Smith, M.A., is completing his doctorate at West Virginia University. He was an intern at the University of MS Medical Center and is currently a staff neuropsychologist at the Pittsburg Veterans Administration Medical Center. His research and clinical interests include the assessment and treatment of tractible seizure disorders and traumatic brain injury.

Danny Wedding, Ph.D., received his doctorate from the University of Hawaii and completed a postdoctoral year of study at the Univeristy of Mississippi Medical Center. He has taught in the medical schools of East Tennessee State University and Marshall University. He currently works for the U.S. Congress where he serves as a legislative aide for Senator Tom Daschle (D-SD). Dr. Wedding's most recent books include *Screening for Brain Impairment* (with Richard Berg and Mike Franzen), *Current Psychotherapies*(with Ray Corsini), and *Behavior and Medicine.*

Betsy L. Williams, Ph.D., received her doctorate in Education (Special Education) from the University of New Mexico in 1982 and did her post-doctoral work in Clinical Neuropsychology with Dr. Lawrence Hartlage in Georgia. She has worked as a School Psychologist and Neurobehavioral Diagnostician in Georgia and as an Educational/Neurobehavioral Diagnostician in New Mexico. Dr. Williams has published articles in the areas of Neuropsychology and School Psychology and is currently in private practice in Albuquerque, New Mexico.

Chapter 1

Life-Span Neuropsychology: An Overview

Arthur MacNeill Horton, Jr. and Antonio E. Puente

INTRODUCTION

The clinical application of human neuropsychology represents a dynamic and growing field. Its practitioners continue to increase in number, and the proliferation of new journals in neuropsychology reflects this trend. While most of the literature focuses on the adult population, there has been continuing success in increasing the survival rate of infants with neuropsychological defects. That development, combined with extended longevity in the geriatric population, makes applied neuropsychology with these age groups the most dynamic and rapidly expanding areas in neuropsychology. Yet, there is a relative lack of applied neuropsychological information, studies, and procedures involving individuals at either end of the life-span. It is the aim of this book to begin to address this gap, as well as to emphasize the usefulness of a developmental approach to applied neuropsychology in general.

DEFINING LIFE-SPAN NEUROPSYCHOLOGY

As Meier (1974) has defined it, "Neuropsychology is the scientific study of brain/behavior relationships." Neuropsychological performance is affected by

---

* Dr. Horton's contribution was in his private capacity and was neither endorsed nor supported by the federal government.

both organic and environmental variables. Some of these variables, both organic and environmental, change systematically as humans age. Life-span neuropsychology, then, explores these systematic changes as they relate to clinical neuropsychological issues. In other words, it is clinically relevant neuropsychological practice using a developmental framework.

At this point, we will examine various organic and environmental variables, consider the ways that some change as a person ages, and finally examine how these changes may influence neuropsychological performance. A general discussion of developmental psychology will lead the way.

THE LESSONS OF DEVELOPMENTAL PSYCHOLOGY

Developmental psychology is the study of age-related cognitive, emotional, and behavioral intraindividual change over the life-span (Baltes, Reese, & Nesselroade, 1977). Development involves two interacting systems. These are biological aspects (e.g., maturation) and environmental factors (e.g., learning) (Baltes, 1983) with both influencing age-related changes in persons.

The various periods of age-related development can be divided many ways. Not least of course were Shakespeare's seven ages of man ("sans teeth, sans eyes, sans every thing"). Less poetically, others would describe infancy, toddlerhood, early childhood, childhood, adolescence, young adulthood, middle age, the young-old, and old-old. Which exact ages correspond to which periods can vary. Eric Erikson, for example, conceptualized development in terms of a sequence of psychosocial tasks.

While certainly, most theoretical categorizations of development would include cognitive, emotional, and behavioral processes, other areas could be added, for example, physical development and social development, personality structure adaption, and memory age-related changes.

Development is not entirely an age-related process. While many conceptions of development have focused on trends toward a state of maturity and general age-related phases, it would be fair to say these conceptions are dated. More contemporary views place emphasis upon the role of the individual as a participant and partner in the developmental process (Baltes, 1983). Put another way, the person's behavior interacts with his or her biological system and environment in a reciprocal fashion (Featherman & Learner, 1985). For example, how long one will live can be modified to a degree by the history of one's parents (e.g., heart attacks at age 50), one's dietary practices (e.g., too much fat), personal safety practices (e.g., wearing seat belts) and where one lives (e.g., in a large city). All of these factors and many others can affect one's developmental status throughout the life-span. Moveover, the factors can interact, creating bidirectional or multidirectional influences.

It would probably be fair to say that the scope of developmental psychology has been expanded over the years. Generally speaking, when one thought of developmental psychology in the 1950s and 1960s one thought of childhood development and adaption to adulthood. Little consideration was given to those over age 30.

In the 1970s and 1980s, factors such as the changing demographics of the United States population (Horton, 1982) focused attention on adulthood and aging (Neugarten, 1969). The field of developmental psychology now encompasses the entire life-span (Baltes, Reese, & Lipsitt, 1980). Along with this paradigm shift has come a focus on life-span changes that are multidirectional and multidimensional (Baltes & Nesselroade, 1979). This means that age-related change can go in any direction and can include abilities and behaviors from a number of categories.

An example is intellectual ability. Earlier, conceptualizations viewed intellectual ability as increasing until about age 16. More recent conceptualizations have posited a differential age-related course of development where some intellectual abilities may continue to increase as one becomes older (Schaie, 1979), i.e., vocabulary skills as measured by the same named subtest of the Wechsler Adult Intelligence Scale-Revised, but other abilities may decline, i.e., psycho-motor speed as measured by the Digit-Symbol subtest of the Wechsler Adult Intelligence Scale-Revised. To a degree, this follows Cattell's (1971) conceptualization of crystallized versus fluid models of intelligence. The clear trend is to move from models such as those by Havinghurst and Piaget, which are childhood focused, to others such as Erikson's which are more life-span oriented. But even Erikson's model fails to account for the wealth of complexity contained in life-span developmental psychology. The notion of bidirectionality and reciprocal influences makes earlier age-related models less applicable as it introduces the idea of individual self-influences on development.

Therefore, life-span developmental psychology moves from a fixed to a multidetermined model. Rather than a single factor (i.e., age) causing development to progress at a steady pace, this new model is open to all sorts of interaction effects. These include, among others, the individual's own active role in his or her development as well as historical and societal influences (Baltes & Nesselroade, 1979). It is clear that a proper model of life-span and developmental psychology would have to include all of these factors (i.e., age-related, individual, historical-social, biological and environmental) to make even a reasonable pretence of comprehensiveness.

NEUROPSYCHOLOGICAL FACTORS

At this point, the focus of the chapter will shift to consideration of neuropsychological factors.

The crucial question to be answered will be the connection between "life-span developmental psychology" and neuropsychology. Put another way, how does psychology's study of development illuminate neuropsychological issues? It should be clear that a conceptual link must be forged between "development" and "neuropsychology"

In order to accomplish this objective, we will first discuss the related concepts of "brain damage" or "cerebral dysfunction" and "organicity."

Brain Damage and Cerebral Dysfunction

A starting point would be to distinguish between the terms brain damage and cerebral dysfunction. Brain damage implies structural injury to brain tissue. A more precise term is "brain lesion," a pathological alteration of brain tissue. Neurodiagnostic methods such as MRI or PET scanners in most cases can identify structural brain lesions. However, classification of changes in brain physiology that are not reflected in structural modification, remain an area where much additional work is needed.

An example would be helpful to clarify this point. Most neuropsychologists would agree an open head injury caused by a blunt instrument results in structural brain damage, yet there are some neuro-toxic conditions that could cause brain damage without obvious structural changes (Hartman, 1988). Sometimes the term "cerebral dysfunction" is used to describe situations where functional changes are clear, but structural changes cannot be verified.

Organicity

Davison (1974) has given a description of organicity as follows

> The concept includes the assumption that any and all kinds of brain damage lead to similar behavioral effects, and that behavioral differences among the brain damaged are due primary to severity of damage and to premorbid personality characteristics. (p. 14)

Historically, the concept of organicity originated in the equipotentiality/localization debate in the early parts of this century. The limitations of organicity have been noted by Horton and Wedding (1984):

> . . . to understand brain damage as existing on a single dimension is as realistic and useful as the assertion that human beings vary on the dimension of height. To be sure, the assertion is true in a general sense, and, in special

> situations, could be quite useful (e.g., college basketball) but in many circumstances there could be a need for additional data with regard to sources of variation. (p. 12).

In spite of the limitations of the concept of organicity, it has developed as a two category (organic vs. functional) diagnostic paradigm that is now decades old. At present, however, the clear trend is the differentiation of organicity into various subtypes. From these subtypes it is possible to envision a more realistic classification system. In a later section there will be a discussion of diagnostic issues related to organic subtype. At this point, however, attention will be devoted to neuropsychological developmental issues.

NEUROPSYCHOLOGICAL DEVELOPMENT ISSUES

As mentioned earlier, an important consideration with respect to life-span neuropsychology is how developmental changes are related to neuropsychological functioning. Perhaps, the best way to approach this very complex issue is to illustrate selected aspects of the problem by considering some of the theoretical ideas of A. R. Luria (Luria, 1966, 1970, 1973). Luria spent his life attempting to validate Volgotsky's Cultural-Historical model of higher cognitive functioning (Horton, 1987). Interestingly, Luria considered childhood and old age as the natural laboratories for understanding human cognitive processes. He postulated that childhood was the situation where higher cognitive processes were built up. By contrast, he saw old age as a situation when higher cognitive process would decline. Both sides of the coin of human mental ability were valuable in understanding higher cognitive process but in opposite ways.

It should be mentioned that there are clear differences between adult cerebral organizations and those of children and the elderly. The brains of children and the elderly, in terms of localization of function, are both less well studied and inherently more difficult to understand than adult brains (Albert, 1981; Horton, & Puente, 1989).

There is much greater degree of variability in the expression of human neuropsychological abilities subserved by a child or senior citizen's cerebral hemispheres. There are good reasons for this. For example, children are in the process of development and are subject to very poorly understood growth spurts, developmental stages, and developmental lags. Similarly, there are numerous changes associated with aging. These can be either primary, nonpathological aging processes (i.e., alterations in sensory functioning) or secondary pathological processes that often occur with aging (i.e., Alzheimer's disease) (Nolan, Swihart, & Pirozzolo, 1986).

As both children and the elderly are either in the process of acquiring or relinquishing academic and daily living skills, it is difficult to accurately determine age appropriate neuropsychological behavior, much less test scores. By contrast, because adult neuropsychological abilities are relatively stable (i.e., between ages 16-50), their brains are easier to understand. In addition, researchers have been studying the neuropsychology of adults for many decades. There is considerably less data available concerning the neuropsychology of aging or the neuropsychology of childhood.

The problem of appropriate normative data is well recognized (Albert, 1981; Hartlage, 1986; Horton, & Puente, 1989; Nolan, et al., 1986). Typical normative scores on standard neuropsychological tests for adults are inappropriate for application with children or the elderly (Horton & Wedding, 1984). Were the problems of life-span neuropsychology limited to devising age-appropriate norms, they would be formidable. Neuropsychological development is even more complex.

There are two important additional issues. The first relates to the influence of environmental and organic variables on neuropsychological development. The second relates to the fact that specific neuropsychological deficits may only be expressed at particular development stages.

As before mentioned, Volgotsky's Cultural-Historical theory, which guided A. R. Luria (Horton, 1987), suggests that cultural, historical, and social influences are important to the integrity of the various brain areas in shaping observed neuropsychological performance. One way that historical influences are reflected in neuropsychological performance is in age-related socialization. In terms of academic skills, for example, there must be an opportunity to acquire them. Children must have had an adequate opportunity to learn to read, spell, write, and do arithmetic before the inability to do these skills can be considered to be a neuropsychological deficit. Similarly, levels of obtained education have been increasing with each generation so one can't hold the elderly to the same academic standards as today's adults. Luria, of course, was famous for demonstrating that the sorts of abstract thought processes that persons in rural areas used were related to education experience (Horton, 1987) Grossly oversimplified, Luria showed that farm workers classified objects by use while school teachers used abstract categories (i.e., "Tools"). A way of understanding the distinction between age-graded biological processes and history-graded environmental influence is to consider the distinction between hardware and software in computer programming (Horton & Puente, 1989). Not all software programs fully exploit the capabilities of a particular computer.

A more formal paradigm of organic influences upon neuropsychological performance might be hemispheric lateralization of function. It is well known that there are morphological differences between the cerebral hemispheres (Geschwind & Levitsky, 1968). It is also well known that the cerebral hemispheres are specialized in terms of the behavioral functions they subserve (Horton & Wedding, 1984). Less well understood are hemispheric lateralization changes that vary with developmental stage (Bryden & Saxby, 1985).

While there is not sufficient space in this chapter to consider this literature in any detail, it might be asserted that there are developmental higher cognitive changes throughout the life-span (Hartlage, 1986; Nolan et al., 1986). Life-span neuropsychology attempts to integrate these insights in terms of understanding unique individual strengths and weaknesses.

The question of whether specific neuropsychological deficits may only be expressed at specific developmental stages is a difficult one. One classic study with brain-damaged children pointed out the complexity of these relationships. Teuber and Rudel (1962) followed a number of groups of brain injured children for a ten-year period to determine the effect of early brain damage on new learning. They postulated three possible patterns could appear: (1) progressive recovering over time; (2) constant stable impairment over time; (3) no discernable deficit at first but over time behavior deficits would arise. The dramatic conclusion was that *all* three patterns were displayed by the brain damaged children, depending on the task assessed.

As noted by Horton and Puente (1989):

> The effects of early brain damage are quite complex. It may depend upon the task under study and the normal developmental sequence of that task, among other factors. It is possible that similar behavioral performances might be accomplished by different groups of neurological structures at different phases of the developmental process. (p. 113)

DIAGNOSTIC ISSUES

While diagnostic issues have been the major focus of neuropsychology for some time, the categorization systems of neuropsychopathology have been little examined. For example, when neuropsychological pioneers such as Ralph M. Reitan, and Arthur Benton, set-up their neuropsychology laboratories at the Departments of Neurology at the Indiana University Medical Center and the University of Iowa Medical Center, respectively, the contribution of the neuropsychologist was solely diagnostic. At that point in time (i.e., 1950s and 1960s), the many neurological diagnostic procedures carried the risk of mortality. Then and now no one has died from a neuropsychological evaluation. With the diagnostic role well established, neuropsychology would profit from attention to the classification system of organic mental disorders and its possible revision. In an earlier section of this chapter the issue of "organicity" was discussed.

Organic Mental Syndromes and Disorders as Defined by DSM-III-R

The development and subsequent revisions of the *Diagnostic and Statistical Manual* (DSM) by the American Psychiatric Association represent the culmination of a number of efforts in working for increased diagnostic accuracy. It is recognized quite clearly that at present, psychiatric and psychological diagnoses of mental syndromes and disorders is an inexact science. Thus, the classification of them is actually a work in progress. Reflecting this, the *Diagnostic and Statistical Manual* has been subject to ongoing revision.

The basic trend in terms of diagnosis of organic mental disorders has been one of increased specification. In the first DSM system of classification, (APA, 1962) there were essentially two categories of brain damage, i.e., acute or chronic. In the second edition of the DSM (APA, 1966), the variable of psychotic or nonpsychotic, acute or chronic, organic brain syndrome was introduced. In DSM-III (1968) there was a greater specification of number of types of organic mental disorders and there was a clear distinction between syndrome and etiology. DSM-III was also more developmentally sensitive as it identified particular groups of disorders that usually arise in infancy, childhood, or adolescence, such as attention deficit disorders or conduct disorders. Also, DSM-III separated clinical syndrome, personality types or specific developmental disorder, and medical problems into Axis I, II, and III respectfully. Specific developmental disorder includes problems with reading, spelling, and math, among others. These are usually first diagnosed in childhood. This three-way classification has many advantages. Syndromes can appear relative to the behavior without regard to etiology, whereas a disorder directly implicates a specific type of neuropathology. It is important to keep in mind that DSM-III-R allows an Axis I diagnosis to be made on behavioral grounds, (i.e., in cases where the etiology of brain dysfunction is unclear). This is important because in a considerable percentage of cases definitive diagnosis of neuropathology is only available after the patient's death. For anyone that has ever been confronted with a behaviorally disordered patient in an emergency room or screening area, such a system of classification has some obvious strengths.

The organic mental syndromes are divided into six major categories. These are as follows:

1. Delirium and Dementia
2. Amnestic Syndrome and Organic Hallucinosis
3. Organic Delusional Syndrome, Organic Mood Syndrome, and Organic Anxiety Syndrome
4. Organic Personality Syndrome
5. Intoxication and Withdrawal
6. Organic Mental Syndrome (not otherwise specified)

Delirium and Dementia are Organic Mental Syndromes in which mental impairment is global. The dividing line between them usually is based on the occurrence of a clouded consciousness or disorders of attention which are present in delirium, but not dementia. Perhaps a simple way to understand dementia is that it appears to be an absence of normal intelligence. Both Delirium and Dementia are most common among the elderly (Albert, 1981). In Amnestic Syndrome and Organic Hallucinosis relatively selective areas of cognitive ability have been compromised. The Amnestic Syndrome refers to impairment of short-term and long-term memory, although, clearly, the history of the syndrome is one which has focussed on impairment of short-term memory and, in Organic Hallucinosis, the hallucinations are the cardinal feature. Organic Delusional Syndrome, Organic Mood Syndrome, and Organic Anxiety Syndrome are syndromes where various aspects resembling schizophrenia, mood disorders, or anxiety disorders exist from organic causes. The diagnostic difficulty is to identify in which cases these is or is not an organic component. Organic Personality Syndrome is a syndrome that is organic in nature and in which the personality is primarily affected. It is important to realize that this category first came into being in order to accommodate the frontal lobe impaired patient. Many characteristics of the syndrome are typical of impairment of the frontal cortex.

Intoxication and Withdrawal Syndromes are clearly related to substance disorders. It is important to realize that these disorders are related to either taking in, or failure to take, a substance which a person is using for psychoactive purposes. The last category, Organic Mental Syndrome not otherwise specified, is essentially an eclectic category for other organic mental syndromes that could not be diagnosed previously. It is, of course, realized that there could be multiple organic mental syndromes existing in the same person; that is to say, a person could have Organic Personality Disorder at the same time as an intoxication Syndrome, etc.

DEVELOPMENTAL ORIENTATION TO DIAGNOSIS

It would appear clear that different sorts of neuropsychological disorders will occur at different points in development. For example, there are a set of disorders which are usually first evident in infancy, childhood, or adolescence. Of this set of disorders, those which are usually diagnosed by neuropsychologists are the Developmental Disorders and the Disruptive Behavior Disorders. Developmental Disorders include Mental Retardation, Pervasive Developmental Disorders (i.e., Autistic disorder), Specific Developmental Disorder (i.e., Academic Skills disorders, Language and Speech disorders, Motor skills disorders, etc.), and Disruptive Behavior Disorder (i.e., Attention-Deficit Hyperactivity Disorder, Conduct Disorder, etc.)

Similarly, there is a set of disorders that usually arise in later years (i.e., senium and proscenium). These include Primary Degeneration Dementia of the Alzheimer's type, Multi-Infarct Dementia and Dementia due to neurodegenerative diseases such as Pick's and Jakob-Creutzfeldt. Clearly, these disorders are age-related.

In cases of disorders in either childhood or old age, a necessary but sufficient condition for diagnosis is the use of age-corrected normative data for the neuropsychological tests used (Albert, 1981; Hartlage, 1986). Appropriate diagnostic practice also includes an understanding of the sort of cognitive changes manifested at particular neuropsychological stages (Hartlage, 1986; Nolan et al., 1986). In addition, one must be sensitive to the distinction between organic (i.e., biological) and environmental (i.e., behavioral) influence upon neuropsychological performances. The final product is a mix of both.

Life–Span Neuropsychology and Other Specialties:

It is important to understand the role and function of the various specialties in order to promote stronger working relationships. The major health care specialties to be considered will, in turn, include neurology and neurosurgery, psychiatry, rehabilitation medicine, pediatric/gerontology, clinical psychology, and health psychology. Two educational specialties which also warrant discussion are school psychology and vocational education.

Neurology and Neurosurgery These specialties have always been intrically related to neuropsychology. It is important to realize that these disciplines, even unto themselves, are not static entities. Neurology, quite clearly over the years, has moved away from a focus on higher cortical functions and toward greater focus on the peripheral nervous system. There are still behavioral neurologists in practice, and many of these behavioral neurologists make important contributions to neurology. Nonetheless, the majority of contemporary neurologists are those that see their interests associated with the spinal cord.

It is interesting to reflect that the initial validation of psychological tests to discern the effect of brain lesions could only have been accomplished with the active assistance of neurosurgeons. At this point, with precise neurological procedures for imaging, there is less of a need for neuropsychologists to aid in preoperative localization assessment. Presently, the role of the neuropsychologist has been one of dealing with the patient postoperatively as well as focusing on ecological issues, such as function, rather than on structure. (Schwartz, Denneral & Lin, 1966)

Psychiatry Clearly, the last few years have shown the increasing interest of psychiatrists in neuropsychological testing. There is great promise in terms of neuropsychologists collaboratively working with psychiatrists in developing better assessment tools and treatment programs for functionally impaired and organically impaired psychiatric patients.

Rehabilitative Medicine This is perhaps one of the areas where neuropsychologists can make impressive contributions. The role of behavioral scientists in rehabilitation is one which is clearly on the assent. Among other areas, head injury is certainly one in which there is a clear mandate for neuropsychologists to aid in the selection of treatment and its skillful implementation. (Seron, DeLoche, Moulard & Rovsller, 1980; Horton, 1979)

Pediatrics/Geriatrics These two medical specialties are concerned with opposite ends of the life-span. With respect to neuropsychology, the application to pediatric problems is well established in the subfield of pediatric neuropsychology (Hartlage, 1986). The pediatric neuropsychologist assesses and treats developmental learning disorders and attentional problems and the sequelae of various medical conditions.

On the other hand, and quite surprisingly, neuropsychology in geriatrics is still in its toddlerhood. In geriatrics neuropsychologists have begun to develop a role in assessment of age associated disorders in which cognitive decline is a key characteristic (i.e., Alzheimer's and Multi-Infarct Dementia). Future efforts might be devoted to increasing the utilization of neuropsychology in developing rehabilitation programs for the cognitively impaired elderly. (Horton, 1979)

Clinical Psychology Although clinical psychology has often provided an umbrella for neuropsychology, it appears that other subdisciplines are currently working to subsume important sections of what had been the clinical psychologist's domain. Neuropsychology, Health Psychology, Clinical Child Neuropsychology, School Psychology are all establishing particular areas of expertise in the delivery of applied services. A working definition of Health Psychology would be "psychology applied to medical complications and specialties" (Horton & Puente, 1986). Neuropsychology would then clearly be considered as the branch of psychology that most clearly interacts with problems of neurologically impaired patients.

Quite clearly in school psychology there is a growing emphasis on neuropsychological assessment of school children who may have developmental disorders (Reynolds, 1981). In addition to children who might have difficulties with reading, mathematics, writing and spelling, some attention has also been directed to the neuropsychological assessment of children with various syndromes of mental retardation.

Emerging Trends and Life-Span Neuropsychology

Education and Training The International Neuropsychological Society and Division 40 of the American Psychological Association formed a joint task force on education, accreditation, and credentialing. Chaired by Dr. Manfred J. Meier, the task force has made major contributions to the development of models for the education and training of neuropsychologists (Meier 1981a, 1981b). Unfortunately, these models have not been widely implemented. These guidelines address training that is generic in nature and life-span developmental issues still remain to be addressed. One hopes that in the coming years more time, energy, and resources would be devoted to these efforts.

Certification and Licensure At present the clinical practice of neuropsychology in most states and provences of the United States and Canada, falls under the generic licensure umbrella of psychology. As far as known to the authors, at present, there is not a specific licensure for a neuropsychologist. With respect to credentialing, the American Board of Professional Psychology (ABPP) has initiated a new specialty in neuropsychology. Under the leadership of Dr. Meier, the American Board of Clinical Psychology (ABCN) has instituted certification procedures for obtaining a diplomate in clinical neuropsychology. In addition, a second board, the American Board of Professional Neuropsychology (ABPN), has also been constituted and that board also offers a diplomate in professional neuropsychology. However, specialization in specific areas of clinical neuropsychology are not presently formally recognized.

Recent Developments In recent years new concepts of subcortical brain damage have been introduced and are expected to make major changes in our current thinking. With an increased ability to image sections of the brain while it is actually in operation one would expect a great elucidation of the role of subcortical brain structures. Rehabilitations and behavior management as earlier noted are emerging areas where there has been an impressive increase in the role of behavioral neuropsychologists. Similarly, there has been an increase in the efforts of neuropsychologists in school settings. The current trends in the treatment of head injury have been toward a greater reliance on behavioral approaches.

New Technology One of the most exciting areas is correlation of neuropsychological tests with neurometric and radiological procedures. The array of neuroradiological procedures available is astounding. Perhaps more than any other, Magnetic Resonance Imaging (MRI) appears to provide the greatest advantage in enhancing various areas of the brain while also staying within the bounds of reasonable cost. One expects that in the near future the cost issue will be controlled, and that even more dramatic representation of brain structure and function will be available.

New Populations Relatively little has been done on neuropsychological toxicology (i.e., the identification and assessment of human neurotoxic syndromes). Such substances as lead, solvents, metals, drugs, pesticides, and alcohol need to be further assessed and the implications for treatment considered (Hartman, 1988). Similarly, many medical disorders, such as cancer and diabetes and a number of others, are currently being explored with respect to their neuropsychological implications.

CONCLUSIONS

In the preceding sections, some major efforts were devoted toward conceptualizing Life-Span Neuropsychology. In addition, there was an attempt to describe some of the major organic related categories of DSM-III-R. In addition, the relationship of Life-Span Neuropsychology with other specialties was briefly reviewed. Finally, a number of important trends in Life-Span Neuropsychology were briefly noted.

REFERENCES

Albert, M. (1981). Geriatric neuropsychology. *Journal of Consulting and Clinical Psychology, 49,* 835–850.

American Psychiatric Association (1987), *Diagnostic and Statistical Manual of Mental Disorders,* Third Edition, Revised (DSM-III-R). Washington, DC: American Psychiatric Association.

Baltes, P. B. (1983). Life-span developmental psychology: Observations on history and theory revisited. In R. M. (Ed.), *Developmental psychology: Historical and philosophical perspectives* (pp. 79–111). Hillsdale, NJ: Erlbaum.

Baltes, P. B., & Nesselroade, J. R. (1979). History and rationale of longitudinal research. In J. R. Nesselroade & P. B. Baltes (Eds.), *Longitudinal research is the study of behavior and development* (pp. 1–39). New York: Academic Press.

Baltes, P. B., Reese, H. W., & Lipsitt, L. P. (1980). Life-span developmental psychology. *Annual Review of Psychology, 31,* 65–110.

Baltes, P. B., Reese, H. W., & Nesselroade, J. R. (1977). *Life-span developmental psychology: Introduction to research methods.* Monterey, CA: Brooks/Cole.

Bryden, M. P., & Saxby, L. (1985). Developmental aspects of cerebral laterialization. In J. E. Obrzut & G. W. Hynd (Eds.), *Child neuropsychology, Vol. 1* (pp. 73–94). Orlando, FL: Academic Press.

Cattell, R. B. (1971). *Abilities: Their structure, growth, and action.* Boston: Houghton

Mifflin.

Davison, L. A. (1974). Introduction. In R. M. Reitan & L. A. Davison (Eds.), *Clinical neuropsychology: Current status and applications* (pp. 1–18). New York: Wiley.

Drotar, D., & Strum, L. (1989). Training psychologists as infant specialists. *Infants and Young Children, 2*(12), 58–66.

Featherman, D. L., & Learner, R. M. (1985). Ontogenesis and sociogenesis: Problematics for theory and research about development and socialization across the life-span. *American Sociological Review, 50*(5), 659–676.

Geschwind, N. & Levitsky, W. (1968). Human brain: Left-right asymmetries in temporal speech region. *Science, 161,* 186–187.

Hartlage, L. C. (1986). Pediatric neuropsychology. In D. Wedding, A. M. Horton, Jr. & J. S. Webster, *The neuropsychology handbook* (pp. 441–455). New York: Springer Publishing Co.

Hartman, D. E. (1988). *Neurpsychological Toxicology.* New York: Pergamon Press.

Horton, A. M., Jr. (1979). Behavioral neuropsychology: Rationale and research. *Clinical Neuropsychology, 1,* 20–23.

Horton, A. M., Jr. (1982). Introduction to psychotherapy for the aging. In A. M. Horton, Jr. (Ed.), *Mental health interventions for the Aging* (pp. 51–66). New York: Praeger.

Horton, A. M., Jr., (1987). Luria's contribution to clinical behavioral neuropsychology. *Neuropsychology, 1*(2), 39–44.

Horton, A. M., Jr., & Puente, A. E. (1986). Behavioral neuropsychology with children. In G. Hynd & J. Obrazut (Eds.), *Child neuropsychology: Clinical practice* (Volume II) (pp. 299–316). Orlando, FL: Academic Press.

Horton, A. M., Jr., & Puente, A. E. (1989). Neuropsychological considerations. In M. Hersen (Ed.), *Innovations in child behavior therapy* (pp. 105–133). New York: Springer Publishing Co.

Horton, A. M., Jr., & Wedding, D. (1984). *Clinical and behavioral neuropsychology.* New York: Praeger.

Jackson, J. H. (1958). *Selected writings of John Hughlings Jackson.* J. Taylor (Ed), New York: Basic Books.

Luria, A. R. (1966). *Higher cortical functions in man.* New York: Basic Books.

Luria, A. R. (1970). The functional organization of the brain. *Scientific American, 222,* (66–78).

Luria, A. R. (1973). *The working brain.* New York: Basic Books.

Meier, M. J. (1974). Some challenges for clinical neuropsychology. In R. M. Reitan & L. A. Davison (Eds.), *Clinical neuropsychology: Current status and application* (pp. 289–323). New York: Wiley.

Meier, M. J. (1981a). Education for competency assurance in human neuropsychology: Antecedents, models, and directions. In S. B. Filskov & T. J. Boll (Eds.), *Handbook of clinical neuropsychology* (pp. 754–781). New York: Wiley.

Meier, M. J. (Ed.). (1981b). Report of International Neuropsychological Society Task Force on education, accreditation, and credentialing. *INS Bulletin,* September, 5–10.

Neugarten, B. (1969). Continuities and discontinuities of psychological issues in adult life. *Human Development, 12,* 121–130

Nolan, B. H., Swihart, A. A., & Pirozzolo, F. J. (1986). The neuropsychology of normal aging and dementia: An introduction. In D. Wedding, A. M. Horton, Jr., & J. S. Webster, *The neuropsychology handbook* (pp. 410–440). New York: Springer Publishing Co.

Puente, A. (in press). Psychological determination of disability. In M. Glancy (Ed.),

Social security law practice guide (Vol. 4). New York: Matthew Bender.

Reynolds, C. R. (1981). Neuropsychological assessment and the habilitation of learning: Consideration in the search for the aptitude treatment interaction. *School Psychology Review, 10,* 342–349.

Schaie, K. W. (1979). The primary mental abilities in adulthood: An exploration in the development of psychometric intelligence. In P. B. Baltis & D. G. Brain, Jr. (Eds.), *Life-span development and behavior (Vol. 3)* (pp. 67–115). New York: Academic Press.

Schwartz, M. C., Denneral, R. D., & Lin, Y. (1966). Neuropsychological and psychosocial predictors of employability in epilepsy. *Journal of Clinical Psychology, 24,* 174–177.

Seron, Z., Deloche, G., Moulard, G., & Rovsller, M. (1980). A computer-based therapy for the treatment of aphasic subjects with writing disorders. *Journal of Speech and Hearing Disorders, 4,* 45–58.

Teuber, H. L., & Rudel, R. G., (1962). Behavior after cerebral lesion in children and adults. *Developmental medicine and child neurology, 4,* 3–20.

Chapter 2

Screening for Brain Damage Over the Life-Span

Richard A. Berg

A primary direction in neuropsychology is, and has been, the differentiation of the brain-damaged patient from all other patients. Past research in neuropsychology has been focused on developing either a single test or a battery of tests that have the ability to make this discrimination with a high degree of validity and reliability. In several clinical settings, there is a need for comprehensive neuropsychological evaluations to aid in the determination of whether cortical dysfunction exists, as well as the extent and nature of the dysfunction.

In some situations, the clinician has the responsibility of assessing unselected cases in order to identify areas where additional evaluation is needed. This typically occurs in psychiatric hospitals, mental health clinics, or private practice situations where psychological screening is routine with each patient to be seen. In these settings, clinicians and examiners do not choose to use a lengthy test battery because of the time and expense involved. A complete neuropsychological evaluation can routinely take as many as six or more hours, and the initial set-up cost can be more than $2000. In addition, many psychiatric hospitals and mental health clinics have neither the personnel nor the space to devote to such lengthy examination procedures. This is especially true in those places where the base rate of neuropsychological dysfunction is low in the screened population.

Many psychologists do not have the formal training in neuropsychological theory and assessment techniques and have neither the time nor the inclination to pursue the post-doctoral training required for proficiency in neuropsychology. However, these same clinicians often recognize a need for additional assessment training to better evaluate those patients who may require referral to either a neurologist or neuropsychologist. It is becoming increasingly apparent and recognized by psychologists that traditional assessment methods, such as the Wechsler scales and the Bender Visual-Motor Gestalt Test, are of limited utility in assessing higher cortical functions and the standard mental status examination may raise as many questions as it answers.

Many workshops have proliferated over the past few years to deal with administration and interpretation of some of the most popular neuropsychological test batteries. A number of highly competent clinicians feel that they can get the requisite training in neuropsychology by attending one of these workshops. However, even those who offer the workshops will admit, and frequently emphasize to those in attendance, that the workshop cannot make one a competent neuropsychologist. From these workshops the clinician can gain a knowledge of the basic administration techniques for a given test battery as well as some basic information about interpretation of the test results. The single or multiple day workshop does not make the clinician expert in the complex subtleties involved in brain-behavior relationships nor is any substantial information typically given concerning the brain functions and their interrelationships that underlie manifest behaviors.

One of the more difficult issues for the practicing neuropsychologist who attempts to work with both children and adults revolves around neuropsychological development and the effects of normal aging. In children, the higher level functions of the nervous system emerge at differing rates across individuals. Although there are some general guidelines, unfortunately there are no hard and fast known rules concerning precisely when a functional capability should be present in a child. Thus, it becomes difficult to determine whether, for example, a certain level of language ability can be considered normal in a four-year-old. As the child matures, the neuropsychologist can begin to feel more comfortable about exactly what the individual should be able to do at a given age. By the age of roughly 16 years, the performance of that individual can be compared with available normative data for adults and an appropriate determination of normal or abnormal functioning can be made.

As the age of the individual begins to reach that point where one is considered to be elderly, a difficulty comparable to that noted in dealing with children emerges. While general guidelines exist as to what can be expected to happen to cognitive functioning with advancing age, there often are no precise markers for indicating what constitutes normal versus abnormal functioning. The practicing clinician must, therefore, have at least some notion as to what constitutes reasonably normal cognitive functioning across the age range.

The screening examination is not an end in itself since the conclusions obtained are usually quite limited. Rather, the experienced clinician can determine whether the possibility of neuropsychological dysfunction exists. The screening techniques discussed in this chapter will not be able to identify the nature of a specific disorder or the primary deficits in the patient's functioning. The neuropsychological screening, as it will be addressed here, can be used effectively and efficiently to identify those individuals whose cases would be clarified through the use of a more comprehensive examination.

The psychologist who uses screening devices can use one of two basic approaches. First, he may employ a variety of tests that are highly sensitive to brain damage in general. Second, she can use a small battery of tests that can be analyzed in much the same fashion as a larger, more comprehensive test battery but without the specificity gained through a rigorous neuropsychological evaluation. The tests in such a battery need to be selected so that each is sensitive to a different type of dysfunction rather that the more global tests appropriate for the first technique. Thus the tests selected for a screening must complement each other with as little redundancy as possible.

The practicing clinician is confronted on an almost daily basis with the need to make decisions about patient care and referral. Often these decisions relate to the cognitive status of patients, and directly or indirectly, to the integrity of the cerebral hemispheres. A number of the questions deal with the patient's ability to function on the job or at home after leaving the hospital. In addition, questions about differential diagnosis are common, and psychological findings are often the basis upon which decision are made about the need for further neurological consultation as part of the work-up of the psychiatric patient. Finally the psychologist often is asked to both predict and postdict—for example, "Was Mrs. Samples able to understand the nature of the law and the consequences of her actions when she agreed to sell her house last April?"

The majority of these questions are best answered after a comprehensive neuropsychological examination and following a detailed assessment of each area of cognitive functioning. However, this can often be impractical as bedfast or nonambulatory patients frequently cannot be conveniently evaluated and patients are often too confused to cooperate fully for the detailed testing to be performed in the neuropsychology laboratory. In addition, the typical 6 to 8 or more hours required for the evaluation can be too draining on the patient, both physically and emotionally. Finally, the typical neuropsychological evaluation can be quite costly for the patient ranging from about $300 to well over $1000, the average being $500 (Seretny, Dean, Gray, & Hartlage, 1986).

Neuropsychological screening for the presence of brain dysfunction can offer a practical alternative to this since they generally do not require much in the way of specialized equipment. Administration and interpretation of screening techniques generally require much less time than that which is required for a more complete evaluation. The cost in terms of materials and personnel as well as space is typically a good deal less. A relatively brief, portable, and easily administered and scored screening exam is much more practical and cost effective in those situations where the primary requirement is to differentiate those individuals who have brain-based pathology from those who do not. Referrals for in-depth examination can then be made on an as-needed basis. It is also worth mentioning that the cost of screenings to the patient is significantly less in terms of time and money.

A good neuropsychological screening technique is designed to minimize the time needed for administration, scoring, and interpretation while maximizing the information gathered by briefly assessing all major cognitive functional areas. These functional areas include: lateral dominance; auditory, tactile, and visual sensation and perception; spatial-perceptual organization; language skills; general information; and memory processes. Furthermore, the tests included in such a screening should have as little redundancy as possible and, ideally, should have been empirically demonstrated to be effective in differentiating brain-damaged from non-brain-damaged individuals. All of the assessment devices should be brief, easily administered, objectively scored, commonly used in clinical settings, and very portable.

MENTAL STATUS EXAMINATIONS

All Ages

In much the same way as a complete neuropsychological evaluation demands too much, the commonly used bedside mental status examination most often offers too little information to be clinically useful. At its worst, it involves a busy physician asking a question or two requiring judgment and then asking the patient to perform a serial subtraction task (usually counting backward from 100 by 7s).

Of somewhat greater value because of slightly more structure is the "Mini-Mental State" (MMS; Folstein, Folstein, McHugh, 1975; Spencer 6 Folstein, 1985). The MMS can be administered in roughly 10 minutes; it provides a quick assessment of orientation to date and place (but not to time or person), or attention, of delayed recall, and of a few select aspects of receptive and expressive language functions. The MMS is reported to have a 24-hour test-retest reliability coefficient of 0.88 in a sample of 22 depressed patients, a 28-day test-retest reliability of 0.98 in a sample of 23 stable impaired subjects, and an interscorer reliability coefficient of 0.83 in a sample of 19 depressed subjects. While the MMS appears to be able to identify cognitive impairment in neuropsychiatric patients and able to differentiate cognitively impaired from nonimpaired subjects, it does not appear to be able to separate organically impaired patients from schizophrenic patients. In general, a score of less that 20 points is probably an indicator of organic impairment, and patients obtaining such a score should be given at least an extended mental status exam or referred elsewhere for more intensive evaluations.

Another standardized mental status examination which can be effective used as part of a screening is the Neurobehavioral Cognitive Status Examination (Mueller, 1984). On average, it requires about 20 minutes for administration and offers quantification for most major cognitive domains. The stimulus items needed for the examination are small, convenient, and portable. The test assesses levels of consciousness, orientation, attention, language (comprehension, repetition, and naming ability), constructional skills, memory abilities, calculation ability, and reasoning (using judgment and Wechsler scale Similarities-type questions).

Much of the efficiency in using this device is achieved through the use of what are referred to as "screens," which are fairly demanding test items requiring moderate skills in the area being assessed. These screens are failed by 10–30% of normal individuals (Mueller, 1984). While failure to pass a screening item does not provide specific evidence of impairment in that particular cognitive domain, it does suggest the need for a more detailed assessment. However, if the patient passes the screening item, the requisite skills are assumed and no additional testing of that particular cognitive function is conducted. For example, the screening for attention involves a digit span-type task involving the recollection of six digits which is the normal (i.e., average) score for the general population. If a patient can correctly repeat six numbers, attention is assumed to be intact. On the other hand, if the patient is unable to correctly repeat the six numbers, the examiner continues with a lengthier and more formal assessment of attention.

The mental status examination can provide a reasonably comprehensive but shallow survey of cognitive functioning. At its best, it will provide the clinician with a high clinical yield at a minimal cost. As Wedding (1988) notes, at its very best, the mental status exam blends into the practice of behavioral neurology. (A comprehensive, behavioral neurology-type mental status exam is detailed in an excellent test by Strub & Black, 1985.)

Because of his or her training in measurement and psychometric assessment, the psychologist is generally the individual best able to supplement the findings of a mental status examination. More comprehensive testing either can expand or negate indications of impairment noted on a mental status exam. Increased testing offers the additional benefit of allowing for assessment of the individual a second time when the clinical picture seen could be quite different as a result of fluctuating clinical conditions, medication effects, adaptation to the hospital environment, and so on. This requires that the psychologist by familiar with a wide range of screening measures. A number of the measures will be briefly discussed here; however, space limitations preclude in-depth discussions or comprehensive listing of all tests available. An extended discussion of these and other assessment devices and techniques can be found in tests by Berg, Franzen, and Wedding (1987) and Lezak (1983). These references also can provide an understanding of the nature of many of the neurologic conditions that can produce impaired test performance. This, in turn, can assist the clinician in appreciating the conditions most likely to be present with psychological symptomatology.

SCREENING FOR ATTENTION

Attention and concentration are prerequisites for all psychological assessment, and their absence makes it extremely difficult even to speculate about other higher-level cognitive processes. If, for example, a patient with a significant attention deficit cannot recall the details of a short story just read to him or her, the patient's performance failure could be secondary to some aspect of deficient memory functioning or strictly to the deficit in attention. Similarly, questions arise regarding the patient's ability to understand complex instructions due to deficits in receptive language functioning or because of an inability to selectively focus attention long enough to listen to the presentation of the task. Thus, attention must be assessed.

Digit Span (4 years through adult)

Attention is often measured by examination of the patient's span for digits, typically using the Digit Span subtest from the age appropriate Wechsler intelligence scales (e.g., Wechsler, 1981) or the Wechsler Memory Scales (1945; 1987). This technique, however, has the complication that there is the possibility of confounding attention and memory functioning. A digit span test, therefore, is best considered as a measure of immediate memory functioning (Wedding, 1988).

Continuous Performance Tasks (15 years and up)

A Continuous Performance Task is one in which the patient is required to attend to a ongoing series of stimuli and respond appropriately when a predetermined contingency occurs. For example, the examiner can require that the patient tap a pencil on a table every time the letter "C" is read from a random list of letters read at a rate of roughly three letters every 2 seconds. If attention is intact, no more than one or two errors in a thirty-second trial should be made by the patient. If the patient cannot meet this criterion, the clinician may wish to reevaluate the patient at a later time.

The clinician can vary the procedure as best fits the situation. Typically, these tests involve the sequential presentation of stimuli (strings of letters or numbers) over an extended time with instructions to the patient to indicate (a tap, raise the hand) when the target stimulus is perceived. The simplest form of this type of task involves only one target stimulus as in the example above. Two or more targets can be used. More complex variations can require the patient to respond only when the target stimulus is preceded by a specific item (e.g., tap when you hear a "B," but only when it follows "D") (Lezak, 1983). As a broad, general rule, the greater the number of errors, the more severe the attention problem.

Cancellation Tasks (6 years through adult)

Cancellation tasks are variations of the Continuous Performance Task (CPT) and require visual selectivity at a rapid speed on a repetitive motor task. They assess a number of functions including the patient's capacity for sustained attention. Visual scanning as well as activation and inhibition of rapid responses are needed to successfully perform cancellation tasks (Lezak, 1983). Lowered scores may reflect a general response slowing and inattentiveness of diffuse brain dysfunction or acute brain conditions or more specific defects of response shifting.

The basic format for these tests follows that of the CPT. It consists of rows of letters or numbers randomly interspersed with a designated target letter or number. The patient is instructed to cross out all target letters or numbers. Performance is scored for accuracy (errors) and time to completion; if there is a time limit, scoring is for errors and the number of targets crossed out within the allotted time limit. The variations on this type of task are almost limitless. For example, Diller and his colleagues (1974) constructed nine different tasks using a variety of stimuli and conditions: two used digits, two used letters, two using easy three-letter words, two using geometric figures (taken from the WISC Coding subtest), and one using simple pictures. The basic task consists of six 52 character rows in which the target stimulus is randomly interspersed approximately 18 times per row.

Lezak (1983) noted that failure on cancellation tasks appears to be associated with "spatial neglect" deficits in patients with right hemisphere lesions. In individuals with left hemisphere brain damage, the problem appears to revolve around the temporal processing of information (Diller & Weinberg, 1977).

Screening for Motor Functions

In a screening examination, it is a good idea to include a measure of manual motor control, speed, and dexterity. These tests tend to be timed speed tests that require an apparatus with a counting device or require a countable response from the patient. Such measures have been found to be useful in the lateralization of brain dysfunction.

Grip Strength (5 years through adult)

Clinicians have realized that intensity or strength of voluntary motor activity can be a reliable indicator of brain functions. Many neuropsychologists use some measure of strength-of-grip in comprehensive evaluations. This can also be done in a screening. A patient's grip strength can be simply and conveniently assessed at bedside by having the patient bilaterally grasp and squeeze the examiner's index fingers which are extended and pointed down in front of the patient (Wedding, 1988). The clinician will want to be sensitive to differences between the two hands, and, with experience, will develop a sense of what are appropriate expectations for grip strength based on age and sex.

A somewhat more sophisticated assessment of grip strength can be accomplished by using a hand dynamometer. Reitan and Davison (1974) established the hand dynamometer as clinically valuable for such purposes. Dodrill (1978) has found that grip strength, as assessed using a hand dynamometer, can effectively discriminate between a control and brain-damaged groups. In the absence of significant brain dysfunction in the region of the brain responsible for motor functions, the grip strength of each hand should be within 5 kilograms (or 11 pounds) of each other with the patient's dominant hand being the stronger.

Finger Tapping (5 years through adult)

Perhaps the most widely used measure of motor functioning is the Finger Tapping Test (Reitan & Davison, 1974. Mechanical devices for assessing finger tapping are widely available. Age and sex-corrected normative data are available; however, most young or middle-aged individuals should be able to tap roughly 50 times with the dominant hand and about 45 taps with the nondominant hand in a ten-second period. Several trials (usually five) are given for each hand with brief rest periods between each trial. The score for each hand is the average across the five trials. The presence of cortical damage tends to have a slowing effect on finger tapping rate. Lateralized lesions may result in a marked slowing in the tapping rate of the hand contralateral to the lesion. However, such effects do not appear with enough frequency or consistency to warrant the use of this test as a screening for lateralized damage. Diffuse damage will lead to a general slowing of the tapping rate of both hands. As a general rule, the clinician can expect to see about a 10% difference in the tapping rates of the two hands, with the dominant hand being the faster.

More complete testing of fine motor functioning is possible with tasks such as the Purdue Pegboard and Wisconsin Pegboard Tests. These tests rarely require more than 5 minutes and the information obtained is usually worth the time required. Full descriptions of these tests can be found elsewhere (Berg, Franzen, & Wedding, 1987).

SCREENING FOR SENSORY DYSFUNCTION

Historically, the sensory examination has been an important part of both neurological and neuropsychological assessment. Portions of this exam can be incorporated into a screening evaluation quite readily. A useful beginning is a simple check of visual acuity. At the patient's bedside this can be done by asking the patient to read from a magazine for suing a Snellen-type eye chart. Once acceptable acuity has been established, it is useful to assess the patient's ability to perceive unilateral and bilateral simultaneous stimulation. The ability to perceive unilateral with subsequent failure to perceive a stimulus on one side when there is bilateral stimulation can be an important clinical sign suggesting the presence of a lesion contralateral to the side of the suppression. Testing for suppressions (also known as extinction) is typically conducted across tactile, auditory, and visual modalities. True suppressions are relatively rare; however, when they occur, it is almost always important and can be considered pathognomonic. Such patients should be referred for neurologic consultation without delay.

It is important to note, however, that at least some training in the administration of this series of tests is essential; they can quite easily be administered improperly, yielding useless findings. The assistance of an experienced neurologist or neuropsychologist can be enlisted or the clinician can take a workshop in which such techniques can be observed and practiced.

A number of other sensory screening measures are available to the psychologist. Stereognosis can be assessed quite simply by having the patient, with eyes closed, touch and identify simple objects such as a key, pencil eraser, coin, or comb. Finger-tip number writing perception can be assessed by seeing if the patient can identify simple numbers written on the fingertips.

The *Reitan-Klove Sensory Perceptual Examination* (Reitan, undated) (ages 9 years through adult) combines much of the traditional neurological exam into a neat package which is comparatively easy for the experienced clinician to administer. A complete description of the test and its instructions is beyond the scope of this chapter. The interested reader is referred to Berg, Franzen, and Wedding (1987) or Reitan and Wolfson (1985).

The first part of the test evaluates the presence of sensory suppressions, using double simultaneous stimulation in the tactile, auditory, and vidual modalities. Tests for the perception of single stimulation are included since suppressions cannot be scored unless it is clear that the patient is able to perceive unilateral stimulation. The remainder of the Sensory Perceptual Examination assesses the more complex tactile perceptual functioning of finger agnosia, agraphesthesia, and astereognosis. The Sensory-Perceptual Examination requires approximately 15–20 minutes for administration on average.

Another important aspect of sensory functioning which should be examined in the course of a screening is two-point discrimination. This can be quickly assessed using what is called an aesthesiometer. These simple devices are inexpensive (about $15.00) and may provide valuable information about the patient's ability to identify and register tactile sensation. Testing involves the determination of the smallest area in which two points can be identified reliably as discrete and separate stimuli. Tactile information of this type is passed through the posterior white columns of the spinal cord and is eventually processed in the parietal regions of the brain. Expected two-point discrimination values range from 0.1 centimeters on the fingertips to 2.0 cm in the palm and heel of the hand. (A slightly modified version of this screening test is available as part of the Reitan-Indiana Neuropsychological Test Battery for Young Children aged 5 through 8 years.)

SCREENING FOR LANGUAGE FUNCTIONS

Assessing language functions is both straightforward and complex. It is straightforward in that patients with adequate educational backgrounds can be expected to be able to read, write, spell, comprehend, enunciate, and repeat. The complexities arise from the fact that language disorders can often be quite subtle and elusive, and because language deficits can clearly exist even in the absence of demonstrable damage to the cerebral cortex.

Language assessment begins with the first verbal interchange between the clinician and the patient. The initial period of "small talk" can be used not only to establish a rapport with the patient but also to provide preliminary information about both the expressive and receptive aspects of the language skills. Fluency and rate of speech are important aspects of speech which can be disrupted in both psychiatric and neurologic disorders. The clinician can evaluate the patient's spontaneous speech ability and assess the relevance of the language used. Speech content also can offer information about the education and intellectual level of the patient. The presence of paraphasias (i.e., word substitutions, using words that are approximately right but not precise, etc.) can provide clues about further directions for the evaluation of language.

Assessment of repetition ability is often omitted from mental status examinations, but it is crucial since some aphasic disorders, such as conduction aphasias in which damage is restricted to the arcuate fasciculus, may spare all other language functions. Patients with minor expressive language deficits typically find it easier to repeat concrete words or phrases than to repeat nonsubstantive items. A statement such as the classic "no ifs, ands, or buts" is preferable to something like "a stitch in time saves nine" as the latter phrase is more concrete and can quite possibly be overlearned.

With a patient of adequate intellectual functioning, it can be useful to assess receptive language skills by asking questions that invert the typical order and logic of sentences (Wedding, 1988). For example, a question from Luria's Neuropsychological Investigation (Christensen, 1975) asks, "are the father's brother and the brother's father the same person or two different people?"

The patient's naming ability can best be assessed through the use of pictures as the use of common objects may prove too simple for the patient with a subtle dysnomia. A test such as the Boston Naming Test (Kaplan, Goodglass, & Weintraub, 1983) or the more readily available Peabody Picture Vocabulary Test-Revised (Dunn & Dunn, 1981) can be employed for this purpose.

Controlled Word Association Test (adult)

Verbal fluency also should be evaluated. This can be accomplished with a task such as the *Controlled Word Association Test.* This test consists of three word naming trials using the letters F, A, and S, respectively. The clinician asks the patient to say as many words as he or she can think of that begin with the given letter of the alphabet, excluding proper nouns, numbers, and the same word with a different suffix. The score is simply the sum of all correct words pronounced in the three one-minute trials, adjusted for age, sex, and education. These adjusted scores are then converted to percentiles. Normative data for this test can be readily found in Lezak (1983) or Berg et al. (1987).

In assessing language functions, the important issue is the selection of a device that can sample a number of aspects of language behaviors (such as listening, speaking, reading, writing, gesturing) quickly and efficiently. While aphasia screening tests are not designed to replace the careful examination of language functions afforded by comprehensive language assessment batteries, they can signal the presence of a disorder and may even call attention to its specific characteristics. It is important to remember that such screenings do not provide for the fine discriminations of more complete test batteries (Eisensen, 1973). However, since these tests do not require technical knowledge of speech pathology for satisfactory administration or interpretation, they can be easily administered and interpreted by clinicians who are not familiar with aphasia syndromes.

Aphasia Screening Test (9 years through adult)

Since its introduction by Halstead and Wepman (1959), the Aphasia Screening Test (AST) or one of its many variations has been incorporated into many formally organized neuropsychological test batteries. Total administration time rarely is longer than 30 minutes and is frequently much shorter. The AST has no rigid scoring standards. Rather, the emphasis of the test is on determining both the presence, and, to a lesser extent, the nature of communications problems. Errors are coded into a diagnostic profile that can provide a description of a patient's language disabilities. Severity of a problem is not assessed; however, the more areas of involvement noted and the more a single area is involved, the greater the severity of the problems.

The more commonly used form of the AST developed by Reitan (undated) consists of 32 items. These items cover all the elements of aphasic disabilities as well as most common language problems with the exception of color agnosias. A complete description as well as instructions and the stimulus materials for this version of the AST can be found in Berg et al., (1987) or in Boll (1981). (A modified version of this screening test is available as part of the Reitan-Indiana Neuropsychological Test Battery for Young Children aged 5 through 8 years.)

SCREENING FOR MEMORY FUNCTIONING

Memory is not a unitary construct. Thus, a screening of memory functioning should cover the span of immediate memory, the addition of new information to recent memory, the extent of recent memory, and the capacity of the individual for new learning (Lezak, 1983). In an ideal situation, these different memory functions would be systematically reviewed through the major input and output modalities (i.e., auditory and visual) with both recall and retrieval techniques. However, in most cases where memory problems do not seem to be primary in nature, thoroughness can be sacrificed for a number of practical considerations such as time, patient cooperation, and fatigue.

If the WAIS-R has been given, this can be a good starting point as it allows the examiner to assess the span of immediate memory as well as the extent of remote memory (via the Information subtest) stored in verbal form. The longer Arithmetic and Comprehension subtest questions also offer the clinician incidental information on the duration and stability of the immediate memory trace. An Extended Mental Status Examination can also augment information gathered from the patient with a delayed verbal memory task (requiring the patient to recall three or four spoken items after five minutes of intervening material) as well as with questions to assess the retention of ongoing experience at the minimum level necessary for independent living. The addition of an immediate memory and retention task, using simple designs, and a test of learning ability will offer a more complete review of the major dimensions of modalities of memory.

When the patient's performance on these tasks is not significantly depressed relative to the best performance on other tasks, and especially when performance on tests of remote memory is not significantly better than the handling of learning tasks, the clinician can assume that memory and learning are reasonably intact. Marked deficits on the general review of memory may suggest the need for a more in-depth memory assessment which involves the systematic comparison between functions, modalities, and the length, type, and complexity of content. This can be done by the clinician conducting the screening if she or he has had the appropriate training and time is available, or it may point up the need for a referral for a comprehensive evaluation of cognitive functioning.

Relative poor performance on tests of immediate memory and learning also may indicate that the patient is severely depressed and may point to the need for such a differential determination. Impaired immediate memory and learning are also common early symptoms of a number of neurologic conditions that ultimately can result in general cognitive deterioration. As the still relatively intact patient with neurological dysfunction experiences his or her failing abilities, he may also be appropriately depressed, a situation that can further compound the differential diagnostic picture.

There are a large number of techniques that can be used to screen for memory and learning problems. If only a limited time is available, the patient can be asked to remember the examiner's name with recall being checked periodically, and corrected if needed. The patient can be asked to learn a list of our items from four discrete categories; the number of trials it takes the patient to learn the simple list is then recorded. Delayed recall can then be assessed by asking the patient to recall the items toward the end of the screening. Cueing can be used if needed, thereby providing a rough assessment of cued recall. If cued recall is poor, the recognition memory can be evaluated by asking the patient to pick out the correct item from a list of four similar items (e.g., crayon, pencil, pen, paintbrush when the item is pen).

Inglis Memory Task (adult)

Wedding (1988) notes that the *Inglis Memory Task* (Inglis, 1959) has been found to be useful particularly with patients suspected of having an early dementing illness. The task simply requires that the patient learn three remotely associated word pairs (cabbage-pen; knife-chimney; sponge-trumpet). After the first presentation trial of all three pairs of words, the initial word of each pair are randomly presented and the patient is asked to respond with the associated word for each pair. The patient is given the correct response after each failure, or positive feedback if the patient's response is correct. The summary score is the sum of the total number of trials required to reach the criterion of three correct responses for each word pair. Scores greater than 20 suggest the presence of dysfunction whereas scores greater than 30 are considered to be indicative of a marked memory deficit.

Rey Auditory-Verbal Learning Test (RAVLT) (6 years through adult)

The RAVLT is an easily administered test that measure immediate memory span, provides a learning curve, elicits tendencies toward retroactive and proactive interference, assesses confusion or confabulation on memory tasks, and measures retention following an intervening activity (Rey, 1964). This test involves the presentation of a list of 15 simple words five times. The number of correct responses is recorded as well as the order of recall after each presentation trial. Following the fifth trial, a second list of 15 words is presented and the number correctly recalled along with the order of recall is again recorded. Finally, the patient is asked to recall as many items as possible from the original list. Normative data for each trial (one through five) are available and are broken down by social class and age. Additional discussions as well as the norms of the RAVLT can be found in Berg et al. (1987).

Wechsler Memory Scale-Revised (age 16+)

The original Wechsler Memory Scale (Wechsler, 1945) was designed to assess a number of aspects of memory functioning and consists of seven subtests. These tests measure orientation, attention, and a variety of nonmemory functions. Russell (1975) reported a modified scoring system for the WMS which included a delayed memory component. The original WMS was limited in its coverage of memory functions believed to be clinically important. Prigatano (1977, 1978) reviews a number of these limitations. The most salient limitations included the fact that the original test includes only one subtest that measures memory for visual material, and thus, the WMS total score reflects

mostly verbal memory. The WMS also was limited in that it assessed only immediate memory. In addition, the single summary score of the WMS permits no differentiation of separate memory functions.

The revised version of the WMS (Wechsler, 1987) addresses a number of these and other problems. The changes incorporated into the new version of the test include normative data which has been stratified at nine age levels (as opposed to the single age level in the original WMS), replacement of the single global summary score with five composite scores (General Memory, Attention/Concentration, Verbal Memory, Visual Memory, and Delayed Recall), addition of new subtests measuring figural and spatial memory, addition of measures of delayed recall, and improved instructions for scoring to increase accuracy in scoring. The administration of the WMS-R is lengthy, it runs roughly 45 minutes on average; however, the test is extremely useful as a comprehensive measure of memory functioning. (The initial validation studies with the WMS-R indicate the presence of some problems with the test, but on the whole the test looks as if the WMS-R can be considered a welcome addition to the clinician's arsenal of testing instruments. For the interested reader, the entire March 1988 issue of *The Clinical Neuropsychologist* (Volume 2, Number 2)was devoted to initial research with the WMS-R.

Randt Memory Test (age 20+)

The Randt Memory Test assesses much the same memory functions as does the original Wechsler Memory Scale; however, the Randt Test offers a few additional measures, such as incidental learning and remote memory, and can be considered comparable in scope to the more recent WMS-R. The test was designed by its developers to be a global survey and evaluation of a patient's memory. Total administration time is comparatively brief (20–25 minutes). The Randt Memory Test is divided into sections that evaluate primary, rote, associative, discourse, and incidental memory. There is also a general information section, a picture recognition section, and a recall feature (Randt & Brown, 1983). The test does not yield information as to possible localization of brain dysfunction and the test was not originally set up for detailed investigations into specific facets of normal memory functioning. Rather, the Randt specifically assesses various aspects of memory, which when taken in the context of a general screening evaluation, can help the clinician make determination as to the presence of brain damage. Details of the test and administration can be found in the test manual or in Berg et al. (1987).

Limited research has been conducted using the Randt Test; the normative data available for the test are limited. With the advent of the WMS-R which covers much of the same ground as the Randt Memory Test and has a stronger normative base, the future of the Randt is uncertain.

Screening for Visual-Spatial Abilities

There are a variety of aspects of visual functioning that can be impaired by brain dysfunction. As a general rule, brain damage that leads to disruption of one visual function will affect a cluster of related visual functions as well. A major division in visual functions occurs between those involving verbal-symbolic material and those dealing with nonsymbolic stimuli. Other stimulus dimensions that may highlight different aspects of visual perception include the degree to which the stimulus is structured, the amount of remote and new memory involved in the task, spatial relationships and the presence of interfacing stimulation. A screening evaluation should be designed to assess this hierarchical structure as efficiently as possible.

One reasonable technique is to use the geometric forms as naming items which are part of the Aphasia Screening Test (Reitan & Wolfson, 1985). The patient is asked to spell, name, and draw the simple geometric forms (square, cross, and triangle). Alternatively, the patient can be asked to draw more complex figures such as a pipe or cube (Wedding, 1988). The patient can be asked to draw these simple or complex figures from command or from a model. Additionally, having the patient draw a standard clock face with the numbers offers valuable information about planning abilities as well as an indication of any unilateral spatial neglect that may be present. These tasks can be performed with individuals of all ages from about five years and older.

Spatial abilities can be more fully assessed by suing selected stimuli from the Hooper Visual Orientation Test (Hooper, 1958) and the Luria-Nebraska Neuropsychological Battery (Golden, Purisch, & Hammeke, 1985) (ages 8 years and older). Although each test is far too long to be used as a screening device, selected items from these measures are quite useful and can provide a rapid assessment of the ability to rotate items mentally in space.

The clinician may wish to use block design tasks, such as can be found in the age appropriate Wechsler scales, to assess the patient's visual-spatial organizational skills. These tasks are sensitive to posterior lesions as well as dementing illnesses. Far lengthier and more complete discourses on available visual perceptual tasks which can be used as apart of a screening battery can be found in Berg et al. (1988) as well as in Lezak (1983).

SCREENING FOR GENERAL COGNITIVE DYSFUNCTION

Dysfunction of higher cognitive processes is not necessarily associated with damage to a specific cortical region. Rather, higher cognitive abilities are generally sensitive to the effects of brain damage regardless of the site of the damage. This is not all that surprising since cognitive abilities always involve at least: (1) an intact system for organizing perceptual information even though specific perceptual abilities may be impaired; (2) an extensive and readily available data base of remembered learned material; (3) the integrity of cortical and subcortical interconnections and interactions patterns that underlie what we commonly refer to as "thought"; and (4) the capacity to process multiple events simultaneously. Additionally, the translation of cognitive activity into overt behavior requires a response modality sufficiently integrated with central activity to transform conceptual experience into manifest behavior and a well-functioning response feedback system for continual monitoring and modulating of output.

There are a number of general measures of cortical integrity that can be routinely included in the assessment of patients with suspected organic dysfunction. These include the *Digit Symbol* subtest from the Wechsler Adult Intelligence Scale or *Coding* from the Wechsler Intelligence Scale for Children-Revised. This is a quick and easily scored and administered test that has been repeatedly demonstrated (e.g., Botwinick, 1977) to be the WAIS subtest that is most sensitive to general cerebral impairment. The WISC-R version is also reasonably sensitive to brain dysfunction although not so much as the adult version.

Stroop Color and Word Test (adult)

The *Stroop Color and Word Test* (specifically the version developed by Golden (1975, 1978) can be used as a measure of verbal fluency as well as a general test of cognitive efficiency. In this test the patient is required to read as quickly as possible from one of three sheets. The first presentation requires the patient to read a list of color words (red, blue, or green) printed in black ink. On the second trial, the patient reads a series of "X's" printed in red, green, or blue ink. On the third and final trial, the patient identifies the color from a page that consists of the words printed on page one printed in colors used on page two; however, a word and the color in which it is printed do not match. Therefore, "red" can be printed either in blue or green ink, "green" in red or blue ink, and "blue" in red or green ink. Good performance on this section of the test requires that the patient repeatedly suppress the dominant response set (reading the color words) and replace it with a less common response (naming the ink color the word is printed in). The score is the number of items correctly finished within the time limit for each page. Markedly poor performance on the third section of the Stroop should alert the clinician to the need for more comprehensive evaluation of higher level cognitive functions.

Trail Making Test (9 years through adult)

The Trail Making Test (Army Individual Test, 1944) has been widely used as an easily administered test of visual-conceptual abilities, visuomotor tracking, and cognitive efficiency (in this case, the ability to shift cognitive set). As is the case with other tests that have a large attentional component, it is highly sensitive to the effects of brain injury in general (Reitan, 1958). In this test, the patient is asked to draw lines connecting consecutively numbered circles on one work sheet (Trails A), and then is asked to connect the same number of consecutively numbered and lettered circles on another work sheet alternating between letters and numbers (Trails B). If the patient makes an error, the error is pointed out to the patient when it occurs so that corrections can be made. Both the item required and the number of errors made are recorded. Age-corrected normative data are available (Davies, 1968). As a general rule, for younger individuals, aged 20 to 39, normal performance item or Trails A should be 50 seconds or less and 79 seconds or less for Trails B. The combined time to complete both parts of the test should be less than 110 seconds. (It must be noted that these criteria, when applied to normal individuals in their 70s, misclassify an average of 91% as being brain damaged. It is important, therefore, to account for the age of the patient and for the distribution of scores achieved by normal older subjects.)

In general, when the time taken to complete Trails A is relatively far less than that needed to complete Trails B, it is likely that the patient has difficulty in complex conceptual tracking or sequencing. Slow performance at any age on one or both parts of the test points to the likelihood of significant brain dysfunction, but does not indicate whether the problem is one of motor slowing, poor coordination, visual scanning difficulties, or conceptual confusion (Lezak, 1983).

TESTS OF CONCEPT FORMATION

Perhaps the most common indicator of cognitive impairment is concrete thinking involving difficulty in forming concepts, categorizing, generalizing from a single instance, or applying procedural rules and general principles. Tests of these functions (concept formation) differ from other tests in that they focus on the quality or process of thinking more than on the specific response content. Thus, there may be no correct answer per se with scoring done through qualitative judgments of the extent to which the response was abstract or concrete, complex or simple.

Tests of interpretation of proverbs are among the most widely used techniques for evaluating the quality of thinking. The Wechsler Scales, the Stanford-Binet Scales, and a standard Mental Status Examination include proverb interpretation. The Proverbs Test (Gorham, 1956) formalizes the task in a standardized format. One version of the test is a multiple choice version containing 40 items, each of which has four alternative explanations for the proverb with only one of the alternatives being appropriately abstract; the remaining choices are either concrete interpretations or common misinterpretations. Scores tend to vary with education and social class (Gorham, 1956; Fogel, 1965).

Wisconsin Card Sorting Test (6 years through adult)

The Wisconsin Card Sorting Test (WCST; Berg, 1948; Grant & Berg, 1948) was devised to study "abstract behavior" and ability to "shift set." The patient is given a pack of 64 cards on which are printed one to four symbols—star, cross, circle, or triangle—in green, red, yellow, or blue. No two cards are identical. The patient's task is to place them, one by one, under four stimulus cards—one red triangle, two green stars, three yellow crosses, and four blue circles—according to a principle that the patient must determine from the pattern of the examiner's responses to the patient's placement of the cards. For instance, if the principle is color, the correct placement of the blue card is under the four blue blocks, regardless of the symbol or number, and the examiner responds accordingly. After the patient has had a run of ten consecutive correct placements, the principle is changed by the clinician. The test begins with color as the first principle, changes to form, then to number, returns to color, and so on. The test continues until the patient has made six runs of ten correct placement, has placed more than 64 cards in one category, or uses 128 cards (Heaton, 1981). Normative data is provided with the test manual and normative data for children have recently been developed (Chelune and Baer, 1986).

A variety of cerebral impairments can result in poor performance on this test. The difficulty may arise in sorting according to category suggesting an impaired capacity for forming abstract concepts. This type of deficit tends to occur most often in patients with frontal lobe dysfunction. Perseveration (difficulty in shifting the principle being used) is another common type of error made by patients with anterior brain damage; such performance also can be seen in patients with a long history of alcohol abuse. Parsons (1975) has also noted a third type of common error which is referred to as "difficulty in maintaining . . . set," in which the patient may be able to form categories easily and shift set readily, but loses track of the current principle after a number of changes in the principle being used.

The Category Test (versions available for ages 5 and older)

The Category Test (Halstead, 1947) is another test of abstraction ability. Stimulus figures, which vary in shape, size, number, intensity, color, and location, and are grouped by abstract principles, are projected on a screen. The patient must figure out the principle relating stimulus subsets and respond by pressing the appropriate key on a simple keyboard. Correct responses are indicated by a bell, which sounds automatically, while incorrect responses result in a harsh buzz. There are 208 items in the test which are divided into seven subsets. The patient is initially told only that each subtest contains a single principle. Correct responses to the first few items are generally a matter of luck. However, the intact patient should quickly learn the pattern of bells and buzzes, and modify responding by developing and testing new hypotheses until the correct principle underlying the subtest is discerned. The patient is told at the end of each subset that a new subtest is about to begin in which the principle to be discerned may be the same or may be different from the last subset.

The test has no time limit and administration time averages about 40–45 minutes. A cutoff score of 50 errors is generally considered to be the point at which cognitive dysfunction is suggested by the test. Lezak (1983) notes that the test is an excellent discriminator between brain-damaged and neurologically intact groups. One problem with the Category test is that the equipment required is both expensive and bulky, and thus, not very easily transportable. This has been remedied to some extent with the advent of a booklet version of the test which appears to be as effective in its discriminative ability as the original version.

An additional problem with the test is the major investment of time (and resulting frustration in the patient who is doing poorly) required when the full 208-item test is administered. A 120 item version has been found to be highly correlated (0.98) with the longer version with a small standard error of estimate (Sherrill, 1985).

SCREENING BATTERIES

The procedures and tests described in this chapter are all useful in assessing the presence or absence of cerebral dysfunction in patients. When a number of these tests are selected and administered together they can constitute a neuropsychological screening battery that will provide a basic assessment of attention, motor and sensory abilities, language and memory functioning, calculation skills, construction abilities, and planning skills which can be performed in an hour or less. The examination will not offer information as to definitive neurodiagnostic questions; rather, it will assist the clinician in identifying those patients who require a more comprehensive and costly neuropsychology evaluation. The screening battery will provide a good deal more information than a standard mental status exam and will do so at only a small increase in the time necessary for administration. Routine administration will permit the clinician to become comfortable with what are considered to be "normal" performance levels, and should provide exposure to a wide range of patients with various neurological conditions.

What follows is an abbreviated listing of different screening batteries that either have been reported in professional journals or discussed at length in professional meetings. All batteries listed have been demonstrated to be effective in assisting the clinician in differential diagnoses. Most of these batteries listed also conform, in large part, to the criteria for a good screening battery noted earlier in the chapter. Since few of these techniques have formal titles, they will be discussed and identified by the names of the battery developers. These batteries are discussed at length in Berg et al. (1987).

Wysocki and Sweet Screening Battery (Wysocki & Sweet, 1985)

Tests and Order of Administration:

1. Finger Tapping Test
2. Logical Memory and Visual Reproduction from Wechsler Memory Scale (use of Russell (1975) delayed recall procedure required)
3. Trail Making—Parts A and B
4. WAIS (or WAIS-R)—Digit Symbol Subtest
5. Stroop Color and Word Test
6. Pathognomonic Scale of the Luria-Nebraska Neuropsychological Battery.
7. Aphasia Screening Test Greek Cross (spatial relations)

Administration Time: 50–55 minutes

Discriminative ability: Using a 6–impaired–performance–out–of–8 decision rule, 68% brain damaged patients were correctly identified, 84% of schizophrenic patients were correctly identified as non-brain-damaged, and 100% of normal control subjects. Similar findings were reported with other patient groups patients in later studies (Altman, Comaty, Hedecker, Davis, Jobe, & Levy, in press; Fisher, Sweet, & Pfaelzer-Smith, 1986).

DeProspero, Lo Presti, and Atkinson Screening System (DeProspero, Lo Presti, & Atkinson, 1983)

Tests:

1. Trail Making, Parts A & B
2. WAIS, verbal-performance IQ score difference
3. Bender Visual-Motor Gestalt using Canter Background Interference Procedure (Canter, 1976)

Administration Time: 75–90 minutes

Discrimination Ability: Using the scoring techniques detailed by the authors (also see Berg et al., 1987), 19 of 20 patients were correctly identified as having cortical impairment.

Barrett, Wheatley, and LaPlant Brief Screening Battery (Barrett, Wheatley, & LaPlant, 1981)

Tests:

1. 1967 Shipley-Hartford Scale
2. Wechsler Memory Scale (Russell 1975 Revision)
3. Name Writing Test (Reitan & Davison, 1974) with both dominant and nondominant hands
4. Reitan-Indiana Aphasia and Sensory-Perceptual Examinations (Wheeler & Reitan, 1962)
5. Spatial Relations Exam—Greek Cross, scored according to the criteria of Russell, Neuringer, and Goldstein (1970).
6. Trail Making Test, Parts A & B
7. Finger Tapping Test
8. Minnesota Multiphasic Personality Inventory-Form R (Hathaway & McKinley, 1967)

Administration Time: 90–120 minutes

Discriminative ability: 92.5% of brain-injured and suspected brain-damaged patients were successfully differentiated from non-brain-damaged individuals. When attempting to discriminate between confirmed brain-damaged and suspected brain-damaged individuals, 80.0 and 80.3% of these respective groups were correctly identified by the battery.

Abbreviated Halstead-Reitan Screening Battery—Version 1 (Golden, 1976)

Tests:

1. Trail Making, Parts A & B
2. Aphasia Screening Test
3. Seashore Rhythm Test (Seashore, Lewis, & Saeveit, 1960)
4. Speech Sound Perception Test
5. Stroop Color and Word Test

From the WAIS

6. Block Design
7. Digit Symbol
8. Similarities
9. Object Assembly

Administration Time: approximately 60 minutes

Discriminative Ability: Golden (1976) reported a hit rate of 71.9% with an amazingly high correct identification rate of 97% of individuals with left hemisphere damage. (It should be noted that there are two reported scoring approaches and that scoring for this screening approach can be complicated. The interested reader is referred to the Golden (1976) or Berg et al. (1987) for more information.)

Abbreviated Halstead-Reitan Screening Battery—Version 2

(Erickson, Calsyn, & Scheupbach, 1978; McNamara, Wechsler, & Munger, 1984)

Tests:

1. Trail Making - Parts A & B
2. Aphasia Screening Test (Russell et al. (1970) scoring)
3. WAIS Block Design
4. WAIS Digit Symbol

Administration Time: much less than one hour

Discriminative Ability: Using the following impairment rating approach, a rating equal to, or greater than 1.55, 84% of the original 90 cases were correctly classified into impaired and nonimpaired groups. McNamara, Wechsler, and Munger (1984) reported similar results.

Determination of Impairment Rating—

Step 1:

Total Impairment Score = 27.338

+ (1.043 × Trail Making A plus B Russell et al., 1970 rating)
+ (−0.655 × Block Design Scale Score)
+ (1.695 × Russell et al., 1970 Aphasia Error Score)
+ (−0.959 × Digit Symbol Scale Score)

Step 2: Average Impairment Rating = Total Impairment Score/12

REFERENCES

Altman, E., Comaty, J. E., Hedecker, D., Davis, J. M., Jobe, T. H., & Levy, D.L. (in press). Neuropsychological test deficits are associated with smooth pursuit eye movement impairment in affective disorders but not in schizophrenia. *International Journal of Clinical Neuropsychology.*

Army Individual Test. (1944). Manual of directions and scoring. Washington, DC: War Department, Adjutant General's Office.

Barrett, E. T., Jr., Wheatley, R. D., & LaPlant, R. J. (1981, February). *A brief clinical neuropsychologic screening battery: Statistical classification trials.* Paper presented at the 19th annual meeting of the International Neuropsychological Society, Atlanta.

Berg, E. A. (1948). A simple objective technique for measuring flexibility in thinking. *Journal of General Psychology, 39,* 15–22.

Berg, R., Franzen, M., & Wedding, D. (1987). *Screening for brain impairment: A manual for mental health practice,* New York: Springer Publishing Co.

Boll, T. J. (1981). The Halstead-Reitan Neuropsychological Battery. In S. B. Filskov & T. J. Boll (Eds.), *Handbook of clinical neuropsychology,* New York: Wiley-Interscience.

Botwinick, J. (1977). Intellectual abilities. In J. E. Birren & K. W. Schaie (Eds.), *Handbook of the psychology of aging* (pp. 580–605). New York: Van Nostrand Reinhold.

Canter, A. (1076). *The Canter Background Interference Procedure for the Bender-Gestalt Test.* Nashville, Tennessee: Counselor Recordings.

Chelune, G. J., & Baer, R. A. (1986). Development norms for the Wisconsin Card Scoring Test. *Journal of Clinical and Experimental Neuropsychology, 8,* 219–228.

Christensen, A. (1975). *Luria's Neuropsychological Investigation.* New York: Spectrum Press.

Davies, A. (1968). The influence of age on Trail Making performance. *Journal of Clinical Psychology, 24,* 96–100.

DeProspero, T., LoPresti, B., & Atkinson, T. (1983, December). *A screening system for neuropsychological testing.* Paper presented at the 17th annual convention of the Associated for Behavior Analysis/World Congress on Behavior Therapy, Washington, D.C.

Diller, L., Ben-Yishay, T., Gerstmann, L. J., Goodkin, R., Gordon, W., & Weinberg, J. (1974). *Studies in cognition and rehabilitation in hemiplegia* (Rehabilitation monograph No. 50). New York: New York University Medical Center Institute of Rehabilitation Medicine.

Diller, L., & Weinberg, J. (1977). Hemi-inattention in rehabilitation: The evolution of a rational remediation program. In E. A. Weinstein & R. P. Friedland (Eds.), *Advances in neurology* (Volume 18). New York: Raven Press.

Dodrill, C. B. (1978). The hand dynamometer as a neuropsychological measure. *Journal of Consulting and Clinical Psychology, 46,* 1432–1435.

Dunn, L. M., & Dunn, L. M. (1981). *Peabody Picture Vocabulary Test-Revised.* Circle Pines, Minnesota: American Guidance Service.

Eisensen, J. (1973). *Adult aphasia.* New York: Appleton-Century-Crofts.

Erickson, R. C., Calsyn, D. A., & Scheupbach, C. S. (1978). Abbreviating the Halstead-Reitan Neuropsychological Test Battery. *Journal of Clinical Psychology, 34,* 922–926.

Fisher, D. G., Sweet, J. J., & Pfaelzer-Smith, E. A. (1986). Influence of depression on repeated neuropsychological testing. *International Journal of Clinical Neuropsychology, 8,* 14–18.

Fogel, M. L. (1965). The Proverbs Test in the appraisal of cerebral disease. *Journal of General Psychology, 72,* 269–275.

Folstein, M. F., Folstein, M. F., & McHugh, P. R. (1975). Mini-mental state: A practical method for grading the cognitive state of patients for the clinician. *Journal of Psychiatric Research, 12,* 189–196.

Golden, C. J. (1975). A group version of the Stroop Color and Word Test. *Journal of Personality Assessment, 39,* 386–391.

Golden, C. J. (1976). The identification of brain damage by an abbreviated form of the Halstead-Reitan Neuropsychological Battery. *Journal of Clinical Psychology, 32,* 821–826.

Golden, C. J. (1978). *The Stroop Color and Word Test: a manual for clinical and experimental uses.* Chicago: Stoelting.

Golden, C. J., Purisch, A. D., & Hammeke, T. A. (1985). *Manual for the Luria-Nebraska Neuropsychological Battery: Forms I and II.* Los Angeles, California: Western Psychological Services.

Gorham, D. R. (1956). A Proverbs Test for clinical and experimental use. *Psychological Reports, 2,* (Supplement 1), 1–12.

Grant, D. A., & Berg, E. A. (1948). A behavioral analysis of degree of reinforcement and ease of shifting to new responses in a Weigl-type card-sorting problem. *Journal of Experimental Psychology, 38,* 401–411.

Halstead, W. C., & Wepman, J. M. (1959). The Halstead-Wepman Aphasia Screening Test. *Journal of Speech and Hearing Disorders, 14,* 9–15.

Hathaway, S. R., & McKinley, J. C. (1967). *Minnesota Multiphasic Personality Inventory.* New York: Psychological Corporation.

Heaton, R. K. (1981). *Manual for the Wisconsin Card Sorting Test.* Odessa, Florida: Psychological Assessment Resources.

Hooper, H. E. (1958). *Manual for the Hooper Visual Organization Test.* Los Angeles, California: Western Psychological Services.

Inglis, J. (1959). A paired associate test for use with elderly psychiatric patients. *Journal of Mental Science, 105,* 440–448.

Kaplan, E., Goodglass, H., & Weintraub, S. (1983). *The Boston Naming Test.* Philadelphia: Lea & Febiger.

Lezak, M. (1983). *Neuropsychological assessment* (Second Edition). New York: Oxford University Press.

McNamara, K. M., Wechsler, F. S., & Munger, M. P. (1984, August). *The Halstead-Reitan versus an abbreviated battery: Feasibility and limitations.* Paper presented at the annual convention of the American Psychological Association, Toronto, Ontario, Canada.

Mueller, J. (1984). The mental status examination. In H. H. Goldman (Ed.), *Review of general psychiatry* (pp.206–220). Los Altos, California: Lange.

Parsons, O. A. (1975). Brain damage in alcoholics: Altered states of unconsciousness. In M. M. Gross (Ed.), *Alcohol intoxication and withdrawal* (pp. 569–584). New York: Plenum.

Prigatano, G. P. (1977). Wechsler Memory Scale is a poor screening test for brain dysfunction. *Journal of Clinical Psychology, 33,* 77–777.

Prigatano, G. P. (1978). Wechsler Memory Scale: A selective review of the literature.

Journal of Clinical Psychology, 34, 816–832.

Randt, C. T., & Brown, E. R. (1983). *Randt Memory Test.* Bayport, New York: Life Science Associates.

Reitan, R. M. (undated). *Instructions and procedures for administering the Neuropsychological Test Battery used at the Neuropsychology Laboratory, Indiana University Medical Center:* Unpublished manuscript.

Reitan, R. M. (1958). Validity of the Trail Making Test as an indicator of organic brain damage. *Perceptual and Motor Skills, 8,* 271–276.

Reitan, R. M., & Davison, L. A. (1974). *Clinical neuropsychology: Current status and applications.* Washington, D.C.: Winston-Wiley.

Reitan, R. M., & Wolfson, D. (1985). *The Halstead-Reitan neuropsychological test battery: Theory and clinical interpretation.* Tucson, Arizona: Neuropsychology Press.

Rey, A. (1964). *L'examen clinique en psychologie* (English chapter summaries). Paris: Presses Universitaires de France.

Russell, E. W. (1975). A multiple scoring method for the assessment of complex memory functions. *Journal of Consulting and Clinical Psychology, 43,* 800–809.

Russell, E. W., Neuringer, C., & Goldstein, G. (1970). *Assessment of brain damage: A neuropsychological key approach.* New York: John Wiley-Interscience.

Seashore, C. E., Lewis, D., & Saeveit, D. L. (1960). *Seashore measures of musical talents* (revised edition). New York: Psychological Corporation.

Seretny, M. L., Dean, R. S., Gray, J. W., & Hartlage, L. (1986). The practice of clinical neuropsychology in the United States. *Archives of Clinical Neuropsychology, 1,* 5–12.

Sherrill, R. W. (1985). Comparison of three short forms of the Category Test. *Journal of Clinical and Experimental Neuropsychology, 7,* 231–238.

Spenser, M. P., & Folstein, M. F. (1985). The mini-mental state examination. In P. A. Keller & L. G. Ritt (Eds.), *Innovations in clinical practice: A source book* (Vol. 4, pp. 305–310. Sarasota, Florida: Professional Resource Exchange, Inc.

Strub, R. L., & Black, F. W. (1985). *The mental status examination in neurology* (Second Edition). Philadelphia: F. A. Davis.

Wechsler, D. A. (1945). A standardized memory scale for clinical use. *Journal of Psychology, 19,* 87–95.

Wechsler, D. A. (1981). *Manual for the Wechsler Adult Intelligence Scale-Revised.* New York: The Psychological Corporation.

Wechsler, D. A. (1987). *Manual for the Wechsler Memory Scale-Revised.* San Antonio, Texas: The Psychological Corporation.

Wedding, D. (1988). Screening for brain impairment: Beyond the mental status examination. In P. A. Keller & S. R. Heyman (Eds.), *Innovations in clinical practice: A source book* (Vol. 7, pp. 217–226). Sarasota, Florida: Professional Resource Exchange.

Wheeler, L., & Reitan, R. M. (1962). Presence and laterality of brain damage predicted from responses to a short aphasia screening test. *Perceptual and Motor Skills, 15,* 783–799.

Wysocki, J. J., & Sweet, J. J. (1985). The use of a brief neuropsychological screening battery to discriminate schizophrenia, brain-damaged, and normal medical patients. *International Journal of Clinical Neuropsychology, 7,* 40–44.

Chapter 3

Neuropsychological Assessment in the Childhood and Adolescent Years

Lawrence C. Hartlage and Betsy L. Williams

Neuropsychological assessment of children and adolescents differs from such assessment of adults on a number of dimensions. Neuropsychological assessment of children and adolescents may have implications for intervention and planning covering longer periods of time, since the life expectancy in this age group is normally quite long. Further, since self-concept and personality styles are in evolutionary stages during this period, neuropsychological assessment which helps support programs for maximizing the child's potential can exert a very important force on facilitating the child's development (Horton, 1974; Lazar & Darlington, 1978; Schweinhart & Weikart, 1980). Both these factors suggest the special importance of valid, reliable, conceptually meaningful approaches toward neuropsychological assessment during this segment of the life span.

Neuropsychological assessment in the childhood and adolescent years presents the clinician with a set of concepts and issues which are both more complex than different from those confronting clinicians who are involved with neuropsychological assessment of adults. In the assessment of central nervous system (CNS) function in adults, it is practical to group 5–10 year age ranges in normative or expectancy tables, and to have interpretive strategies which encompass these 5–10 year age ranges as being more or less functionally equivalent. With children, it is not possible to work in such crude age ranges. A three-year-old child must be assessed quite differently than an eight-year-old child, and quite different interpretive strategies must be applied to findings from evaluation of children at the ends of this five-year continuum.

The complexity surrounding normative expectancy sensitivity to relatively small age increments is compounded when considering the interpretation of discrepancy values. In an eight-year-old child with intelligence quotient 75, is motor function two years below age expectancy a sign of significant discrepancy, or within the normal range of expectancy based on mental ability level? For an adult, a "two-year age discrepancy" would not be a consideration in interpreting neuropsychological assessment findings. Further, children are qualitatively different from adults on a number of neuropsychologically relevant measures to the extent that an interpretive strategy valid for adults may be less valid with children, especially at younger ages. Such issues as rate or extent of frontal lobe maturation can play roles of differing importance in neuropsychological functions at different ages in children and adolescents. Adult interpretive strategies may be totally invalid for use with children who may use different strategies to produce apparently similar performances on given test items.

Finally, neuropsychological assessment in childhood and adolescence is more demanding in terms of both knowledge of age-appropriate developmental milestones and range of clinical skills than what is required for adequate neuropsychological assessment of adults. With an adult who has completed three years of apprentice training and worked successfully as an electrician, a finding of visuospatial memory in the borderline retarded range on neuropsychological assessment may be sufficient to raise the question of possible decline in functional level; answer to such a question could be approached by reviewing school records or other indices of prior mental functional level. A child six years of age with age-expectancy finding of borderline function on this same scale has no paper trail of school or vocational history. The clinical neuropsychologist must be able to assess the child's developmental milestones as part of the determination concerning whether this (borderline) level of function may represent a decline from prior levels.

In cases of suspected degenerative disorder, or in forensic cases wherein it is important to determine etiology of impairments found on neuropsychological assessment, the knowledge of appropriate neurodevelopmental skills and their relationship to neuropsychological assessment findings becomes a requirement additional to those required for adult assessment. The range of clinical skill requirements is greater in child neuropsychological assessment for the simple reason that, to a considerable extent, a different assessment battery may be required at different age levels, involving such age ranges as early childhood, preschool, primary grades, middle grades, and adolescence. Affective phenomena can be measured in adults with objective instruments like the Minnesota Multiphasic Personality Inventory (MMPI), but there are no comparable objective instruments for use with younger children. As a result, factors such as depression, which can obviously influence performance on some neuropsychological measures, needs to be recognized from clinical clues, and their potential influence on test scores evaluated without support of T scores or other empirical estimates of extent of depression.

Thus neuropsychological assessment in the childhood and early adolescent years, while representing a segment of the life-span with perhaps greatest potential for meaningful intervention, is more challenging in terms of conceptual issues. It is also more demanding in terms of range of both test and developmental knowledge. It is more difficult due to the child's having a narrower repertoire of abilities which can be assessed for purposes of developing a comprehensive neuropsychological profile based on objective test data.

Perhaps in recognition of the complexities included in neuropsychological assessment of children, the traditional approach used in such assessment has involved the downward extension of items used for neuropsychological assessment of adults. Venerable scales from the Halstead-Reitan Battery, such as the Categories Test or Trail Making Test, have been made simpler either by deleting difficult categories or shortening the length of the test. Similarly, the children's version of the Lucia-Nebraska Neuropsychological Battery is a shorter version of the Adult Battery. Whether the adaptation of adult battery for use with children was accomplished by intuitively simplifying the task, or empirically determining which (adult) items could not be processed by children, the apparent assumption inherent in such modification was that an adult model of neuropsychological assessment was equally appropriate for use with children.

In recent years it has been argued that children are not just small adults. The utilization of assessment models developed for use with adults, no matter how well validated with adults, may not be sufficiently sensitive to capture the full range of variability of neuropsychological organization found among children of differing ages (Hartlage & Telzrow, 1986). Thus, while there is no consensus concerning the best approach to neuropsychological assessment of children and adolescents, there is a need for such assessment to serve as the basis for appropriate intervention and planning for the children involved. Because the need for such assessment will typically have slightly different foci at different ages, the focus of this chapter follows the sorts of neuropsychological assessment issues common to given ages, from early childhood through early adolescence. Obviously, some issues, such as head injury, can occur at any given age; while others, such as learning disorders, may not arise much before school age, but may continue throughout adolescence. In cases where a given issue or problem is likely to appear at more than one age interval, it will be mentioned at each age level in which a different assessment or interpretive strategy may be required.

NEUROPSYCHOLOGICAL ASSESSMENT IN THE PRESCHOOL YEARS

Perhaps reflecting the adult assessment origins of human clinical neuropsychology, applications to children in this youngest age segment have tended to be the latest in development. One of the earliest papers addressing preschool neuropsychological assessment was at an International Neuropsychological Society meeting in the present decade (Telzrow & Hartlage, 1981), making preschool neuropsychological assessment the youngest focus area both in patient age and duration of focused clinical and research interest. That the topic of preschool neuropsychology is now recognized is to some extent reflected in its being the topic of both invited and regular chapters in books dealing with psychological and educational issues of children (e.g., Hartlage & Telzrow, 1982; 1983a; 1983b; 1986) and as an invited topical paper in the National Association of School Psychologists' *Preschool Interests* (Hartlage, 1987).

The sorts of issues or questions which preschool neuropsychological assessment may address are essentially the same as those involving older patients: i.e., to what extent, if any, are problems attributable to neurological impairment; and what are the appropriate and meaningful interventions. Assessment differs on a number of variables, relative to both conceptual and methodological factors which require unique strategies for assessment of children in this age range.

It is especially important that the neuropsychologist working with very young children be at least moderately knowledgeable concerning the biological components of behavior in early years of life. In premature infants, for example, the calculation of the child's age, based on gestational age vs. chronological age, can produce quite different estimates of level of mental development; when determining the child's age at time of examination both such age measures should be included (Hartlage, Aziz, Mains, & Noonan, 1981; Hartlage & Stovall, 1980). Presence of physical limitations on performance of motor tasks and depression are examples of conditions which can affect the child's performance on early are neuropsychological assessment measures, in ways more global and difficult to detect than would be the case with assessment of older patients.

Since depression cannot be fully evaluated by objective behavior scale (like the MMPI) or conversation with young children, knowledge of such possible correlates as failure to thrive, retarded weight relative to age, or other biological phenomena may be needed to assess possible presence of depression as an influence on neuropsychological test performance. Limitations on performance of motor tasks, such as might result from spinal dysraphisms or mild cerebral palsy, may suggest false positive symptoms of global developmental delay to the child neuropsychologist. The neuropsychologist must be sensitive to the relationships between reflexes, or gross and fine motor function of given extremities as clues to the meaning of given types of impaired performance on specific motor tasks (Hartlage & Telzrow, 1982).

History and Observation

History and observation, while important components of the neuropsychological examination of patients at any age, are especially important in the early preschool years. Since the young child's repertoire of objectively measurable behaviors is much smaller than that of an adult or even an older child, those indices of development which can be determined through non-test procedures are much more crucial for formatting a comprehensive diagnostic picture. Some of the historical components with special attention in this age group include:

1. *Prenatal and perinatal information.* Gestational age-chronological age discrepancies in the case of premature infants can influence developmental/expectancy level quotients at early ages. Significant illness or trauma sustained by the mother during given stages of pregnancy may provide clues to the presence of given types of problems. Duration or conditions of labor can provide clues to potential anoxia or subsequent motor problem. Extended periods of separation from mother in the neonatal period, such as might be precipitated by sustained neonatal intensive care in hospital, may prevent normal mother-child bonding and introduce a personal/social phenomenon to be considered.
2. *Neonatal information.* Seizures, infections, intraventricular hemorrhage, or related insults to the central nervous system can have significant implications for brain-behavior relationships in the very young child (Hartlage, Stovall, & Hartlage, 1980; Hynd, Hartlage, & Noonan, 1984; Klonoff, Low, & Clark, 1977). Medical disorders of nonneurological origin can be associated with generalized mental development delay, in much the same configuration as might be found in diffuse neurological impairment, and so need to be taken into consideration (Hartlage, 1980).
3. *Developmental information.* Ages at which a child reaches developmental milestones in motor or language spheres are extremely important factors in differentiating whether any neuropsychological deficits found on examination are acquired or developmental in nature. Comparison with sibl-

ings on these same milestones can be one approach to helping rule out possible sociocultural factors in developmental anomalies. Occult traumatic head injury is not uncommon during the early years of life: young children may be dropped or otherwise injured by siblings or babysitters who are afraid to acknowledge their negligence, and covert child abuse is another etiology which needs to be considered in the neuropsychological assessment of young children. It is during this post-neonatal period that familial socioeconomic and educational variables can exert a special influence on rate and type of mental development (Hartlage, 1980; 1981a; Hartlage, Catterton, Noonan, & Proefrock, 1982; Hartlage, DeFilippis, Noonan, & Shaw, 1982; Hartlage, DeFilippis, Noonan, Shaw, & Snow, 1982), and careful attention must be paid in relating these factors to findings of psychomotor instruments when making neuropsychological interpretations.

4. To some extent related to developmental history, some items of *family history* can be relevant to the understanding of test data concerning the neuropsychological status of the child in this age period. If an older sibling, or a parent, had a history of late development of verbal or motor skills but is unimpaired in later years, positive findings of delay on these variables in the child may relate to genetic rather than disease or traumatic causes. Developmental disorders such as dyslexia may have a strong familial pattern, and may present, in preschool years with less specific patters of deficit. Problems such as hyperactivity in siblings can be of relevance for helping resolve the issue of whether increased activity levels in the patient may reflect CNS damage, or family behavioral/childrearing patterns. For this same purpose, comparing the child with siblings in terms of developmental milestones can be contributory. Positive family history for syncopal episodes, seizure disorders, motor tics, tremor, or related neurological disorders are obviously relevant at this as in any age, for helping consider alternative neuropsychological interpretations of test findings.

Observation, while clearly an important component of the pediatric neurological examination, tends to be much less a part of the pediatric neuropsychological examination, even though data from this source can help in the identification of a number of underlying neuropsychological disorders (e.g., Hartlage & Telzrow, 1986; Rosenberg & Weller, 1973; U. S. Department of Health, Education, and Welfare, 1968; Waldrop & Halverson, 1971; Waldrop, Pederson, & Bell, 1968). Although visualization of the ventricular system is necessary for definitive diagnosis, hydrocephalus typifies a developmental neurological disorder in which observation may suggest a CNS condition. Observation of the child's height, weight, and occipital-frontal circumference (OFC) of the head can suggest not only hydrocephaly or microcephaly, but also general developmental state. Neuropsychological test data placing a young child at the 2nd percentile on given neurocognitive tasks may suggest different interpretations in a child at the 2nd percentile on height, weight, and OFC than for a child around the 50th percentile on these physical developmental variables.

Since with children in the preschool age it is typically much more difficult to obtain formal test data in a structured examination format, the data from observations can assume proportionately greater importance than such observations may provide at later ages. Careful clinical observation can suggest clues not only relevant to general developmental level, but also to lateralized sensory or motor problems. Alertness to whether the child attends or responds better to visual or verbal stimuli on the right or left sides can provide indicators of unilateral sensory problems. Observation of size of right vs. left upper and lower extremities, whether walking is straight or tends to veer to one side, and whether one hand is used more for transfer to the other can all suggest motor asymmetries. The clinician need not wait passively to observe these sorts of phenomena. By systematically presenting stimuli to one vs. another side, these observations can be a part of the interactive observational process throughout all stages of the examination. Watching the child ascend/descend steps or attempt to put together Lego blocks may be the sorts of observational clues to lower or upper extremity motor asymmetry which can help in the interpretation of more standardized test data.

One relatively powerful neuropsychological assessment approach with young children involves comparisons of the functional efficiency of the two sides of the body. Of course, as with adults, it is necessary to separate functions, mediated contralaterally at the level of the cerebral cortex, from those functions innervated ipsilaterally by lower central or peripheral nervous systems loci. Given attention to these caveats concerning the necessity for pretest appraisal, it is worth reviewing some of the assessment devices or procedures which can help evaluate the comparative functional efficiencies of the contralateral cerebral hemispheres in very young children.

One of the most sensitive of these approaches involves the measurement of reaction time and measurement time. A reaction time device of the type developed by Jensen (1980), which has been found to relate to such neurologically relevant measures as evoked potential (Jensen, Schafer, & Crinella, 1981), and psychometrically relevant measures such as IQ and academic achievement (Jensen, 1980; Vernon, 1981; 1985), have been found to be useful with preschoolers as young as 2 years of age (Telzrow, 1983). Such a procedure allows the comparison of reaction time to stimuli presented to the right vs. to the left, as well as providing opportunity to compare movement times of right vs. left hands. Other reaction timing devices such as the Lafayette (Model 63035) visual choice reaction time apparatus are available commercially, and can provide highly reliable measurement (Hamsher & Benton, 1977).

For those clinicians or researchers who do not have access to such refined measurement instrumentation, tests such as the pegboard task from the Bayley Scale can be used to compare motor speed by having the child complete the pegboard using first one and then the other hand. Tests such as the Binet cube stacking can be compared for right vs. left hand performance. In the drawing or copying of simple figures, as in the human figure drawings of older preschoolers, systematic hemispace (sensory) neglect or (motor) asymmetry can provide clues to possible developmental or acquired asymmetry of function (Telzrow & Hartlage, 1983). Since with the young preschool child much of the developmental assessment depends on motor skills, it is important to avoid false positive errors in classifying as retarded those young children with motor delay (Kearsley, 1981). Conversely, in many cases of neurologic impairment in young children, delays may be found in a wide range of skill areas (Hartlage & Telzrow, 1986); unique care needs to be taken in this age range to separate the effects of diffuse neurological impairment from the impairments of developmental delay of non-neurological origin.

The complexities of this area have been recognized for many years, since early research demonstrated that unilateral cerebral insult occurring at very young ages may not present with the same lateralizing findings as might occur following later age insult (Fitzhugh, Fitzhugh, & Reitan, 1962). One clue to neurologically determined delay may be found in the developmental profiles from such scales as the Minnesota Child Development Inventory (MCDI), whose 320-item, parent-completed, forced-choice format provides developmental age scores for seven domains, as well as a total score. Uneven levels of development among the various domains may provide the initial clue that more detailed investigation of possible neurological etiology may be contributory to an accurate diagnosis. In cases where low parental reading level may preclude their valid completion of the MCDI, the Adaptive Behavior Scales (VABS) interview format can be substituted, although this scale provides standard scores for only four major domains.

With older and younger children, both the comparison of language and nonlanguage abilities and the unilateral sensory and motor abilities can provide useful information concerning neuropsychological status. In younger children, however, the measurement approaches and instructions differ. Perhaps the main difference between assessment of young preschoolers and older age children involves the dimension of flexibility vs. standardization. While neuropsychological clinicians recognize the value of standardization in test administration, those who venture into the challenging world of assessment of young children must recognize the range of deviations from standardized administration which is compatible with valid data collection. They must be capable of judging which interpretive strategies may need to be modified to deal with the data obtained from less than standardized administration.

Such behaviors as refusal to take a test or test item are not uncommon in this age range, and the examiner must be willing to do such evaluation as the child will permit in the sequence in which the child is willing to perform, and sometimes for the duration which the child will address to a given test item. Thus the examiners must abe prepared for a test or subtest to be partially completed then refused. They will have to judge whether reintroduction at a later stage in the examination will be accepted by the child and, if accepted, how such interruption may affect validity or interpretation. It is often not possible for the examiner to complete the battery of tests that had been intended, so that flexibility in substituting other tests or in dealing with less than the hoped for test data may be real considerations. When feasible, arranging for more than one examination session, and ending the first session with the use of a task the child enjoys, may help increase the likelihood that a complete data base can be collected.

Moving from approaches to instruments suited to this age range, classification by use may be of help to those planning to work with children in this age group. Due to resistance, distractibility, or other causes, a child may not be able or willing to cooperate on a given test, making it necessary to have in mind alternative scales measuring the same general ability. For general cognitive ability, the Bayley, McCarthey, Kaufman, Leiter, Woodcock Johnson, Stanford Binet, or even Wechsler Preschool scales may be appropriate, depending on the child's age and developmental level. Basic language skills can be evaluated by: the Receptive-Expressive Language Scale, Language Sample of 50 Utterances, Preschool Language Scale, Clinical Evaluation of Language Functions, Revised Peabody Picture Vocabulary Test, Expressive One Word Picture Vocabulary Test, Test of Early Language Development, or Test for Auditory Comprehension of Language. (Publishers for these scales and those mentioned in the remainder of this section on preschool assessment are cited in Hartlage and Telzrow, 1986, pp. 114–115.) Motor ability may be measured by: the motor domain scales of MCDI or VABS, or Battele Developmental Inventory, with Bayley Scales of Infant Development, the Developmental Test of Visual Motor Integration, finger tapping (Telzrow & Hartlage, 1983), grip strength (Reitan & Davidson, 1974), or pegboard task done with either hand (Annett, 1973). Sensory ability may be assessed by the Motor Free Visual Perception Test by symbol writing (Hartlage, 1982), hand-face test (Telzrow & Hartlage, 1983), visual field comparisons via reaction time, or dichotic listening measures adapted for very young children (Lewkowicz & Turkewitz, 1982).

When combined with history and behavioral observations, such data sources will normally suffice to sample a sufficient range of behaviors to permit interpretive statements concerning the neuropsychological functional status of the young preschool child. For the somewhat older preschool child, discrete scales from existing batteries have been postulated for use at different ages, and may be of interest to the clinician interest in an abbreviated battery type approach for neuropsychological assessment in preschool years (Hartlage & Telzrow, 1981).

SCHOOL AGE YEARS

Although neurological disorders and neuropsychological problems of numerous types are present throughout all childhood ages, some such disorders and problems tend to have greater incidence or implications for the child during certain life stages. Among school age children, neuropsychological deficit from traumatic head injury, and problems related to developmental learning disorders and seizures can present special diagnostic challenges, and will be addressed separately.

Traumatic Head Injury

Traumatic head injury represents perhaps the highest neuropsychological risk phenomenon in this age group (Lezak, 1983). With an estimated ten million head injuries occurring each year in the United States, and the large percentage of these head injuries occurring in the school age years, there is a statistical likelihood that each school age child may suffer head injury (Hartlage, in press).

Among certain groups the incidence may be greater than others: Barth and his coworkers (Barth, Alves, Ryan, Macciocchi, Rimel, Jane, & Nelson, 1989) have found up to a 40% head injury rate due to football injuries alone. While in cases of more severe head injury there may be longer term problems involving social adjustment and transition into adult life (Kriel, Krach, Bergland, & Panser, 1988), the majority of cases of head injury are comparatively mild, to the extent that they are likely to go untreated and even undetected unless fairly careful neuropsychological evaluation is done (e.g., Caveness, 1977; Hartlage, 1984a).

Identification of head injury as being etiological in poor academic performance or impaired social adjustment in school age children can be important for a number of reasons. The identification of specific neuropsychological substrates of academic difficulties can be an important first step toward helping the child receive appropriate academic intervention. For behavioral or social adjustment problems secondary to CNS insult, the identification of their etiology can provide the therapist or educator with realistic goals based on the child's (potentially) limited adaptive capacity, and help identify those treatment approaches and behavior management strategies most complementary to the child's situation. In cases where liability may be involved, as in auto torts, the identification of the neurologic bases of the child's impairments can be crucial in helping the child receive damages or compensation. For academic planning and career choice decisions, knowledge of the status of intact and impaired CNS functional systems can help avoid frustration and failure from injudicious interventions choices and help enhance the likelihood of realistic treatment choices and goals.

Testing considerations for children with head injury involve likelihood of mental fatigability and decreased stamina, and possible confounding of psychometric profiles by variable or decreased attention span. Memory is likely to be affected, therefore special attention to assessment of various aspects of memory (e.g., short vs. long term; verbal vs. visuospatial content) is important. Fortunate from the standpoint of neuropsychological assessment, the child of school age is typically experienced in taking tests, and also has (depending on age and mental ability level) a fair repertoire of "old" acquired knowledge, which can be assessed by academic skill measures such as the Wide Range Achievement Tests or similar scales which have good norm-referenced data bases. Comparison of findings on these tests with prior non-referenced school achievement scales can provide clues concerning how such skills may have been compromised. The comparison of such skill levels with current intellectual and memory abilities can suggest the extent to which current mental functioning may be compromised from prior levels. A child whose current academic skill levels in fourth grade are at grade placement expectancy (i.e., with standard scores around 100) but whose current IQ is around 80 has arguably suffered a fair amount of decline in presumed mental ability; normally a child with a current IQ at the 80 level would not be expected to have maintained extended academic performance at the level of expectancy 20 points higher. If some sort of litigation is involved, as in the case of car accident, a loss of this magnitude can have rather striking economic implications. A loss in the range of 10 IQ points for a child in the average IQ range could rule out the child's potential for successful performance of more than 6000 job categories, including many which have high projected growth rates in the next decade (Lees-Haley, 1987).

The timing of tests within the evaluation session needs to take into account the possible effects of stamina on test performance. Tests which depend on speed (e.g., reaction time) or sustained concentration (e.g., Symbol Digit, Digit Symbol) may be moved to early portions of the session, while tests of personality (e.g., Rorschach) or fund of information (e.g., Information, Vocabulary subscales or word recognition/reading) may be deferred until later in the examination. When feasible, testing on more than one occasion can help obviate the effects of decreased mental stamina on test scores.

On occasion, it may be necessary to terminate some tests in order to help prevent frustration, decreased motivation, or anger from contaminating test results. In the cases of tests like the Category Test from the Halstead-Reitan Neuropsychological Battery, for example, the child may be confronted repeatedly with feedback indicative of failure, and may become resistive, angry, or extremely frustrated over inability to solve the conceptual task required for successful test performance. This can affect rapport and subsequent test performance. In such cases, discontinuance after the child has reached or exceeded the error score considered necessary for meeting classificatory criteria can help keep the child's interest and motivational levels operative for subsequent test performance. Obviously in cases wherein the child is experiencing frustration, extra encouragement and support can help alleviate the child's frustration without invalidating test results.

The choice of tests for use in neuropsychological assessment with this age group is relatively broad, since well standardized and normed measures of a wide range of neuropsychologically relevant abilities are available. Indeed, surveys of practicing neuropsychologists have fairly consistently revealed a diversity of approaches (e.g., Hartlage & Telzrow, 1980; Hartlage, Chelune, & Tucker, 1981; Seretny, Dean, Gray, & Hartlage, 1986), ranging from a use of standardized battery such as the Luria-Nebraska and Halstead-Reitan, to an idiosyncratic admixture of diverse discrete tests in many combinations and permutations. In this regard, matters such as examiner experience with given tests, specific abilities to be assessed, age/mental level of the child, time available for examination and purpose of the neuropsychological assessment may all exert different influences in given situations. These may make it difficult to identify an absolute "best" test battery or collection of tests which will be equally responsive to all questions or amenable for use across all ages with the school age child. It is the authors' premise that the individual examiner will likely do the best child neuropsychological evaluation by assessing all relevant aspects of neuropsychological function with the tests, observations and assessment procedures with which he or she is more familiar (whether those measures are from a standardized battery or an individually assembled collection of different tests).

It is important to remember that the neurobehavioral sequelae of head injury in children can be more devastating than the neurocognitive sequelae. This is the case insofar as effects on longer term adjustment are concerned, whatever the tests used for neurocognitive assessment following childhood head injury.While it may be possible to successfully modify academic or vocational planning to take into account reduced mental ability levels, it is much more difficult for schools, peers, and families to accept someone who is angry, agitated, cross, depressed, easily upset, impatient, irritable, and short tempered. However, those behaviors have been found to occur in a majority of cases ($p < .01$), following head injury, among individuals who had not been that way prior to the head injury (Lewis & Hartlage, 1986; Hartlage & Williams, 1989). Whatever the assessment procedure, be it self-report, projective report by others, objective personality assessment, or other means, a behavioral assessment following head injury is necessary for completing the neurodiagnostic picture of the child.

Learning Disability

Learning disability is increasingly recognized as a condition with neuropsychological substrates, and as a condition in which comprehensive neuropsychological assessment can be of value for the development of appropriate intervention strategies. At least since the enactment and implementation of Public Law 94–142 (Cohen, Semmes, & Guralnick, 1979), the search for processes involve, at least informally, the sorts of investigative procedures, techniques, and tools traditionally considered to be within the realm of child clinical neuropsychology. Training in neuropsychology, typically through continuing education programs provided by professional associations and by practicing neuropsychologists, has been popular among school psychologists who evaluate children with learning disabilities and clinical psychologists whose practice includes children with suspected learning disabilities. While there has been controversy concerning the actual criteria necessary for the establishment of a diagnosis of learning disability (e.g., Algozzine & Ysseldyke, 1981; 1986), there has been comparatively little question that neuropsychological assessment can make important contributions toward helping understand the child with symptoms of learning disability, and relating the child's intact abilities to an educational program (Hartlage & Telzrow, 1983c; 1986).

To help put the role of neuropsychology as it relates to learning disability in perspective, a brief overview of the conceptual basis of learning disability may be helpful. In essence, the concept of learning disability is based on a discrepancy between a child's ability (e.g., measured by IQ test) and academic achievement (e.g., as measured by achievement test). In order to meet requirements for classification as learning disabled, there must be a certain magnitude of discrepancy between "ability" and "achievement" (the magnitude may vary with educational system and with time), in the absence of sensory impairments (e.g., reduced vision or hearing) or motivational problems. Thus the very criteria necessary for classification as learning disabled tend to exclude many or even most factors other than central nervous system dysfunction, to the point where it is not unreasonable to consider learning disability to be almost synonymous with neuropsychological impairment.

A major problem with such a discrepancy formula for determining learning disability involves the possibility of false positives for children who have moved often or who have subtle home problems, unknown to school personnel and unadmitted by parents, which may be affecting achievement. The possibility of false negatives exists for children who have had intense tutoring or have learned to compensate just enough not to have the "magic" number of standard score points difference to qualify for learning disability services. Another problem with the discrepancy formula is that it tends to penalize children with dull normal IQ, their baseline IQ level is sufficiently low that a discrepancy, between it and achievement quotient, which is sufficient for classification as learning disabled, would require that they be almost hopelessly behind academically before being eligible for special help.

A final problem with discrepancy requirements relates to age. It is difficult for a child in first or even second grade to be sufficiently discrepant to meet criteria. The opportunity for early intervention is typically precluded by the operational aspects of the criteria necessary for the diagnosis of learning disability.

A neuropsychological approach to the assessment of learning disability can help sort out external factors, which may be affecting achievement, from cognitive processing deficits, which may be affecting learning. A simple example of how this might be approached would be the inclusion of two quick and informal neuropsychological procedures when assessing a child. Halstead's finger tapping test and fingertip writing test assess contralateral posterior frontal and anterior parietal areas of the brain, respectively. Upon administration, should these tests reveal asymmetry or lateralizing effects, then the examiner could formulate hypotheses as to the nature of the problem and begin to test them out against other test findings with lateralizing implications. It is not likely that a recent divorce, frequent moves, unstable home environment, or other situational factors would cause the lateralizing effects which might be picked up by careful neuropsychological examination.

Extensive testing for specific strengths and weaknesses relative to the brain-behavior relationships also has a most valuable product; the results are easily translatable to educational programming in the form of individual educational plans (IEP's). Not only is the academic deficit documented but the probable reason for it is determined, in a manner which should facilitate remediation. Perhaps of greatest benefit to the child, a neuropsychological assessment approach can help avoid the frustrations and failure engendered by well-intentioned efforts to remediate the weakness of focusing educational attention on the central processes which are impaired. This teaching to dead tissue approach popular with educators is replaced by neuropsychological determination of the child's most intact processing, storage, and retrieval skills and building the educational intervention around them (Hartlage & Reynolds, 1981).

To a considerable extent, the actual test instruments required for learning disability classification are mandated in fairly specific fashion by the public school systems. A typical minimum assessment battery required by schools in most localities involves measures of intelligence, achievement, and psychomotor or perceptuomotor function. Usually, this will include the age appropriate Wechsler scale, an achievement battery such as the Wide Range, and a design copying test such as the Bender Gestalt or Beery Visual Motor Integration scales. While there has been interest in assessment of learning disabled (or suspected learning disabled) children with formal neuropsychological batteries such as the Halstead-Reitan (D'Amato, Gray, & Dean, 1987; Strom, Gray, Dean, & Fisher, 1987), or Luria-Nebraska Children's scales (Snow, Hynd, Hartlage, & Grant, 1983), such batteries typically add to or complement rather than replace the minimum battery required by most schools. Therefore, they have a number of practical limitations for routine use in learning disability evaluation. The addition of specific neuropsychological measures related to lateralizing sensory and motor functions can be an important step toward development of a data base with potential neuropsychological implications, when added to the intelligence, psychomotor, and skill measures in the context of a good developmental history and careful observation during examination. This represents one parsimonious approach toward meeting school system requirements while screening for neuropsychological problems in a time efficient approach (Hartlage & Telzrow, 1986).

Seizure Disorders

While by no means confined to school age children, seizure disorders probably exert their most deleterious effect during childhood in the school age years. The social, cognitive, and psychological implications of seizures during the school years intrude into essentially all aspects of the child's life, especially in cases where the seizures are poorly controlled. Further, early age of onset is generally related to greater impairment of cognitive-intellectual abilities (Dikmen, Matthews, & Harley, 1977), to significantly increased levels of dependency (Hartlage & Offutt, 1972) and depressed communicative and social skills (Hartlage & Green, 1971), making epilepsy in the school age child a particularly vexatious problem. Estimates of the incidence of epilepsy in the United States suggest that up to a million children in this country may be affected (Hartlage & Telzrow, 1984).

While no definitive research has determined the relative effects on the child resultant from the different types of the epilepsies, it seems probable that the generalized tonic-clonic type (formerly referred to as grand mal) seizure is more upsetting to the child and frightening to the child's peers. The potential for urinary or bladder incontinence, physical harm, and post-ictal confusion or lethargy must be a cause for concern to the child with epilepsy. Peers commonly reject or ridicule the child who has had such seizures in their presence. While usually less violent, the partial complex (formerly often called temporal lobe or psychomotor) seizure pattern may cause the child to be seen as "weird" by peers, and again be a source of possible rejection or ridicule. The absence type (formerly called petit mal) seizure, while less striking in manifestation, can give the child the appearance of being "spaced out" or "out of it" during attacks. Although typically brief, the attacks may occur hundreds or thousands of times each day.

In addition to the obvious risk of social problems from seizures, sustained attention or concentration on school matter may be limited by the seizure, by the underlying brain pathology which causes the seizure, or by a combination. Whatever the type of seizure, the medication commonly used for its control can further impair mental alertness and even impede mental development (Camfield, Chaplin, Doyle, Shapiro, Cummings, & Camfield, 1979; Hartlage & Hartlage, in press). Indeed, since most children with epilepsy who are seen for neuropsychological evaluation are likely to be receiving anticonvulsant medication, the very results of neuropsychological evaluation need to be interpreted with caution due to the selective effects of anticonvulsant medication on specific measures (Hartlage, 1981b; 1984b). In general, the barbiturates (and drugs which metabolize as barbiturates, such as Mysolene) tend to impair speeded motorperformance (e.g., rate of finger oscillation, reaction time) and psychomotor function (i.e., Digit Symbol, Symbol Digit), and attention/memory (e.g., Digit Span) to an extent greater than most other neurocognitive abilities; although, it has also been reported that full scale IQ in children with epilepsy has been reported as being up to a standard deviation lower than average (Whitehouse, 1971). It is not clear whether this lowered IQ in epilepsy may have reflected functional deficits of impaired brain tissue or the sedative effects of anticonvulsant medication. This issue is further clouded by findings that, with increased seizure frequency, there is a corresponding decreased mental ability level in adults (Dikmen & Matthews, 1977).

Neuropsychological assessment in the child with epilepsy, perhaps unlike many other conditions, is rarely done for the purpose of establishing a diagnosis. Typically, the child with epilepsy who is referred for neuropsychological evaluation is already known to have epilepsy, and the evaluation may be requested more for purposes of establishing a baseline or for evaluation of neurocognitive and neurobehavioral status relative to therapy than for diagnostic purposes. In a sense perhaps this is fortunate, in that there does not appear to be a neuropsychological pattern or profile which is either diagnostic of or unique to epilepsy. There is much more homogeneity among children with given types of seizure disorders, than among children with epilepsy in general, in terms of intellectual deficit. The greatest deficit is more common in children with generalized tonic-clonic seizures than among children with absence type seizures, although there is overlap among seizure types even on this general IQ dimension (Hartlage & Hartlage, in press). Further, findings on even comprehensive neuropsychological assessment of children with epilepsy do not suggest much ability to differentiate, either between children with and without epilepsy or among children with different types of epilepsy (Farwell, Dodrill, & Batzell, 1985; Reitan & Davidson, 1974).

In light of the sensitivity of such neuropsychological measures as reaction time, memory, psychomotor function, and motor dexterity to anticonvulsant medications, the inclusion of measures of these functions into a neuropsychological evaluation of the child with epilepsy can be important for two purposes. First, of course, is to help the clinician partial out those diagnosed findings which vary with serum anticonvulsant levels from those which may more likely reflect dysfunctional brain tissue. Perhaps of more practical consequence, by relating performance of given test items to anticonvulsant titrations, the neuropsychologist can assist the neurologist to achieve optimal seizure control with minimal side effects by relating neurocognitive status to anticonvulsant medication tritation. Thus the neuropsychologist helps the child attempt schoolwork without the additional limitations imposed by sedation from too high levels of medication.

There are, of course, many other problems involving the child of school age for which neuropsychological involvement can be helpful. Hopefully, by introduction of some concepts and research findings relevant to neuropsychological involvement in three of the more common problems in which neuropsychologists are likely to be involved, this may stimulate extrapolation to the diverse other areas in which neuropsychological contributions to school age children have not yet been so well developed.

ADOLESCENT YEARS

Adolescent years continue to be at years of risk for head injury as a new phenomenon, and for continued manifestations of problems resultant from learning or seizure disorders. The focus of neuropsychological assessment in this age range tends to move from academic planning toward career planning. There is a corresponding shift from interest in matching the child's neuropsychological status to academic instruction toward matching the adolescent's intact abilities to curricular and job training goals in which the value of the intact abilities is most likely to be maximized.

Independent of the level of residual mental ability, the basis for adolescent's future rule out considerations of which career choices are precluded by neuropsychological limitations, while increasing focus on goals compatible with intact abilities. An adolescent with very high verbal ability but very poor visuospatial abilities would probably not do well as a neurosurgeon, but could possibly expect to succeed in another branch of medicine like psychiatry. An adolescent with epilepsy who had good manual dexterity might well be suited to a career in crafts or assembling, but unsuited to work as a steelworker working at heights. As at any age, a neuropsychological evaluation oriented toward identifying strengths is helpful; in adolescent years it can be extremely helpful for purposes of helping avoid pitfalls resultant from pursuit of goals which are not realistically within the individual's repertoire.

Many years ago, Halstead determined that, by somewhere around the age of 14, adolescents generally processed information in ways indistinguishable from adults. He concluded that from about that age onward the same neuropsychological assessment procedures used with adults would be appropriate for use with adolescents. Since that time there has been no compelling reason to doubt his conclusions. There is, however, one aspect of neuropsychological functioning in adolescence beyond the age of 14 which differs from that of adulthood, even though its effect on neuropsychological test performance may not be egregious. Specifically the qualitative aspects of performance related to maturation of the frontal lobes, perhaps most easily measured by ability to deal with complex relations among obstructions (Fischer & Silvern, 1985), continue to evolve, with different rates for boys and girls (Waber, 1976). Behavioral observations suggest that girls may reach mature levels of neuropsychological functioning by late teenage years, while boys may be beyond the teen years before such full maturation of frontal lobe function is reached, and there is evidence of some similarity among longer term impairment patterns among youngsters in the 14-18 year age range compatible with this observation (Kriel, Krach, Bergland, & Panser, 1988). This issue is worth consideration in situations involving head injury among the adolescent years, since damage to frontal cortical areas may not become fully manifest until the early adult years. It is possible to become falsely optimistic over a lack of strongly positive neuropsychological findings in an adolescent suffering head injury, and conclude no impairment has occurred; but follow-up over several years will often reveal that the apparently normal adolescent never quite seemed to reach full levels of functional maturity. Comments from parents, employers, or friends are often along the lines of "he never quite seemed to get it together," or "I don't know whether he'll ever really grow up," following head injury in adolescence; this makes the phenomenon worth keeping in mind when evaluating head trauma in this age range with an eye toward developing prognostic statements.

CONCLUSION

Neuropsychology has been recognized as a specific scientific and clinical specialty for only a short period, with refinements involving school age children developed for an even shorter period, and with applications to preschool children still being in its infancy. The excitement of discovery in a new science is tempered by a need for caution while travelling new and unexplored ground. It is our hope that this chapter has, in some small way, helped capture the sense of excitement and challenge and encouraged the reader to extrapolate to new areas while keeping in touch with the realities of research and its implications for practice.

REFERENCES

Algozzine, B., & Ysseldyke, J. E. (1981). Special education services for normal children: Better safe than sorry? *Exceptional Children, 48,* 238–243.

Algozzine, B., & Ysseldyke, J. E. (1986). The future of the LD field: Screening and diagnosis. *Journal of Learning Disabilities, 19*(7), 394–398.

Annett, M. (1973). Laterality of childhood hemiplegia and the growth of speech and language. *Cortex, 9,* 4–33.

Barth, J. T., Alves, W. M., Ryan, T. V., Macciocchi, S. N., Rimel, R. W., Jane, J. A., & Nelson, W. E. (1989). Mild head trauma in sports: Neuropsychological sequelae and recovery of function. In H. Levin, A. Benton, & H. Eisenberg (Eds.), *Mild head injury.* Cambridge: Oxford Press.

Camfield, C. S., Chaplin, S., Doyle, A. B., Shapiro, S. H., Cummings, C., & Camfield, P. R. (1979). Side effects of phenobarbitol in toddlers: Behavioral and cognitive aspects. *Journal of Pediatrics, 95*(3), 361–365.

Caveness, W. (1977). Incidence of cranio-cerebral trauma in the United States. *Transactions of the American Neurological Association, 102,* 136–138.

Cohen, S., Semmes, M., & Guralnick, M. J. (1979). Public law 94–142 and the education of preschool handicapped children. *Exceptional Children, 45*(4), 279–285.

D'Amato, R. C., Gray, J. W., & Dean, R. S. (1987, March). The Halstead-Reitan neuropsychological battery and the WISC-R with L-D children: Support for a neuropsychological approach in service delivery. Paper presented at National Association of School Psychologists.

Dikmen, S., & Matthews, C. G. (1977). Effect of major motor seizure frequency upon cognitive-intellectual functions in adults. *Epilepsia, 18*(1), 21–29.

Dikmen, S., Matthews, C. G., & Harley, J. P. (1977). Effects of early versus late onset of major motor epilepsy on cognitive-intellectual performance: Further considerations. *Epilepsia, 18*(1), 31–36.

Farwell, J. R., Dodrill, C. B., & Batzell, L. W. (1985). Neuropsychological studies of children with epilepsy. *Epilepsia, 26,* 395–400.

Fischer, K. W., & Silvern, L. (1985). Stages and individual differences in cognitive development. *Annual Review of Psychology, 36,* 613–648.

Fitzhugh, K. B., Fitzhugh, L. C., & Reitan, R. M. (1962). Wechsler-Bellevue comparisons in groups with "chronic" and "current" lateralized and diffuse brain lesions. *Journal of Consulting Psychology, 26,* 306–310.

Hamsher, K. D., & Benton, A. C. (1977). The reliability of reaction time determinations. *Cortex, 13*(3), 306–310.

Hartlage, L. C. (1980, March). Factors influencing longitudinal mental development. Paper presented at Southeastern Psychological Association, Washington, DC.

Hartlage, L. C. (1981a, October). Neurological sequelae of perinatal insult. Paper presented at National Academy of Neuropsychologists.

Hartlage, L. C. (1981b). Neuropsychological assessment of anticonvulsant drug toxicity. *Clinical Neuropsychology, 3,* 20–22.

Hartlage, L. C. (1982). Neuropsychological assessment techniques. In C. Reynolds, & T. Gutkin (Eds.), *Handbook of school psychology.* New York: Wiley.

Hartlage, L. C. (1984a). Unsuspected consequences of apparently insignificant head injuries. *Auto Torts, 7,*187–191.

Hartlage, L. C. (198b, August). False positive lateralizing signs related to anticonvulsant medications. Paper presented at American Psychological Association, Toronto.

Hartlage, L. C. (1987). Preschool neuropsychology. *Preschool Interests, 3*(1), 1–2.

Hartlage, L. C. (in press). *Neuropsychological evaluation of head injury.* Sarasota, FL: Professional Resource Exchange.

Hartlage, L. C., Aziz, E., Mains, M., & Noonan, M. (1981, February). Longitudinal neuropsychological sequelae of prematurity and low birth weight. Atlanta: International Neuropsychological Society.

Hartlage, L. C., Chelune, G., & Tucker, D. (1981, August). Survey of professional issues in the practice of clinical neuropsychology. Paper presented at American Psychological Association, Los Angeles.

Hartlage, L. C., & Green, J. B. (1971). Comparative performance of epileptic and nonepileptic children and adolescents on tests of academic, communicative, and social skills. *Diseases of the Nervous System, 32*(6), 418–421.

Hartlage, L. C. & Hartlage, P. L. (in press). Neuropsychological aspects of epilepsy. In C. Reynolds (Ed.), *Handbook of clinical child neuropsychology.* New York: Plenum.

Hartlage, L. C. & Offutt, L. (1972). Dependency in epileptic children. *Epilepsia, 13*(1), 27–30.

Hartlage, L. C., & Reynolds, C. R. (1981). Neuropsychological assessment and the individualization of instruction. In G. W. Hynd, & J. E. Orbzut (Eds.), *Neuropsychological assessment and the school-aged child: Issues and procedures.* New York: Grune & Stratton.

Hartlage, L. C., & Stovall, K. W. (1980, April). Age/test validity interactions in preschool assessment. Southeastern Psychological Association, Washington, DC.

Hartlage, L. C., Stovall, K. W., & Hartlage, P. L. (1980). Age related neuropsychological sequelae of Reye's syndrome. *Clinical Neuropsychology, 2,* 83–86.

Hartlage, L. C., & Telzrow, C. F. (1980). The practice of clinical neuropsychology in the U.S. *Clinical Neuropsychology, 2*(4), 200–202.

Hartlage, L. C., & Telzrow, C. F. (1981). Neuropsychological assessment of young children. *Clinical Neuropsychology, 3*(3), 41–43.

Hartlage, L. C., & Telzrow, C. F. (1982). Specific preschool medical findings which predict specific learning outcomes. In W. Cruickshank, & J. Lerner (Eds.), *The best of ACLD* (pp. 36–44). Syracuse, NY: Syracuse University Press.

Hartlage, L. C., & Telzrow, C. F. (1983a). Assessment of neurological functioning. In

K. Paget, & B. Bracken (Eds.), *Psychoeducational assessment of preschool and primary aged children.* New York: Grune & Stratton.

Hartlage, L. C., & Telzrow, C. F. (1983b). Evaluation and programming for infants and preschoolers with neurological and neuropsychological handicaps. In C. Reynolds, & J. Clark (Eds.), *Assessment and programming of children with low incidence handicaps.* new York: Plenum.

Hartlage, L. C., & Telzrow, C. F. (1983c). The neuropsychological basis of educational interventions. *Journal of Learning Disabilities, 16,* 521–528.

Hartlage, L. C., & Telzrow, C. F. (1984). Neuropsychological aspects of childhood epilepsy. In R. Tarter, & G. Goldstein (Eds.), *Advances in clinical neuropsychology* (pp. 159–179). New York: Plenum.

Hartlage, L. C., & Telzrow, C. F. (1986). *Neuropsychological assessment and intervention with children and adolescents.* Sarasota, FL: Professional Resource Exchange.

Hartlage, L. C., & Williams, B. L. (1989, January). Neuropsychological assessment and management of behavioral sequelae of head injury. Presented at International Head Injury Symposium, Sarasota, FL.

Horton, K. B. (1974). Infant intervention and language learning. In R. Schiefelbusch, & L. Lloyd (Eds.), *Language retardation and interventions.* Baltimore, University Park Press.

Hynd, G., Hartlage, L., & Noonan, M. (1984). Intracranial hemorrhage in neonates: Data on cognitive development. *International Journal of Clinical Neuropsychology, 6*(2), 111–115.

Jensen, A. R. (1980). Chronometric analysis of intelligence. *Journal of Social and Biological Structures, 3,* 103–122.

Jensen, A. R., Schafer, E. W., & Crinella, F. M. (1981). Reaction time, evoked brain potentials, and psychometric *g* in the severely retarded. *Intelligence, 5,* 179–197.

Kearsley, K. B. (1981). Cognitive assessment of the handicapped infant: The need for an alternative approach. *American Journal of Orthopsychiatry, 51,* 43–54.

Klonoff, H., Low, M. D., & Clark, C. (1977). Head injuries in children: A prospective five year follow-up. *Journal of Neurology, Neurosurgery and Psychiatry, 40,* 1211–1219.

Kriel, R. L., Krach, L. E., Bergland, M. M., & Panser, L. A. (1988). Severe adolescent head injury: Implications for transition into adult life. *Pediatric Neurology, 4,* 337–341.

Lazar, I., & Darlington, R. B. (1978). *Lasting effects after preschool.* (DHEW Publication No. OHDS 79–30178). Washington, DC: Office of Human Development Services.

Lees-Haley, P. C. (1987). Mild brain injury: Proving lost earnings. *Trial, 11,* 83–86.

Lewkowicz, D. J., & Turkewitz, G. (1982). Influence of hemispheric specialization in sensory processing on reaching in infants. *Development Psychology, 18,* 301–308.

Reitan, R. M., & Davidson, L. A. (1974). *Clinical neuropsychology: Current status and applications.* New York: Wiley.

Rosenberg, J. B., & Weller, G. M. (1973). Minor physical anomalies and academic performance in young school children. *Developmental Medicine and Child Neurology, 15,* 131–135.

Schweinhart, L. J., & Weikart, F. P. (1980). *Young children grow up: The effects of the Perry Preschool Program on youths through age 15.* Ypsilanti, MI: Monographs of the High/Scope Education Research Foundation.

Seretny, M. L., Dean, R. S., Gray, J. W., & Hartlage, L. C. (1986). The practice of clinical neuropsychology in the United States. *Archives of Clinical Neuropsychology, 1*(11), 5–12.

Snow, J. H., Hynd, G. W., Hartlage, L. C., & Grant, D. H. (1983). The relationship between the Luria-Nebraska neuropsychological battery children's revision and the Minnesota perceptuo-diagnostic test with learning disabled students. *Psychology in the Schools, 20,* 415–419.

Strom, D. A., Gray, J. W., Dean, R. S., & Fischer, W. E. (1987, March). The incremental validity of the Halstead-Reitan neuropsychological battery in predicting achievement for learning disabled children. Paper presented at National Association of School Psychologists, New Orleans.

Telzrow, C. F. (1983). Making child neuropsychological appraisal appropriate for children: Alternatives to downward extension of adult batteries. *Clinical Neuropsychology, 5,* 136–141.

Telzrow, C. F., & Hartlage, L. C. (1981, February). Neuropsychological assessment of preschool children. Paper presented at Internal Neuropsychological Society, Atlanta.

Telzrow, C. F., & Hartlage, L. C. (1983). Evaluation and programming for infants and preschoolers with neurological and neuropsychological impairments. In C. Reynolds, & J. Clark (Eds.), *Assessment and programming for children with low incidence handicaps* (pp. 43–118). New York: Plenum.

U. S. Department of Health, Eduction, and Welfare (1968). *Mental retardation syndromes: Visual diagnosis of facies and physical findings.* Washington, DC: U. S. Government Printing Office.

Vernon, P. A. (1981). Reaction time and intelligence in the mentally retarded. *Intelligence, 5,* 345–355.

Vernon, P. A. (1985). Individual differences in general cognitive ability. In L. Hartlage, & C. F. Telzrow (Eds.), *The Neuropsychology of individual differences: A developmental perspective* (pp. 125–150). New York: Plenum.

Waber, D. P. (1976). Sex differences in cognition: A function of maturation rate? *Science, 192,* 527–574.

Waldrop, M. F., & Halverson, C. F. (1971). Minor physical anomalies and hyperactive behavior in young children. In J. Hellmuth (Ed.), *The exceptional infant* (Vol. 2, pp. 343–380). New York: Brunner/Mazel.

Waldrop, M. F., Pederson, F. A., & Bell, R. Q. (1968). Minor physical anomalies and behavior in preschool children. *Child Development, 39,* 391–400.

Whitehouse, D. (1971). Psychological and neurological correlates of seizure disorders. *Johns Hopkins Medical Journal, 129,* 36–42.

Chapter 4

Neurological Disorders in the Elderly

Danny Wedding and Steven Cody

Neurological problems and concerns are common in the elderly who are at greatly increased risk to experience CNS dysfunction. While there are clear neurological changes that occur with normal aging, many others develop secondary to disease.

The neurological effects of normal aging include: age-related sensory decline across sensory systems, with particularly salient losses of vidual acuity and of the ability to perceive high frequency sounds; mild decrements in motor functioning including loss of strength, diminished sense of balance, and loss of agility; and a general behavior slowing which is frequently present in the elderly. In contrast, cognitive functions, in the absence of disease, tend to remain relatively stable up to about the age of 60 when there is a typical pattern of cognitive decline in those tasks which require mental flexibility and the ability to process information rapidly in novel situations. This results in a characteristic pattern of performance on the Wechsler Adult Intelligence Scale-Revised (WAIS-R) in which verbal subtest scales require minimal corrections to adjust for the effects of aging while performance subtests, presenting novel tasks and greater speed demands, require marked adjustment to offset the effects of aging. (For example, a total of 31 points is required to earn a Performance IQ of 101 at the age of 70; the identical performance in a 25-year-old only earns a Performance IQ of 76.) We believe it is helpful to conceptualize these differences in terms of the concepts of fluid and crystallized intelligence (Horn & Cattell, 1967).

The specific neurological diseases to which the elderly are heir are legion. They include diseases which affect cognitive function directly through damage and deterioration at the neuronal level (e.g., the dementias) and disorders which affect the brain indirectly (e.g., vascular insufficiency). In addition, the elderly are at increased risk for closed head injury due to an increasing frequency of motor vehicle accidents and falls; this problem is exacerbated by the fact that there is typically a more fragile vascular structure in the elderly person. Finally, older adults are at greater risk for neoplastic disease, in the form of both primary CNS tumors and metastic lesions. This chapter will survey the major categories of neurological disorders found in the elderly. More detailed and comprehensive reviews are available in standard neurological textbooks and in speciality texts devoted to each of the areas we discuss.

THE DEMENTIAS

Dementia can be defined as acquired, persistant and diffuse deterioration of cognitive ability secondary to brain dysfunction (Nolan, Swihart, & Pirozzolo, 1986). The term has historically connoted an insidious onset with an irreversible progression; however, more contemporary usage includes reversible dementias (e.g., those linked with neurotoxin exposure). Some possible causes of reversible dementias are listed in Table 4.1.

We believe it is unfortunate that current psychiatric nomenclature (i.e., the Diagnostic and Statistical Manual of the American Psychiatric Association, DSM-III-R) uses the term dementia to refer to *any* disorder which produces global cognitive impairment and loss of memory ability. This practice lumps together a wide variety of neurological disorders with dramatic differences in etiology and outcome and lacks the specificity necessary to be useful in a scientific taxonomy.

Alzheimer's Disease

Senile dementia of the Alzheimer's type is the most common of the dementias. It affects approximately 1 individual in 25 over the age of 65; by the age of 80, approximately one person in four is affected with the condition. It is the fourth leading cause of death in the United States with a mean survival rate of about two and one-half years after onset of the illness (Kwentus, Hart, Lingon, Taylor, & Silverman, 1986). However, these statistics mask tremendous variability: many patients with Alzheimer's disease live for a decade or more and there are few illnesses that exact a higher toll in human suffering. It has become almost a cliché to point out that these problems will only worsen in a population with a gradually increasing mean age and an ever

Table 4.1 Causes of Reversible Dementia

- Intracranial conditions
  - Meningiomas
  - Subdural hematomas
  - Hydrocephalus
    - Communicating
    - Noncommunicating
  - Epilepsy
  - Multiple sclerosis
  - Wilson's disease
- Systemic illness
  - Pulmonary insufficiency
  - Cardiac arrythmia
  - Severe anemia
  - Uremia
  - Hyponatremia
  - Portosystemic encephalopathy
  - Porphyria
  - Hperlipidemia
- Deficiency states
  - B12 deficiency
  - Pellagra
  - Folate deficiency
- Endocrinopathies
  - Addisons disease
  - Panhypopituitarism
  - Myxedema
  - Hypoparathyroidism
  - Hyperparathyroidism
  - Recurrent hypoglycemia
  - Cushings disease/steroid therapy
  - Hyperthyroidism
- Drugs
  - Methyldopa and haloperidol
      Clonidine and fluphenazine
  - Disulfiram
  - Lithium carbonate
  - Phenothiazines
  - Haloperidol and lithium carbonate
  - Bromides
  - Phenytoin
  - Mephenytoin
  - Barbituates
  - Clonidine
  - Methyldopa
  - Propranolol hydrochloride
  - Atropine and related compounds
- Heavy metals
  - Mercury
  - Arsenic
  - Lead
  - Thallium
- Endogenous toxins and industrial agents
  - Trichloroethylene
  - Toluene
  - Carbon disulfide
  - Organophosphates
  - Alcohol
- Infections
  - General paresis
  - Chronic meningitis
  - Cerebral abscess
  - Cysticercosis
  - Whipple's disease
  - Progressive multifocal leukoencephalopathy
- Collagen-vascular and vascular disorders
  - Systemic lupus erythematosus
  - Temporal arteritis
  - Sarcoidosis
  - Carotid artery stenosis
- "Potentially recoverable dementia"
  - Cerebral anozia
  - Trauma
  - Excessive electroconvulsive therapy
  - Encephalitis

Adapted from Cummings, J., Benson, F., & LoVerma, S. (1980). Reversible dementia: Illustrative cases, definition, and review. *JAMA, 243*, 2434–2439.

greater proportion of its citizens represented in the ranks of the elderly.

The brains of patients who develop Alzheimer's disease are characterized by neurofibrillary tangles, neuritic plaques, and granulovacuolar degeneration. Selective neuronal loss may occur in the basilar forebrain (e.g., in the nucleus basalis of Meynert) and in brainstem nuclei. Losses in these nuclei, particularly in the nucleus basalis of Meynert, appear to be responsible for the deficits in the neurotransmitter acetycholine which are associated with Alzheimer's disease. Plaques and tangles are found primarily in the cortex; although both are associated with the development of Alzheimer's, tangles are more highly correlated with the clinical severity of the illness.

Diagnosis of Alzheimer's disease is made using clinical data and inferential reasoning; the diagnosis is only made after other equally compelling possibilities have been ruled out and it is confirmed only at autopsy. Mild cortical atrophy may be present on computed tomographic evaluation in patients with Alzheimer's disease; however, this is a common finding in the normal, unimpaired elderly population and should not be overinterpreted. Likewise, electroencephalographic evaluation is likely to be normal or to exhibit only equivocal slow wave activity—another ordinary finding in the older patient. Evoked potentials and cerebral blood flow studies may yield more valuable information, but memory decline tends to precede demonstrable physiological change. Neuropsychological tests remain the most sensitive assessment measure in the early stages of Alzheimer's.

Insidious, progressive memory loss is perhaps the most common early sign of Alzheimer's disease. Many prople are aware of this fact and present clinically with considerable concern about what they perceive to be failing mnestic functions. However, *benign senescent forgetfulness* is a common occurrence in the elderly and most typically it is *not* the harbinger of impending disease. Formal neuropsychological investigation of memory abilities is often sufficient to reassure the worried patient. However, the patient with genuine Alzheimer's disease will experience considerable difficulty with the types of novel learning required by neuropsychological tests and tasks like paired-associate learning may be impossible or exceedingly difficult.

Impaired visuospatial abilities are also frequent early signs of Alzheimer's disease and may reflect selective loss of parietal lobe functioning in the disease. Language abilities, in contrast, are relatively spared and the patient may retain considerable social skill in the early stages of the illness. With progression of the disorder, naming ability and verbal fluency will begin to decline with relatively good retention of comprehension and repetition abilities. In the final stages of the disorder both language production and comprehension are lost.

A variety of systems have been proposed for staging the clinical phenomena associated with the progression of Alzheimer's disease. Strub and Black

(1988), for example, propose a useful three stage system for classifying patients with Alzheimer's disease. However, in our own clinical experience we have found the FAST Functional Assessment Staging of Alzheimer's Disease) system developed by Barry Reisberg and his colleagues at New York University Medical Center to be the most clinically useful system currently available. The FAST is applicable to all dementias and is especially helpful in differential diagnosis: it readily points out those situations in which an atypical progression of deterioration is occurring and underscores the need for a redoubled search for treatable causes of the dementia. The defining characteristics of the FAST system are listed in Table 4.2.

In the early FAST stages the patient with a psychiatric illness (e.g., depression) is most likely to be misdiagnosed as demented. In the later stages the patient with a major medical condition (e.g., stroke, tumor, normal pressure hydrocephalus) is most at risk for being mislabeled as having Alzheimer's disease.

One advantage of the scale is its relatively clean ordinal relationship. Each of the scales should occur in an invariant order and the early occurrence of any sign outside of its expected precedence signals the likelihood of a treatable

Table 4.2 FAST Stages and Characteristics

FAST Stage	Characteristics
1	No subjective or objective functional deficits
2	Complaints of forgetting location of objects; subjective work difficulties
3	Decreased functioning in demanding work settings evident to coworkers; difficulty traveling to new locations
4	Decreased ability to do complex tasks (e.g., balancing a checkbook)
5	Requires assistance in selecting appropriate clothes; may require coaching to bathe
6a	Difficulty dressing properly
6b	Requires assistance bathing; fears bathing
6c	Difficulty with mechanics of toileting
6d	Urinary incontinence
6e	Fecal incontinence
7a	Vocabulary limited to one to five words
7b	Intelligible vocabulary lost
7c	Ambulatory ability lost
7d	Ability to sit lost
7e	Ability to smile lost
7f	Ability to hold up head lost; ultimately stupor or coma

Adapted from Reisberg (1986).

dementia. For example, language is typically preserved until stage 7: therefore, an early occurring aphasia suggests focal left posterior pathology. Likewise, urinary incontinence (6d) and loss of ambulatory ability (7c) should be late occurring features of Alzheimer's and their early presence is a red flag indicating that normal pressure hydrocephalus may be present.

It is quite interesting to observe that the progression of deterioration reflected on the FAST reverses the order in which skills are acquired in the newborn (e.g., the child smiles before she sits, speaks before she develops bowel and bladder control, and learns to bathe independently before more complex cognitive skills are acquired).

Pick's Disease

Pick's disease is an age-related progressive dementia which is characterized by selective atrophy of the frontotemporal lobes. It can be distinguished from Alzheimer's disease during its initial stages by its clinical features but this distinction is largely academic since neither disorder has a specific treatment. Because of its frontal focus, patients with Pick's disease tend to lose social graces earlier in the disease process and they tend to retain mnestic abilities longer. Parietal lobe functions are relatively spared in Pick's and few of these patients develop apraxias. The patient with Pick's is more likely to develop urinary incontinence and is not likely to have any significant awareness of his or her failing mental prowess. However, as the disease progresses the differences between it and Alzheimer's blur and both diseases eventually produce total loss of higher cortical functions.

In a neurology residency, one is sometimes taught the following clinical dictum: When the patient could care less about how he looks, diagnose Pick's; when the patient dresses better than you do, diagnose Alzheimer's. However, when the clinician is unsure of the diagnosis but suspects either Pick's or Alzheimer's, the latter diagnosis should always be given preference, simply because the prevalence of Alzheimer's is 50–100 times greater than the prevalence of Pick's disease (Strub & Black, 1988). The disease appears to be approximately equally represented across males and females, unlike Alzheimer's disease in which one finds a greater incidence among women.

Subcortical Dementias

A number of diseases which produce dementias in the elderly have a selective pathological locus in the basal ganglia and other subcortical structures. For example, the substantia nigra is specifically affected in Parkinson's disease while the caudate nucleus is the primary area of degeneration in cases of Huntington's disease. Both disorders can produce a variety of psychological symptoms including lethargy, confusion, forgetfulness, impaired mental flexibility, and personality change (Strub & Black, 1988).

By the age of 75, approximately 1 person in 50 is affected by Parkinson's disease. The disorder is characterized by resting tremor, muscular rigidity, and bradykinesia. Additional clinical signs include a "masked" facial expression, diminished swinging of the arms when walking, and stooped posture. Gait is usually shuffling. The tremor is often unilateral in the early stages of the illness and is especially likely to be present when the patient is walking. It is frequently of the "pill rolling" type. Parkinson's disease occurs most often between ages 50 and 70 and can be either idiopathic of secondary to arteriosclerosis, neurotoxins, trauma, syphilis, or cerebrovascular accidents.

James Parkinson did not initially believe that cognitive decline was part of the clinical presentation of the disease that now bears his name. However, recent studies have demonstrated that a substantial percentage of patients with Parkinson's disease will go on to develop cognitive deficits similar to those observed in the early stages of Alzheimer's (Passafiume, Boller, & Keefe, 1986).

VASCULAR DISORDERS

The incidence of vascular disease increases dramatically and exponentially with age. In addition to increasing age, other risk factors have been identified and include hypertension, atherosclerosis, and smoking.

Vascular disease can be quite focal in its effects. It can involve the entire convexity of a hemisphere, or it may be diffuse in nature and involve virtually the entire brain due to widespread atherosclerosis. Chusid (1985) reports that severe narrowing of the cerebral vessels sufficient to cause vascular insufficiency occurs in 6-8% of people between the ages of 60-70.

Cerebrovascular accidents (CVAs) or strokes are focal neurological events that comprise the third leading cause of death in the United States. (Given their clear association with diet, habit, and lifestyle, it is probably a misnomer to refer to these events as "accidents.") Strokes can be hemorrhagic in nature and blood can be sprayed into the brain with surprising force. These hemorrhages produce extensive neurological damage and death is usually imminent. The prognosis is somewhat better with cerebellar hemorrhages and with subarachnoid hemorrhages resulting from rupture of arterial aneurysms (Kaufman, 1985).

Cerebral *infarctions* occur when the normal flow of blood is blocked or significantly reduced. This can result from a thrombus or an embolus. A thrombus occurs when atherosclerotic plaque builds up sufficiently to obstruct the passage of blood; the thrombus is most likely to occur at the point of bifurcation of a vessel. The resulting CVA is typically painless and frequently occurs during sleep. Cerebral embolism occurs when the lumen of a vessel becomes occluded by a small clot of blood or by a piece of fat or a similar substance. In the elderly, cerebral emboli are frequently sequelae of atrial fibrillation and coronary thrombosis. Both types of infarctions result in necrosis of the cortical area supplied by the vessel and softening of the surrounding neural tissue.

The effects of cerebrovascular events are often partially attenuated by collateral circulation in the healthy brain. The cerebral vasculature itself is intricate and exquisitely engineered and a basic knowledge of it topography is often adequate to help the clinician localize vascular lesions. For example, most CVAs involve one of the middle cerebral arteries which supply the convex surface of each hemisphere. The clinical consequences of a middle cerebral artery infarct include contralateral hemiparesis and contralateral sensory loss. Lesions of the dominant cerebral hemisphere often produce aphasia, and hemi-inattention and neglect frequently result from right middle cerebral artery infarcts. The anterior cerebral artery supplies the medial surface of the frontal lobes and loss of its blood supply results in marked lower extremity motor impairment with relative sparing of contralateral sensory abilities and upper extremity motor functions. Posterior cerebral artery infarctions frequently produce a contralateral homonymous hemianopsia. In a similar way, brainstem infarctions can often be isolated with considerable precision simply by knowing something about the relationship between clinical syndromes and vascular morphology.

Robinson, Lipsey, and Price (1985) developed a model for explaining the relationship between stroke and depression. They argue that unilateral strokes produce major depression in about 60% of patients with left hemisphere stroke and in about 15% of patients who have right hemisphere lesions. They argue that the severity of the resulting depression varies *inversely* with the distance of the lesion from the frontal pole in the left hemisphere while it varies *directly* with distance from the frontal pole in the right hemisphere. Their data is provocative; however, other investigators have reported difficulty in replicating these findings.

Repeated emboli from atheromatous plaques can result in the development of multi-infarct dementia. This is a disorder which occurs most commonly in the late sixties and early seventies in hypertensive men and women. There has often been a history of transient ischemic attacks (TIAs). There is characteristically a history of stepwise cognitive deterioration which stands in marked contrast to the insidious development of Alzheimer's dementia. Focal neurological signs are common and memory functions are frequently better preserved than are speech functions (Strub & Black, 1988). Hachinski, Iliff, and Zihka (1974) have developed a clinical scale for assessing the likelihood of multi-infarct dementia.

NEOPLASTIC DISEASE

The risk for tumors of the central nervous system, like the risk for cancer in general, increases with age. Cancer is the second leading cause of death among persons over 65, surpassed only by heart disease, (Crawford & Cohen, 1984). In addition to tumors arising from primary sites in the central nervous system, such as gliomas and meingiomas, metastatic lesions occur secondary to malignancies at other sites. The more common of these malignancies—cancers of the lung, breast, gastrointestinal tract, kidney, and prostate, for example—are themselves more common with advancing age.

The effects of neoplastic disease in the elderly are essentially the same as in other age groups and depend on characteristics of the tumor such as type, location, and rate of growth. Extrinsic tumors do not infiltrate neural tissue but occupy intracranial space and exert their destructive effects by direct physical pressure on nearby structures and by increasing intracranial presssure. Intrinsic tumors invade brain tissue and produce both direct necrosis and indirect interference with the functioning of the invaded structures. Metastatic lesions most often involve multiple tumors; treatment is complicated in these cases and prognosis is poor (Kolb & Wishaw, 1985). Increases in intracranial pressure can be massively destructive affecting not only cortical function but also causing herniation of brain tissue and damage to the midbrain and brainstem. In some cases, skull films will reveal bone damage and resulting hyperostosis (Reitan & Wolfson, 1985).

While increased intracranial pressure may result in acute confusional behavior and generalized cognitive impairment, the focal nature of the lesion will often manifest in more circumscribed and focal symptoms depending on the specific location of the mass. Specific sensory or motor losses may be noted, as may specific dysphasias, dyspraxias, and so on. In the case of many frontal or temporal lobe tumors, psychiatric symptoms are initially observed. Common early symptoms of brain tumors include headache, particularly headaches which are worse in the morning and precipitated or exacerbated by exertion, and the presence of seizures.

Neoplastic disease is an important alternative to consider when confronted with psychiatric symptoms in an elderly patient with no prior psychiatric history, or with seizures in a patient with no prior history of seizure disorder. Likewise, complaints of headache need to be carefully evaluated and those patients may require further neuroradiological examination. In general, the diagnosis of tumor should be documented by available brain imaging technology rather than surmised on the basis of the clinical examination.

DEPRESSION AND PSEUDODEMENTIA

Differentiating between irreversible senile dementia and treatable illness is one of the most important and most challenging tasks of the clinician working with an aged population. The term *pseudodementia* is typically used to refer to cognitive and intellectual impairments which give the appearance of dementia but are in fact due to a primary psychiatric disorder (Nolan et al., 1986). The psychiatric illness most frequently associated with pseudodementia is depression.

Several factors contribute to the clinician's diagnostic dilemma. First, the elderly are more vulnerable to both dementing illness and depression than are persons in other age groups, and it appears that the elderly are more vulnerable to the cognitive dysfunctions associated with affective disorder (Donnelly, Waldman, Murphy, Wyatt, & Goodwin, 1980). Depression is described as the most prevalent functional disorder of later life, and estimates of the prevalence of depression among the aged are consistently higher than estimates of prevalence among younger persons (Chaisson-Stewart, 1985a). Second, the cognitive deficits associated with depression to some extent overlap with the deficits observed in dementia, particularly in the earlier stages. Impairment of memory function, for example, is one of the most consistently documented cognitive deficits associated with depression (McAllister, 1981). Third, dementia and depression are not mutually exclusive and often coexist, particularly in the earlier stages of a dementing illness when symptoms are the most ambiguous. Fourth, there is the suggestion that depression is in some cases an early warning for progressive neurological disease. In one prospective study of 225 patients referred to a dementia clinic over a three-year period, more than half of those initially believed to be depressed and nondemented subsequently developed a frank dementia (Reding, Haycox, & Blass, 1985). Finally, impairments associated with either depression or dementia must be distinguished from the normal (and considerable) variability in cognitive functioning among the elderly, and from normative age-related declines (Kaszniak, Sadeh, & Stern, 1985). Caine (1986) summarized the clinician's challenge in terms of discriminating among (a) the intellectually intact depressed elderly, (b) impairment which is reversible when affective disorder is treated, and (c) progressive neurological disease accompanied by depression.

Complicating the task further is the fact that the elderly are less likely than others to recognize depression for what it is and are more likely to present their discomfort and distress in physical rather than in emotional or psychological terms (Chaisson-Stewart, 1985b). Partly in consequence, depression in the elderly may reach more malignant proportions before it receives appropriate attention. Early complaints of insomnia, fatigue, or decreased sexual interest may be dismissed as inevitable results of aging; irritability may be dismissed as "cantankerousness." Lack of concern about grooming or hygiene, or reduced variability of facial expression in dementia may resemble the apathy or loss of pleasure associated with depression. Furthermore, depression may be precipitated by other conditions—anemia, malnutrition, diabetes, myocardial infarction, cerebrovascular accident, or thyroid dysfunction, for example. These in turn can contribute to or be responsible for cognitive impairment.

The clinician will find that a careful history and attention to the nature and presentation of memory complaints are often helpful in making the necessary distinctions. Dementia is more likely to involve a gradual and insidious progression of symptoms, while depression is more likely to involve a rapid and precipitous deterioration of cognition. The depressed patient is likely to present sooner after the onset of cognitive dysfunction, and family members are less likely to recall earlier incidents overlooked at the time but seen in retrospect to be early expressions of dementia. Depressed patients are also more likely to have a prior history of psychiatric illness and treatment.

The patient with depressive pseudodementia is more likely to present with extensive and well-described complaints of memory failure, and more likely to be distressed about the problem. In contrast, the dementia patient more commonly does not complain of cognitive dysfunction, presents problems more vaguely, and is more inclined to attempt to conceal or rationalize disabilities (Kaszniak et al., 1985). The behavior of the demented patient and that patient's test results are more often consistent with the extent of memory dysfunction. Formal memory testing of depressed patients often fails to document impairment relative to age-appropriate expectations (Kahn, Zarit, Hilbert, & Niederehe, 1975).

When tested, elderly depressed persons are more likely to give up easily, display less effort, and exhibit inconsistent preformance across tasks of similar difficulty. Dementia patients are more likely to struggle and tend to perform more consistently (Wells, 1979). In general, it appears that memory deficits in depression are more evident when "effortful" rather than "automatic" processes are called upon, while performance on both types of tasks is impaired in dementia (Caine, 1986; Cohen, Weingartner, Smallberg, & Murphy, 1982). A useful summary of these differences may be found in Zarit and Zarit (1983).

We have found it useful to include the modification of the Wechsler Adult Intelligence Scale -Revised (WAIS-R) Digit Symbol subtest proposed by Hart, Kwentus, Wade, and Hamer (1987) in our assessents of elderly patients. This modification requires noting the subject's progress after 90 seconds as in the conventional administration; however, the subject is required to complete the entire subtest and the total time necessary for completion of all items is also noted. Subjects are then asked to recall as many symbols and symbol-number pairs as they possibly can. The required completion of all items insures that all subject shave similar exposure to test stimuli and, since subjects are not anticipating the recall demand, their performance offers a good measure of incidental learning. Hart et al. (1987) provide practical and clinically useful scores for groups of depressed, demented, and control subjects.

With some patients, objective assessment of cognition and memory will be sufficient to illuminate the depressive etiology of an apparent dementia. With others, history will clearly suggest either dementia or depression. In many instances, however, even complex batteries will not provide the clinician with clear guidelines for diagnosing and treating individual patients. Indeed, it has been suggested that pseudodementia per se is less frequent than many texts imply, and that the more common finding is coexisting depression and dementia (Christison & Blazer, 1988). We may indeed find that cognitive deficits persist after resolution of affective problems, but the wise clinician will err on the side of caution; a fatalistic diagnosis can be deferred while treatment for affective symptoms is initiated (Jenike, 1988). Resolution of the depression, even when cognitive impairment persists, is important in reducing "excess disability" (Kahn & Tobin, 1981) and can meaningfully enhance the quality of life for patients with dementing illness.

MEDICATION EFFECTS AND IATROGENIC ILLNESS

Medication issues figure prominently in the care of the aged, who use far more medications than persons in other age groups (Nolan & O'Malley, 1988). Psychotropic medications, including antipsychotics, antidepressants, anxiolytics, and hypnotics, are second in frequency of prescription only to those drugs prescribed for cardiovascular disorders and pain (Salzman, 1984). Age-related changes in response, overmedication, undesirable interactions between medications, and drug usage errors all contribute to the potential for alterations in cognitive status secondary to drugs.

G. D. Cohen (1988) identified two major pharmacokinetic changes associated with the aging process: (a) there are alterations in the way drugs are absorbed, distributed in the body, metabolized, and excreted, and (b) there are changes in central nervous system sensitivity with increasing age. Most commonly, the influence of these changes is to be found in the risk of adverse reactions at dosage levels which would not have the same effect on younger persons, and in the greater potential for accumulation of a substance to toxic levels. Older persons have roughly double the risk of younger persons of experiencing an adverse drug reaction (Friesen, 1983; Stewart & Cluff, 1972). In addition, the relationship between use of a medication and the development of untoward effects is in many cases obscured by the gradual nature of the accumulation; it may take so long to reach toxic levels that clinicians are discouraged from considering medication as a likely cause for current cognitive disturbances.

Problems of reactivity are compounded by the frequency with which the elderly take multiple medications, suffer from a number of concomitant physical conditions, take over-the-counter medications in addition to what is prescribed (often without informing their physician of these extra medications), and either err or fail to comply in using medications as instructed. Drug intoxication is described as one of the primary causes of acute confusional states (ACS) in the elderly; in addition to psychoactive medications, drugs associated with ACS include a variety of cardiac medications, antihypertensives, analgesics, anti-inflammatories such as the corticosteroids, and over-the-counter drugs including cold remedies, sleep aids, stimulants, and antinauseants (Albert, 1988).

Confusional behavior can also be induced by hospitalization in general and surgery in particular. Elderly patients who must undergo general anesthesia in conjunction with major surgery can display confused behavior for weeks postoperatively. Cardiac surgery, particularly intracardiac procedures such as valve replacements, involves particular risk (Strub & Black, 1988). Patients in intensive care units following surgery also commonly have periods of confused behavior, probably attributable to the combination of sensory deprivation and unusual environmental conditions (Kornfeld, Zimberg, & Malm, 1965).

SUMMARY

There are few patient groups more interesting and more challenging than the elderly. They present with complex diagnostic problems and their symptoms often reflect the confluence of medical, personal, social, and sometimes psychiatric issues. A basic knowledge of neuropathology in the elderly is essential for adequate assessment and care of older patients since so many of their problems have their basis in altered CNS functioning. However, equally compelling is the need for patience in assessment and a genuine interest in, and respect for, the geriatric patient. Like many clinicians, we have frequently found ourselves too busy to do the extensive and careful analysis our elderly patients required; however, when we have taken the time, the returns have been enormous.

REFERENCES

Albert, M. S. (1988). Acute confusional states, In M. S. Albert & M. B. Moss (Eds.), *Geriatric neuropsychology* (pp. 100–114). New York: Guilford.

Caine, E. D. (1986). The neuropsychology of depression: The pseudodementia syndrome. In I. Grant & K. M. Adams (Eds.), *Neuropsychological assessment of neuropsychiatric disorders* (pp. 221–243). New York: Oxford University Press.

Chaisson-Stewart, G. M. (1985a). Depression incidence: Past, present and future. In G. M. Chaisson-Stewart (Ed.), *Depression in the elderly: An interdisciplinary approach* (pp. 3–17). New York: Wiley.

Chaisson-Stewart, G. M. (1985b). The diagnostic dilemma. In G. M. Chaisson-Stewart (Ed.), *Depression in the elderly: An interdisciplinary approach* (pp. 18–43). New York: Wiley.

Christison, C., & Blazer, D. (1988). Clinical assessment of psychiatric symptoms. In M. S. Albert & M. B. Moss (Eds.), *Geriatric neuropsychology* (pp. 82–99). New York: Guilford.

Chusid, J. G. (1985). *Correlative neuroanatomy and functional neurology* (19th ed.). Los Altos, CA: Lange.

Cohen, G. D. (1988). *The brain in human aging*. New York: Springer Publishing Co.

Cohen, R. M., Weingertner, H., Smallberg, S. A., & Murphy, D. L. (1982). Effort and cognition in depression. *Archives of General Psychiatry, 39*, 593–597.

Crawford, J., & Cohen, H. J. (1984). Aging and neoplasia. *Annual Review of Gerentology and Geriatrics, 4*, 3–32.

Donnelly, E. F., Waldman, I. N., Murphy, D. L., Wyatt, R. J., & Goodwin, F. K. (1980). Primary affective disorder: Thought disorder in depression. *Journal of Abnormal Psychology, 89*, 315–319.

Friesen, A. J. D. (1983). Adverse drug reactions in the geriatric client. In L. A. Pagliaro & A. M. Pagliaro (Eds.), *Pharmacologic aspects of aging* (pp. 257–293). St. Louis: C. V. Mosby.

Hachinski, V. C., Iliff, L. D., & Zihka, L. (1975). Cerebral blood flow in dementia. *Archives of Neurology, 32*, 632–637.

Hart, R. P., Kwentus, J. A., Wade, J. B., & Hamer, R. M. (1987). Digit symbol performance in mild dementia and depression. *Journal of Consulting and Clinical Psychology, 55*, 236–238.

Horn, J. L., & Cattell, R. B. (1967). Age differences in fluid and crystallized intelligence. *Acta Psychologica, 26*, 107–129.

Jenike, M. (1988). Depression and other psychiatric disorders. In M. S. Albert & M. B. Moss (Eds.), *Geriatric neuropsychology* (pp. 115–144). New York: Guilford.

Kahn, R. L., & Tobin, S. S. (1981). Community treatment for persons with altered brain function. In N. E. Miller & G. D. Cohen (Eds.), *Clinical aspects of Alzheimer's disease and senile dementia*. New York: Raven Press.

Kahn, R. L., Zarit, S. H., Hibert, N. M., & Niederehe, G. (1975). Memory complaint and impairment in the aged. *Archives of General Psychiatry, 32*, 1569–1573.

Kaszniak, A. W., Sadeh, S. H., & Stern, L. Z. (1985). Differentiating depression from organic brain syndromes in older age. In G. M. Chaisson-Stewart (Ed.), *Depression in the elderly: An interdisciplinary approach* (pp. 161–192). New York: Wiley.

Kaufman, D. M. (1985). *Clinical neurology for psychiatrists* (2nd ed.). Orlando, FL:

Grune & Stratton.

Kolb, B., & Wishaw, I. Q. (1985). *Fundamentals of human neuropsychology* (2nd ed.). New York: W. H. Freeman.

Kornfeld, D. S., Zimberg, S., & Malm, J. R. (1965). Psychiatric complications of open heart surgery. *New England Journal of Medicine, 273*, 287–292.

Kwentus, J. A., Hart, R., Lingon, N., Taylor, J., & Silverman, J. J. (1986). Alzheimer's disease. *The American Journal of Medicine, 81*, 91–96.

McAllister, T. W. (1981). Cognitive functioning in the affective disorders. *Comprehensive Psychiatry, 22*, 572–586.

Nolan, B. H., Swihart, A. A., & Pirozzolo, F. J. (1986). The neuropsychology of normal aging and dementia. In D. Wedding, A. M. Horton, Jr., & J. Webster (Eds.), *The neuropsychology handbook: Behavioral and clinical perspectives* (pp. 410–440). New York: Springer Publishing Co.

Nolan, L., & O'Malley, K. (1988). Prescribing for the elderly, Part I: Sensitivity of the elderly to adverse drug reactions. *Journal of the American Geriatrics Society, 36*, 142–149.

Passafiume, D., Boller, F., & Keefe, N. C. (1986). Neuropsychological impairment in patients with Parkinson's disease. In I. Grant & K. M. Adams (Eds.), *Neuropsychological assessment of neuropsychiatric disorders* (pp. 374–383). New York: Oxford University Press.

Reding, M., Haycox, J., & Blass, J. (1985). Depression in patients referred to a dementia clinis: A three-year prospective study. *Archives of Neurology, 42*, 894–896.

Reisberg, B. (1986). Dementia: A systematic approach to identifying reversible causes. *Geriatrics, 41*(4), 30–46.

Reitan, R. M., & Wolfson, D. (1985). *The Halstead-Reitan Neuropsychological Test Battery: Theory and clinical applications*. Tucson, AZ: Neuropsychology Press.

Robinson, R. G., Lipsey, J. R., & Price, T. R. (1985). Diagnosis and clinical management of post-stroke depression. *Journal of Clinical Psychiatry, 26*, 769–778.

Salzman, C. (Ed.). (1984). *Clinical geriatric psychopharmacology*. New York: McGraw-Hill.

Stewart, R., & Cluff, L. (1972). A review of medication errors and compliance in ambulatory patients. *Clinical Pharmacologic Therapy, 13*, 463.

Strub, R. L., & Black, F. W. (1988). *Neurobehavioral disorders: A clinical approach* (2nd ed.). Philadelphia: F. A. Davis.

Wells, C. E. (1979). Pseudodementia. *American Journal of Psychiatry, 136*, 895–900.

Zarit, S. H., & Zarit, J. (1983). Cognitive impairment. In P. M. Lewinsohn & L. Teri (Eds.), *Clinical geropsychology* (pp. 38–80). New York: Pergamon.

Chapter 5

Clinical Neuropsychology and Older Populations

Michael D. Franzen and Paul R. Rasmussen

As people age, the reasons why they might be seen by a clinical neuropsychologist change. For school-aged patients, the referral reason is likely to be related to academic performance. For the young adult, the reason is most likely to be related to head injury. For older populations, the reasons are most likely to include cerebrovascular disease, central nervous system effects of medical disorders, or progressive dementias. Older adults are also more likely to experience the "pseudodementia" effects of affected disorders than are younger patients.

There are qualitative as well as quantitative changes in the neuropsychological performance of people as they age. Therefore, it is important for the clinical neuropsychologist to be familiar both with the normal changes associated with the aging process and with the changes associated with, or characteristic of, abnormal processes. This chapter will review the changes thought to be associated with the normal aging process from both the neuropsychological and developmental perspective. The clinical presentation of the more common disorders will be discussed. The differences between dementia and pseudodementia will be highlighted. Finally, some basic suggestions regarding treatment will be offered.

NORMAL AGING

Early conceptions of aging have persisted in the popular culture. For example, we are all familiar with the stereotype of the aged individual who is hard of hearing and who has a faulty memory. Although both peripheral sensory loss and memory deficits can be associated with aging, memory loss is not part of the normal aging process. However, aging is associated with a greater prevalence of certain disorders that can cause memory loss. Other early conceptions of aging involved hypotheses regarding fairly uniform decline in neuropsychological skill as the result of aging. These conceptions turn out to be as misleading as the idea of memory decline.

The early conceptions of the effects of aging on neuropsychological functioning involved an assumption that aging was accompanied by a general decline in skill level. This belief was congruent with the notions of aging in the popular culture; namely, that the older individual experiences declines in sensory functions as well as in mental functions. Under this view as the person ages, eyesight becomes less acute, hearing becomes less sensitive, reflexes slow, memory becomes inaccurate, complex problem solving becomes less skilled, and judgment falters. The stereotypical image of the older individual with a hearing horn who gets into humorous situations as the result of poor memory or hearing has been in so many public portrayals that this image has become almost a cultural icon of the comedy sketch writer. However, the actual case is far from the popular image.

Two decades ago, Reitan (1967) described a decline in cognitive function in the elderly and ascribed this decline to a lifetime accumulation of cortical insults and injuries. The decline was not consistent across all cognitive functions tapped by the Halstead-Reitan Neuropsychological Battery (HRNB), a pattern that had been originally pointed out by Reed and Reitan (1963). The decline existed primarily for skills requiring active problem solving and, to a lesser extent, for skills requiring access to old information. In comparing young (mean age = 28 years) and old (mean age = 53 years) subjects, none of whom were suspected of a neurological disorder, Reed and Reitan (1963) reported significant differences on scores on the Category Test, the Tactual Performance Test, the Block Design subtest of the Wechsler-Bellevue scales, and on Trails. Interestingly, the older subjects were significantly better on the Seashore Rhythm Test. The older subjects also had superior performance on the Vocabulary, Arithmetic, and Comprehension subtests of the Wechsler-Bellevue, but these differences were not statistically significant. Fitzhugh, Fitzhugh, and Reitan (1964) reported a similar pattern in a sample of epileptic subjects who had been divided at the median age of 35 years.

One of the limitations of the above studies is that although the topic matter was the aging process, several of the subjects in the "older" groups could actually be considered to be young (aged 35 years). Similarly, even for the older subjects, there may be differences between "old" old and "young" old subjects. Bak and Greene (1980) investigated this possibility with a sample of 15 subjects between the ages of 50 and 62 years and 15 subjects between the ages of 67 and 86 years. These researchers found significantly better performance in the younger subjects for the Trails, the Tactual Performance Test, the Fingertapping Test, the Block Design and Digit Symbol subtests of the WAIS, and for both the Visual Reproduction and Delayed Visual Reproduction subscales of Russell's revision of the Wechsler Memory Scale (WMS). This evidence suggested that something more than just active problem solving was affected by aging.

This point was more fully investigaged by Benton, Eslinger, and Damasio (1981) who administered several neuropsychological tests to 162 normal volunteers between the ages of 65 and 84 years, divided into four age groups (five years each group). The authors reported declines on Digit Span and on the Logical Memory and Associate Learning subtests of the WMS but only for the subjects over 80 years of age. There was a general decline in Digit Sequence Learning and on the Benton Visual Retention Test across the ages, and a decline in the Facial Recognition for subjects over 70 years and in the Judgment of Line Orientation Test for subjects over 75 years.

Theories of the Effects of Aging

The apparent differential effects of aging on neuropsychological functioning raised two important questions: first, do the effects of aging obscure the effects of brain pathology? and second, do different areas of the brain age differentially? Investigating the first question, Golden and Schlutter (1978) found significant effects for age and diagnosis but no significant effect for the interaction of the two variables on HRNB performance in a sample of 171 healthy and brain impaired subjects.

In an elaboration of this study, Marvel, Golden, Hammeke, Purish, and Osmon (1979) evaluated performance on the Luria Nebraska Neuropsychological Battery (LNNB) in 269 subjects across two age groups (20–40 years and 50–70 years), three levels of education (grade school, high school, and post-high school), and three diagnostic groups (normal controls, schizophrenics, and brain impaired subjects). They found significant effects for diagnosis and education on each of the clinical scales and significant effects for age on all of the scales except Reading, Writing, and Arithmetic. Again there were no significant interactions involving age. These results indicated that aging may not override or obscure the effects of brain pathology. Another study concluded that although aging did not obscure the effects of brain pathology, the effect of age was substantially reduced in a brain impaired population (Hamsher & Benton 1978).

Investigating the second question Goldstein and Shelly (1981) examined the HRNB performance of 1,247 subjects divided into groups pertaining to the six decades between 20 and 80 years old. These researchers reported a larger decline in performance on right hemisphere tasks than on left hemisphere tasks. However, to state that the right hemisphere ages more quickly than the left is problematic because of the greater reliance on complex problem solving skills in the right hemisphere tasks (Botwinick, 1977). Recent research has focused on the role of health status among the elderly. For example, Willis, Yeo, Thomas, and Garry (1988) reported that although there were age-related changes in memory function as measured by the WMS Logical Memory and Visual Reproduction subscales, there were no age-related changes in performance on the Halstead Category test that were instead related to health status.

One hypothesis proposed to explain age related declines involves a general slowing of cognitive processing and motor processes (Mahurin & Pirozzolo 1986). More than one researcher has suggested that declines in measured intelligence are related to a slowing of cognitive processes. A complication arises in individual assessment because slowing is a prominent feature of dementias. The apparent conflict can be resolved when it is remembered that as well as slowing, demented inviduals will also show qualitative signs such as constructional deficits and paraphasias. In fact, this differential can be useful in assessment situations. If the patient can perform accurately when extra time is allowed, we would be less sure that dementia is present. On the other hand if extra time makes no difference in performance, dementia may be the reason.

Regardless of the reason for age related changes in neuropsychological performance, the data suggest that age related norms are necessary for the clinical evaluation of aged individuals. Bornstein, Paniak, and O'Brien (1987) evaluated the use of the regular cut-off scores in classifying 228 older subjects on the basis of their HRNB results. The classification rates for normal subjects ranged from only 67% using Trails A to only 2% using the preferred hand Fingertapping score for the female subjects. Several interpretation strategies use an examination of pattern of scores rather than the absolute level of scores; because of this Thompson, Heaton, Matthews, and Grant (1987) evaluated age differences in the accuracy of classification by left-right comparisons in the manual tasks of the HRNB. The only age effect was found in the Tactual Performance Test in which the expected improvement was not found from the preferred hand to the non-preferred hand.

Only a few of the shorter neuropsychological tests, such as the Purdue Pegboard, have norms for older subjects (Agnew, Bolla-Wilson, Kawas, &

Bleecker 1988). For the HRNB, the limited sample norms of Bak and Greene (1980), and the somewhat larger sample (N = 85) of Australian elderly on a few selected HRNB subtests given by Ernst (1988) are helpful, although still nonoptimal. Although MacInnes, Gillen, Golden, Graber, Cole, Uhl, and Greenhouse (1983) found reasonable accuracy of classification using the age adjusted critical level of the LNNB in a sample of 78 healthy elderly, the false positive rate of 8% may be undesirable in a clinical situation. Interestingly, 59 of these subjects were retested after four years, and the false positive rate decreased to 2% at that time (MacInnes, Paull, Uhl, & Schima 1987). Similarly, Spitzform (1982) found a 7% false positive rate using the LNNB in a sample of 14 healthy elderly. What is needed is large sample clinical norms for these standard tests or else specialized tests such as the Kendrick Cognitive Tests for the Elderly (Gibson & Kendrick 1982) that are specifically designed for use with older subjects.

VARIABLES AFFECTING PERFORMANCE

Affective Functioning

Anxiety and depression have been assumed to exert an influence on neuropsychological performance. The effects have not been seen uniformly in all subjects for all tasks. However, it appears that, at least for memory and for tasks that require cognitive processing of effort, anxiety may inhibit performance. This topic has been addressed in a theoretical fashion for humans using animal data. For example, Gray (1982) posits a neurochemical mechanism by which subjective states of anxiety may affect neuropsychological performance. Not all of the data regarding this point is derived from animal studies. Miller, Richardson, Jyu, Lemay, Hiscock, and Keegan (1988) reported the results of an investigation in which eighteen elderly patients undergoing surgery received low dose scopalamine resulting in low levels of serum anticholinergic activity and subsequent cognitive impairment. It may be that the elderly are more sensitive to the neurochemical effects of anxiety.

Medical Disorders

Medical Disorders with Central Nervous System Effects As people age, the threat of developing any of a large number of medical disorders increases. Beyond the immediate risk of the medical condition is the possibility of central nervous system effects as a consequence of that illness. Although the central nervous system's vulnerability to the effects of the medical disorder may not be unique to the older population, the elderly are more at risk of developing medical disease, leaving them more susceptible to the neurological concomitants of the medical condition.

Research has demonstrated that symptoms similar to the social and cognitive impairments characteristic of dementia are often caused by a degeneration of the cerebral cortex in response to such disease states as hyper- and hypoadrenalism (Jefferson & Marshall, 1981). Additionally, disorders of the thyroid gland are often accompanied by impairments in cognitive processing skills and memory abilities (Jellinek, 1962; Golden, Strider, Ariel & Golden, 1986).

Diabetes is a significant endocrinopathy affecting the central nervous system. In a study conducted by Skenazy and Bigler (1984), using the Halstead-Reitan Neuropsychological Test and the Wechsler Memory Scale, it was demonstrated that patients with diabetes mellitus perform worse than normals on tests of somatosensory examination, motor strength and motor speed, compared to nondiabetic normals. Deficits were also noted on Trails, the Category test, and on performance IQ, as assessed by the WAIS-R. In a study by Strider (1982), these deficits were demonstrated to occur at a greater rate in patients with later-onset diabetes mellitus, relative to diabetic patients who developed diabetes at an early age.

Perhaps one of the greatest fears people experience as they grow older is that of developing heart disease. As a result of the brain's reliance upon the heart for metabolic processes, it is highly susceptible to damage as an outcome of disease of the cardiovascular system. As people age, because of the normal aging process or because of deleterious lifestyle effects, heart disease and heart failure become significantly greater risks, as does the risk of central nervous system impairments.

Risk of developing neuropsychological impairments as a result of cardiovascular disease is not limited to the immediate effects of heart or vascular insufficiency. Golden and his colleagues (1986) suggest that the treatment of cardiovascular disease has potential iatrogenic effects on neurological functioning, ranging from the effects of post-operative infections to hypoxia following a toxic reaction to anesthesia.

Older individuals also experience a decline in functioning of their autoimmune system as they age and therefore are more vulnerable to infectious illness. The possible number of organisms that can infect the body and produce central nervous system effects is enormous. Infection can invade the central nervous system by both direct invasion and by secondary systemic effects (Jefferson & Marshall, 1981). Most noticeable in the aged population are infections by viruses such as viral meningitis, lupus and influenza, which can produce behavioral symptoms consistent with symptoms of dementia or psychoses (Spittle, Fliegnar, & Faed, 1977).

Of all neuropsychological conditions among the elderly population, perhaps one of the most common syndromes is delirium. Lipowski (1980) reports that the group at the highest risk for developing delirium are people aged 60 years or over. This increased incidence in the aged population results from the vast number of known and potential causes of delirium and the elderly population's increased susceptibility to these illnesses. For instance, the states of disease noted above all have delirium as a possible neuropsychological outcome. As a result, with the increased susceptibility to these various medical disorders, the risk of delirium increases. Delirium is also associated with additional medical disorders such as closed head injury, metabolic changes, toxin and drug exposure, and essential element deficiencies (Wise, 1987).

Other Influences on CNS Function Another important point revolves around the possibility that older individuals have central nervous systems (CNS) that are more sensitive to various extraneous influences. We have already discussed how older individuals are more likely to exhibit the signs of delirium under conditions of medical disorders. There is likely to be more variability in the cognitive functioning of older individuals both in terms of variability across individuals and variability in the same individual across time. For example, proper nutrition is thought to play a role in adequate neurotransmission. However, it is usually thought that nutrition does not grossly affect cognitive functioning in the adult unless chronic deficiencies of certain vitamins (B12), electrolytes (potassium), or proteins are present.

A study by Goodwin, Goodwin, and Garry (1983) indicates that this may not be the case for the elderly. These investigators recruited 304 volunteers over the age of 60 years. A complete medical history and physical examination with laboratory tests excluded 24 subjects as having some form of previously undiagnosed medical disorder. Eleven other subjects were deleted because of incomplete data. Data regarding levels of specific nutrients (folate, riboflavin, Vitamin B12, and Vitamin C) were obtained on the basis of both self-report nutrition diaries and on the basis of blood levels. Protein intake was measured only using the nutrition diary. All subjects were administered the Russell revision of the Wechsler Memory Scale and the Halstead Category Test. There were significant differences between the subjects in the lowest 10% of the nutrient levels and the subjects in the top 90% for both tests. These results are all the more impressive because they were derived from a sample of healthy, independently living individuals. Nutrition apparently plays a large role in the neuropsychological functioning of older individuals.

Pharmacological Treatment of Older Individuals Because older individuals are more likely to have a variety of medical conditions, they are also more likely to be receiving pharmacological treatments. This is an extremely important consideration for the clinical neuropsychologist because many drugs have effects on central nervous system functioning, even if the intended main effect of the drug is on some other organ system. Pharmacokinetics are not stable across the life-span, and older people may be more susceptible to the side effects of certain medications because of age-related changes in the absorption, distribution, metabolism, and elimination of the drug. Additionally, older individuals may be maintained on multiple drug schedules that have been initiated separately by different care providers, raising the possibility of drug interactions. Therefore, it is extremely important for the clinical neuropsychologist, evaluating an older patient, to obtain a complete medication history. Because many older individuals do not always remember the names and doses of drugs that they are taking, the neuropsychologist can request that the patient bring a complete list of drugs to the evaluation appointment. This information should always be corroborated.

The neuropsychologist who uncovers a memory deficit in an older patient on medication has a responsibility to evaluate the ability of the patient to follow the prescribed medical regimen. In cases of minor memory impairment, the use of a behavioral prosthetic such as a medication diary or large type reminders taped to the medicine cabinet can be useful in helping to insure accurate compliance. More severe memory impairments may necessitate supervision by another individual in the environment. The method chosen to ensure compliance should be designed under the twin principles of maximizing health and maximizing the independence of the patient.

If no memory complaints are uncovered, but the patient is still reported to forget the medicine instructions, further investigation is warranted. It may be possible that the memory assessment instruments used were not sensitive to the type of memory complaint. Most memory assessment instruments involve the evaluation of specific verbal or visual memory. Following a medical regimen or remembering whether the regimen has been followed that day may involve episodic memory. Another possibility is that failure to comply with the medical regimen is not related to a memory problem but rather to a problem in motivation. One older individual with whom we are familiar had complained of not being able to remember whether or not she had taken her arthritis and heart medication but was not found to have a memory deficit. The suggested use of a medication diary was also not successful. Further interview with the individual indicated that she had always been healthy until after her seventieth birthday. She was having a difficult time accepting the need for medication even though she could articulate the reasons. The successful intervention involved brief counseling to help her accept the changes her body was going through as she aged.

Dementia

Dementia is not a unitary construct, and in fact is not a single disorder with a solitary cause. In general, dementia refers to a decline in cognitive functions. Dementias may be found in all age groups, but they have their highest concentration in the elderly. Some dementias are caused by medical conditions and may therefore be reversible as the medical condition is adequately treated. As a result, it is extremely important that the clinical neuropsychologist evaluating an older individual be aware of the behavioral, qualitative signs that differentiate the dementias so that a patient is not diagnosed as having a progressive, irreversible dementia and be wrongly excluded from curative treatment. It also helps to remember that irreversible dementias are not untreatable, they are merely incurable. Alzheimer's patients deserve the best palliative treatment available given their own and the community's resources.

Just as dementia has multiple manifestations, so may a single type of dementing disease take different forms. For example, there is some debate as to whether Alzheimer's disease represents a single disorder or multiple disorders. Albert and Moss (1984) have argued that there are three major types of Alzheimer's disease. The first type is characterized by early impairment in memory with associated deficits in abstract reasoning and cognitive flexibility. The second type is characterized by early signs of aphasia, and the third type is characterized by early signs of visual spatial impairment. Considered together, these three constitute a triad of clinical features present in all Alzheimer's patients at middle stages of the progression. On the other hand, Schwartz (1987) argues that the different temporal relations among appearances of these symptoms reflect individual variability in the manifestations of a single disorder. For example, a breakdown in semantic memory processes is thought to be a fairly consistent feature of Alzheimer's disease (Salmon, Shimamura, Butters, & Smith, 1988). The appearance of deficits in individuals with Alzheimer's may be partly related to the learning history of the individual. For example, Cummings and Zarit (1987) reported the case of a professional artist who developed Alzheimer's disease. Although the artist's paintings showed a decline in quality, his performance on standard tests of visuoconstructive skill remained relatively stable.

Discrimination of Dementia from Benign Senescent Forgetting and Pseudodementia A common problem for neuropsychologists in their dealings with the elderly population arises when confronted with the differentiation of dementia from benign senescent forgetting and from pseudodementia. If the differential diagnosis is inaccurately performed, the care of the elderly individual is seriously compromised (Gurland & Toner, 1983). The clinical features of diagnosable dementia have been identified above.

Dementia, in all of its forms, is characterized by a gradual, insidious onset. Typically, it is difficult for either the patient or close family members to pin-point a date or period of onset. As a result of this gradual onset, often over the course of several years, both the patient and family are unaware of the severity of the deficits experienced by the patient. As the disease has progressed, the family has adapted to the patient's impairments and has attributed noted impairments to plausible events in the environment or to the expected effects of aging. Often the deficits are ignored by the family, with the hope that the difficulties will "clear-up" and go away. There may be no history of a psychiatric disturbance in the patient's past, and as a result, family members and possibly trained caregivers, are less inclined to attribute signs of diminished cognitive abilities to a psychiatric condition.

Pseudodementia, although partly characterized by a sequelae of symptoms similar to dementia, is also characterized by symptoms unique to dementia, is also characterized by symptoms unique to this syndrome. In pseudodementia, an approximate date or period of onset can often be pin-pointed. Because of the rapid onset, family members are often aware of the accompanying deficits and are quicker to seek medical assistance with the disorder. Often, unlike "true" dementias, the patient has a known history of psychiatric difficulties, frequently consistent with depressed characteristics (Wells, 1979). These disorders are also characterized by unique behavioral manifestations. For example, the patient may display disorientation to time, but display prompt arrival to desirable appointments such as mealtime, or the patient may exhibit deficits on tests of memory, but be able to look up numbers in the phonebook and recall them for dialing (Wells, 1979).

Consistent with identifiable differences is onset, there are attempts by demented patients to incorporate compensatory strategies in order to cope effectively with the changes associated with the disease process. Such attempts often include a greater reliance on calendars, notes and the reminders provided by others in the environment. The patients may deny and complain very little of difficulties and may be unable to clearly articulate the nature of the deficits. However, the patient is confronted with impairments and must struggle to maintain functional abilities. Particular difficulties are experienced in tasks that require attention/concentration skills and complex cognitive abilities. These patients will typically retain remote memory skills, but will experience difficulties with recent memory. In an attempt to compensate for these deficits, the demented patient is likely to rely on confabulatory behavior to cover-up and deny his/her impairments. Frequently, it is the confabulatory behavior that indicates to family members that the patient is functioning at an impaired level. Indentified deficits are usually consistent across tasks of similar difficulty. Depending upon the stage of disease progression, these patients become more prone to disorientation and may be more likely to experience confusion. Often, during later stages of the disease, the patient experiences the sundown effect, characterized by an exacerbation of symptoms during the evening hours and by occasional night wandering. Social skills remain relatively intact, and the presence of social skills adds to the general unawareness of the deterioration by others.

Psuedodemented patients, on the other hand, are much less likely to rely on compensatory strategies and become much more dependent upon others. They typically complain a great deal about their inabilities, draw attention to these deficits and make reduced effort to maintain independent functioning. Often others in the environment become somewhat resentful of the patient's symptoms and will initiate treatment in an attempt to gain relief from these complaints. Attention/concentration skills are only mildly impaired, but the patient is likely to respond to inquiries with an "I don't know" reply. Global deficits are typically noted in memory skills, and the patient often reports loss of memory for specific events, both recent and remote. Deficits are typically inconsistent across similar tasks with unexpected abilities occurring during times of need. Along with a general decrease in functional abilities, the pseudodemented patient experiences a significant decrease in social functioning. Typically there is no evidence of the sundown effect characterized by the patient. Emotional symptoms are also different for these two disorders.

The emotional responses of demented patients are typically blunted, although often quite labile. They often appear relatively unconcerned with emotionally-laden events in their environment, and prone to laughter or sadness at seemingly inappropriate times. Additionally, their emotional reactivity is more labile than prior to the disease onset. Pseudodemented patients, however, appear to be generally more depressed in affect and more anxious. Responses to environmental events are often either blunted, as in depression, or overly reactive as in catastrophizing. Frequently, pseudodemented patients have a history of psychiatric disorders.

Although the characteristics of these disorders appear unique, it is difficult to make a differential diagnosis without thorough and careful assessment. It is important that a complete history be obtained from both the patient and close family members. In particular, the neuropsychologist should assess the parameters of the onset of the disorder, the behavioral manifestations, cognitive impairments experienced by the patient, the social and emotional features and the impact on, and awareness of the persons, in the patient's environment. Additionally, complete psychological and neuropsychological assessments will aid in the differential diagnosis. Consistent with the above discussion, the neuropsychologist can expect to identify more consistent neuropsychological deficits in the demented patients and less consistent deficits in pseudodemented patients on tests of neuropsychological functioning. Additionally, the neuropsychologist can expect to see increases on measures of affective disturbance on tests of current psychological functioning. The risk of misdiagnosis is significant, and attempts should be made by the neuropsychologist to be complete and rely on various strategies to insure correct diagnostic conclusions.

Benign Senescent Forgetting A term first used by Kral (1962) to describe the memory deficits resulting from the normal aging process is "benign senescent forgetfulness" (BSF). BSF is characterized by a general inability to recall the specific aspects of a situation, while being able to recall the episode itself (Jolles, 1986). It is suggested that as people age they become less able to organize the content of short term memory and experience a significant deterioration in recall memory (Craik, 1977), with a relative maintenance of recognition performance. As a result of these memory deficits, elderly individuals often appear forgetful and confused. Although the impairments are not severe and fluctuate in frequency of occurrence, they often appear suggestive of a developing dementia.

Types of Dementia

Alzheimer's Dementia The most common and the most well known form of dementia is Alzheimer's disease. Approximately 65% of all cass of dementia in the elderly may be the result of Alzheimer's (Crook, 1987). Alzheimer's disease is actually a post-mortum diagnosis. It is characterized by the presence of senile plaques, neurofibrillary tangles, and granulovacuolar degeneration. Cerebral atrophy may also be present in Alzheimer's, but is not considered to be indicative of the disease because cerebral atrophy is associated with several other disorders (Bigler 1987). Vacuolar changes are also found in Creutzfeldt-Jakob disease, however, in Alzheimer's these changes are limited to the medial temporal cortex and the amygdala (Smith, Anwer, DeGirolami, & Drachman 1987).

Alzheimer's disease has generated a huge amount of interest and sizable numbers of investigations in all related fields: basic neuroanatomy and physiology, psychiatry, neurology, and neuropsychology. It is beyond the scope of this chapter to provide a comprehensive review of this research. However, a few points relevant to clinical diagnosis of probable Alzheimer's are in order. Although the exact etiology of Alzheimer's is unknown, it appears that early signs of it may include hypometabolism of the parietal regions (Duara, Grady, Haxby, Sundaram, Cutler, Heston, Moore, Schlageter, Larson & Rapoport, 1986). It is a progressive disorder that is fatal, following progression to a bed-ridden, incontinent state. The memory deficits seen in Alzheimer's disease may be related to reduced levels of thiamine (Gibson, Sheu, Blass, Baker, Carlson, Harding & Perrino, 1988). The general areas of decline in clinical presentation include, deficits in lexical/semantic access, difficulty in the transfer from short-term to long-term memory, and visual construction deficits.

Because the disease is slowly progressive, a patient is usually not seen by a neuropsychologist until fairly far along in the early stages. In fact, this information can help make a differential diagnosis between Alzheimer's dementia and dementia secondary to depression. The onset of symptoms in Alzheimer's can rarely be dated with any certainty, and the patient may engage in confabulation in order to cover his/her deficits. In depression, the patient is aware of the deficits, can date their onset fairly well, and calls attention to the deficits because of his/her concern over them.

Multi-Infarct Dementia Multi-infarct dementia (MID) is also a progressive disorder, but the course of progression is qualitatively different from that of Alzheimer's. In MID, the patient shows a pattern of abrupt changes in discrete areas of neuropsychological function followed by gradual, slight improvements and subsequent abrupt declines in some other neuropsychological function. This scalloped or "step-wise" decline is due to the nature of the etiology. In MID, there are multiple small strokes in different areas of the brain. Eventually, the patient is demented, but at first, there are only pockets of impairment. The areas of impairment are related to the location, extent, and number of small infarcts (Cummings & Zarit, 1987). The diagnosis of MID should be considered in individuals who have a history of high blood pressure.

Pick's Dementia Pick's dementia is usually described as being rare, however recent evidence indicates that Pick's dementia, or dementia of the frontal lobe type is more common than was previously thought to be the case (Neary, Snowden, Northen & Goulding, 1988). There appears to be a genetic component to Pick's disease (Heston, White & Mastri, 1987). Pick's disease involves atrophy of the frontal and temporal lobes and the presence of Pick bodies in neurons. The clinical picture includes disinhibition, unconcern, and personality change with variable memory impairment and an absence of visual-spatial impairment (Neary et al., 1988). The patient with Pick's dementia will show signs of frontal lobe involvement with inappropriate laughter and possibly with sexual or aggressive acting out. This is in contradistinction to Alzheimer's where social skills may be maintained far into the course of the disease. Although Lishman (1987) reports a greater prevalence of Pick's disease among women than among men, an investigation by Heston, White, and Mastri (1987) reported that men are at greater risk than are women. The onset of Pick's disease is typically later than for Alzheimer's (Lishman, 1987).

Normal Pressure Hydrocephalus

Another disease process characterized by neuropsychological signs similar to other forms of dementia is Normal Pressure Hydrocephalus (NPH). NPH occurs most often as a result of either a blockage of cerebral spinal fluid (CSF) within the subarachnoid space or as a result of a reduction in the amount of

CSF uptake by the venous sinuses, resulting in a decrease flow of CSF to the frontal lobes (Barth & Macciocchi, 1986; Merritt, 1973). NPH is characterized by a progressive onset occurring over several weeks to several months. The degenerative symptoms include a progressive triad of dementia and confusion, fait disturbances, and urinary incontinence (Prockop, 1984). NPH is distinguished from Alzheimer's dementia via lumbar puncture and CT scan results. On CT scans, patients with NPH exhibit ventricular enlargement without cortical atrophy, while Alzheimer patients exhibit similar ventricular enlargement, but with cortical atrophy. Additionally, NPH is characterized by a decrease in CSF circulation, while this circulation remains normal in Alzheimer's diseas (Martin & Black, 1987). Accurate diagnosis of NPH is critical considering that this form of dementia is nearly 100% correctable with early detection. Recommended treatment is the placement of a ventricular shunt to correct abnormal flow patterns of CSF (Vorstrup, Christensen, Gjerris, Sorensen & Thomsen, 1987; Prockop, 1984).

The Evaluation of Dementia

The Use of Neurodiagnostic Techniques Objective neurodiagnostic techniques, such as the Computerized Tomographic (CT) scan and Magnetic Resonance Imaging (MRI) have been useful in the diagnosis of several dementias only to the extent that they can rule out other etiologies, such as cerebral tumors. The structural changes in progressive dementias may be microscopal and therefore undetectable by current imaging techniques. Eslinger, Dimasio, Graff-Radford, and Damasio (1984) reported that there were no significant correlations between CT results and neuropsychological testing in a sample of 64 individuals who had been referred to a neurology service for evaluation of possible dementia. When 26 of those patients were matched for age, sex, and education to normal subjects, there were significant but moderate correlations between the two sets of variables. The canonical correlation between the CT and neuropsychological variables was .725, indicating that they shared 53% of their variance. Apparently, CT results in a sample of possibly demented individuals do not accurately predict actual functioning.

Measures of cerebral metabolism may have more promise for the diagnosis of Alzheimer's disease. Friedland, Budinger, Brant-Zawadski, and Jagust (1984) reported that although there were no abnormalities of CT or MRI in two patients with Alzheimer's, both patients showed hypometabolism in the temporal-parietal cortex on the PET scan. Subsequent work with the PET scan confirmed the hypometabolism in the parietal and temporal regions and indicated that early signs of hypometabolism may precede both the appearance of deficits on psychometric testing and the appearance of behavioral signs of cognitive decline (Foster, Chase, Mansi, Brooks, Fedio, Patronas, and

DiChiro, 1984). Data obtained by deLeon, George, Ferris, Rosenbloom, Christman, Gentes, Resiberg, Kricheff, and Wolff (1983) indicates that the hypometabolic changes are correlated with decrements in performance on neuropsychological tests. There is some recent data to suggest that single photon emission CT (SPECT) may be helpful in the differential diagnosis of Alzheimer's from MID (Gemmell, Sharp, Besson, Crawford, Ebmeier, Davidson, and Smith, 1987). However, as of yet, the diagnosis of Alzheimer's disease is still a clinical diagnosis conducted with the help of a neuropsychological evaluation.

The Use of Neuropsychological Tests Standardized neuropsychological testing can be useful in the early stages, batteries such as the LNNB or HRNB can provide information regarding the probable diagnosis by specifying the areas of relative strength and weakness in order to determine if the model profile for a given disorder is present. Additionally, the batteries can provide information regarding the optimal level of supervision needed for the individual to function. More specific tests of individual functions, such as the Randt Memory Test or Fuld Object Memory Test, may be useful here to determine the level of skill present. As the individual moves into the middle stages of the dementia, the value of the standardized battery decreases because the scores may begin to show a floor effect. By the time the individual reaches the late stages, standardized testing may not offer useful information. A behavioral assessment of the individual's ability to meet the demands of the environment is more appropriate at that point.

The Treatment of Dementia

Many dementias are due to medical causes and may therefore be reversible. These reversible dementias are primarily due to infections, endocrine disorders, and systemic disease. It is important to remember that even if the dementia is not reversible, treatment is possible.

Pharmacologic Treatment of Dementia Perhaps one of the most controversial topics in the treatment of patients with Alzheimer's is the use of cholinergic drugs or of drugs that affect blood supply to the brain. The general classes of drugs used experimentally to treat Alzheimer's disease include psychostimulants, cholinergics, vasodilators, and opioid antagonists (Goodnick & Gershon, 1984).

Because of the understandably large interest of the general public in such drug treatments, there is often a large amount of publicity surrounding announcements of even modest gains in memory or cognition as the result of such drug treatments. Unfortunately, there is not often replication of these promising results. Even in the studies that do find positive effects of drugs, there appears to be a complex set of relations among the characteristics of the subjects, the type of cognitive skill tested, and the dose of the medication. For example, McCaffrey, Steckler, Gansler, Roman, and Holub (1987) found that doses of 450 mg of Suloctidil, but not doses of 600 mg or placebo, improved performance on the Boston Naming Test, but not on Trails or the Grooved Pegboard. A therapeutic window for lecithin was also thought to have been responsible for the results of a double-blind investigation by Little, Levy, Chuaqui-Kidd, and Hand (1985) where doses in the middle range showed treatment effects not present at either extreme.

Summers, Majovski, Marsh, Tachiki, and Kling (1986) reported beneficial effects of oral tetrahydroaminoacridine on the results of a global assessment, the Orientation test, and the Alzheimer's Deficit Scale in 17 subjects with Alzheimer's disease. Further evidence for the effectiveness of cholinergic potentiation comes from Muramoto, Sugishita, and Ando (1984) who found temporary (≤ 60 minutes) improvement in three of six patients given physostigmine. As mentioned above, the results of these and other studies can rarely be replicated, and must therefore be cautiously interpreted. For now, the safest conclusion is probably that offered by Dysken (1987), namely, that there is not evidence to support clinical use of drug therapy to reverse of halt the progression of deficits in Alzheimer's, but that several of the drugs still bear promise for future investigation.

Psychological Treatment of Dementia One of the most important considerations in the treatment of dementia is in the provision of a supportive environment. The elderly person is going through a period of change, the velocity of which has not been experienced since adolescence. The older person's body does not perform as well as it had in the past. There are new pains and limitations. The older person also has new limitations in his/her cognitive efficiency. Memory is not as accurate as it once was. The act of problem solving may require more effort and time than it did previously. Because cognition is somewhat less efficient, adaptation to change may be harder to achieve.

Additionally, the social environment changes drastically as a person becomes older. There are fewer people who are older and who have more experience and on whom one can rely for advice. The network of friends and relatives becomes attenuated as these individuals die or move. Offspring may become less available as their own children enter adolescence or young adulthood. In our current culture, we no longer have the extended family domicile. Older members of our families often live alone. The older individual is forced to cope with a lessened set of supportive resources. The neuropsychologist can help to develop a supportive environment by exploring the acceptability and feasibility of different options such as joining a peer support group of encouraging daily check-ins by a family member and then providing reinforcement for these behaviors. The older individual may resent having someone check everyday and the neuropsychologist may have to help negotiate a reasonable solution. For more independent individuals, referral to volunteer organizations such as adoptive grandparent programs or retired business volunteer organizations may help the older person maintain a sense of independence and personal worth.

The clinical neuropsychologist can help provide information used to determine the level of supervision needed by the patient. If the neuropsychologist uncovers deficits in calculation or judgment, supervision of financial affairs may be necessary. If deficits in memory are uncovered, supervision of compliance with the medical regimen may be necessary. Deficits in visual spatial perceptual skills will make it necessary to review the driving privileges of the patient. Because clinical neuropsychological assessment is by nature analog assessment, the results of an examination must be evaluated against information derived from behavioral observations by the clinician and by others in the patient's environment.

There is a long gap between completely independent living and hospitalization. The clinical neuropsychologist can make suggestions regarding the appropriate level of supervision and care needed in individual cases. The ideal, even in cases of progressive degeneration, is to maintain the highest level of independence. Simply conducting a psychometric evaluation is insufficient. The clinical neuropsychologist should also obtain information regarding the requirements for functioning in the patient's current environment as well as information regarding the current level of success in meeting those requirements. The level of complexity in the environment should be titrated to meet the level of skill shown by the patient.

Changes in the environment should be instituted carefully with the full knowledge of the patient. Supervisors should be alerted to the fact that changes in the environment, even simplifications, may induce temporary exacerbations in the level of confusion exhibited by the patient. Progressive dementias generally occur over a period of several years, allowing time for the patient to develop compensatory behaviors or to rely on overlearned adaptive skills. Changing the environment strips the patient of these compensatory mechanisms and potentiates the appearance of symptoms. Sometimes changes are necessary, and the temporary exacerbation should be predicted and explained to the caregiver or supervisor with suggestions on how to minimize it by explaining and practicing new compensatory behaviors with the patient.

Specific Treatments for Symptoms of Dementia Because several of the forms of dementia are irreversible, our thinking may become focused on the lack of a cure rather than on the presence of a palliative treatment. It is true that the memory deficits associated with Alzheimer's may become worse over time, but it is also true that the deficits may become lessened slightly by behavioral treatment. The use of behavioral prosthetics may increase the functional aspects of memory performance without actually improving memory skills themselves. Daily orientation of the patient and the placement of a large calendar in the patient's room, whether at home or in a care facility, can help keep the person aware of change in time. Constant repetition and overlearning can also help compensate for memory difficulties.

In some cases, older persons with dementias may show paranoid behavior. This is not the same as a paranoid thought disorder. The paranoid-like behavior and speech of the older impaired individual is secondary to his/her limits in processing verbal information or in forming memories. The patient with Alzheimer's disease may not remember a particular conversation, and when two other family members or staff concur with the original statement, it might begin to resemble a conspiracy. Fear or suspicion of losing one's financial resources to younger family members may be partially realistic given that the family may be trying to institute supervision of the patient's finances. Here, treatment consists of attempts to remediate the primary deficit. The information from important conversations should be repeated, and where possible, documented in a written form that the patient can keep in his/her own possession.

Another common problem found in Alzheimer's disease patients is that of wandering, especially when associated with disturbances in the sleep/wake cycle. Many Alzheimer's patients are at their most confused in the evening or early night. This has been called the sun-downing effect. There are few treatments other than supervision, but explaining the phenomenon to family members can make a large difference. It is also possible that wandering may occur during the daylight hours. Supervision can be supplemented by sewing explicit identification and instructions for contacting a family member in the clothing of the patient.

Family Treatments in Dementia The patient is not the only individual who can benefit from treatment. The family or other caregivers can also derive improvement from the application of psychological treatment methods. First, education as to the disorder's mechanisms and prognosis can relieve their anxiety and increase their understanding of the patient. The family can be trained to be effective behavioral managers of the patient. This will require extra effort on their parts and is not likely to be maintained independently. The clinician can provide positive reinforcement to family members in order to help maintain the desired behaviors.

The family may also be in need of group counseling or family therapy. Each member of a family occupies a unique position in that family system. When a member of the family becomes less able to fulfill his/her role, the nature of relationships change and other family members must take on some of the patient's role duties. Families, like most other systems, are conservative and are resistant to change. The family may require intervention in order to navigate the changes. Additionally, witnessing a family member become demented may remind other members of their vulnerability and mortality, necessitating exploration and resolution of the resulting affective responses.

Finally, taking care of a demented patient is a full-time job, exhaustive both emotionally and physically. It is very difficult to maintain the level of activity needed. Families would benefit from respite care; temporary placement of the patient in a care facility or having a supervisor or caregiver come into the house on a weekly basis. One common impediment to utilizing respite care is the presence of guilt in the family. Many organizations and even some public agencies offer respite care programs, but a family member may feel guilty over having a stranger provide care for even a short period of time. Brief counseling can help the family member accept the benefits of respite care by pointing out the long-term positive effects of short breaks.

REFERENCES

Agnew, J., Bolla-Wilson, K., Kawas, C. H., & Bleecker, M. L. (1988). Purdue Pegboard age and sex norms for people 40 years old and older, *Developmental Neuropsychology, 4*, 29–35.

Albert, M., & Moss, M. (1984). The assessment of memory disorders in patients with Alzheimer's disease. In L. R. Squire & N. Butters (Eds.) *Neuropsychology of Memory* (pp. 236–246). New York: Guilford.

Bak, J. S., & Greene, R. L. (1980). Changes in neuropsychological functioning in an aging population. *Journal of Consulting and Clinical Psychology, 48*, 395–399.

Barth, J. T., & Macciocchi, S. N. (1986). Dementia: Implications for clinical practice. In S. B. Filskov & T. J. Boll (Eds.), *Handbook of Clinical Neuropsychology* (Vol. 2, pp. 398–425). New York: Wiley.

Benton, A. L., Eslinger, P. J., & Damasio, A. R. (1981). Normative observations on neuropsychological performances in old age. *Journal of Clinical Neuropsychology, 3*, 33–42.

Bigler, E. D. (1987). The clinical significance of cerebral atrophy in dementia. *Archives of Clinical Neuropsychology, 2*, 177–190.

Bornstein, R. A., Paniak, C., & O'Brien, W. O. (1987). Preliminary data on classification of normal and brain-damaged elderly subjects. *The Clinical Neuropsychologist, 1*, 315–323.

Botwinick, J. (1977). Intellectual abilities. In J. E. Birren & K. W. Schaie (Eds.), *Handbook of the Psychology of Aging,* (pp. 214–241). New York: Van Nostrand Reinhold.

Craik, F. I. M. (1977). Age differences in human memory. In J. E. Birren & K. W. Schaie (Eds.), *Handbook of the Psychology of Aging,* (pp. 178–192). New York: Von Nostrand Reinhold.

Crook, T. (1987). Dementia. In L. L. Carstenson & B. A. Edelstein (Eds.), *Handbook of Clinical Gerontology*. New York: Pergamon.

Cummings, J. L., & Zarit, J. M. (1987). Probable Alzheimer's disease in an artist. *Journal of the American Medical Association, 258*, 2731–2734.

deLeon, M. J., George, A. E., Ferris, S. H., Rosenbloom, S., Christman, D. R., Gentes,

C. I., Reisberg, B., Kricheff, I. I., & Wolf, A. P. (1983). Regional correlations of PET and CT in senile dementia of the Alzheimer type. *American Journal of Neurological Research, 4*, 553–556.

Duara, R., Grady, C., Haxby, J., Sundaram, M., Cutler, N. R., Heston, L., Moore, A., Schlageter, N., Larson, S., & Rapoport, S. I. (1986). Positron emission tomography in Alzheimer's disease. *Neurology, 36*, 879–887.

Dysken, M. (1987). A review of recent clinical trials in the treatment of Alzheimer's dementia. *Psychiatri Annals, 17*, 178–191.

Ernst, J. (1988). Language, grip strength, sensory-perceptual, and receptive language skills in a normal elderly sample. *The Clinical Neuropsychologist, 2*, 30–40.

Eslinger, P. J., Damasio, H., Graff-Radford, N., & Damasio, A. R. (1984). Examining the relationship between computed tomography and neuropsychological measures in normal and demented elderly. *Journal of Neurology, Neurosurgery, and Psychiatry, 47*, 1319–1325.

Fitzhugh, K. B., Fitzhugh, L. C., & Reitan, R. M. (1964). Influence of age upon measures of problem solving and experiential background in subjects with long-standing cerebral dysfunction. *Journal of Gerontology, 19*, 132–134.

Flicker, C., Ferris, S. H., Crook, T., Reisberg, B., & Bartus, R. T. (1988). Equivalent spatial-rotation deficits in normal aging and Alzheimer's disease. *Journal of Clinical and Experimental Neuropsychology, 10*, 387–399.

Foster, N. L., Chase, T. N., Mansi, L., Brooks, R., Fedio, P., Patronas, N. J., & DiChiro, G. (1984). Cortical abnormalities in Alzheimer's disease. *Annals of Neurology, 16*, 649–654.

Friedland, R. P., Budinger, T. F., Brant-Zawadski, M., & Jagust, W. J. (1984). The diagnosis of Alzheimer-type dementia. *Journal of the American Medical Association, 252*, 2750–2752.

Gemmel, H. G., Sharp, P. F., Besson, J. A. O., Crawford, J. R., Ebmeier, K. P., Davidson, J., & Smith, F. W. (1987). Differential diagnosis in dementia using the cerebral blood flow agent 99mTc HM-PAO: A SPECT study. *Journal of Computer Assisted Tomography, 11*, 398–402.

Gibson, A. J., & Kendrick, D. C. (1982). *The Kendrick Cognitive Test for the Elderly*. London: NFER-Nelson Publishing Company Ltd.

Gibson, G. E., Sheu, K-F. R., Blass, J. P., Baker, A., Carlson, K. C., Harding, B., & Perrino, P. (1988). Reduced activities of thiamine-dependent enzymes in the brains and peripheral tissues of patients with Alzheimer's disease. *Archives of Neurology, 45*, 836–840.

Golden, C. J., & Schlutter, L. C. (1978). The interaction of age and diagnosis in neuropsychological test results. *International Journal of Neuroscience, 8*, 61–63.

Golden, C. J., Strider, M. A., Ariel, R., & Golden, E. E. (1986). Neuropsychology and medical disorders. In S. B. Filskov & T. J. Boll (Eds.), *Handbook of Clinical Neuropsychology*, (Vol. 2). New York: Wiley.

Goldstein, G., & Shelly, C. (1981). Does the right hemisphere age more rapidly than the left? *Journal of Clinical Neuropsychology, 3*, 65–78.

Goodnick, P., & Gershon, S. (1984). Chemotherapy of cognitive disorders in geriatric subjects. *Journal of Clinical Psychiatry, 45*, 196–209.

Goodwin, J. S., Goodwin, J. M., & Garry, P. J. (1983). Association between nutritional status and cognitive functioning in a healthy elderly population. *Journal of the American Medical Association, 249*, 2917–2921.

Gray, J. A. (1982). *The neuropsychology of anxiety*. New York: Oxford Press.

Gurland, B., & Toner, J. (1983). Differentiating dementia from nondementing conditions. In R. Maycus & W. G. Rosen (Eds.), *Advances in neurology: The de-*

mentias pp. 43–52). New York: Raven Press.

Hamsher, K. deS., & Benton, A. L. (1978). Interactive effects of age and cerebral disease on cognitive performances. *Journal of Neurology, 217*, 195–200.

Heston, L. L., White, J. A., & Mastri, A. R. (1987). Pick's disease. *Archives of General Psychiatry, 44*, 409–411.

Jefferson, J. W., & Marshall, J. R. (1981). *Neuropsychiatric Features of Medical Disorders*. New York: Plenum.

Jellinek, E. M. (1962). Fits, faints, coma, and dementia in myxodema. *Lancet*, (No. 2) 1010–1012.

Jolles, J. (1986). Cognitive, emotional, and behavioral dysfunctions in aging and dementia. *Progress in Brain Research, 70*, 15–22.

Kral, V. A. (1962). Senescent forgetfulness: Benign and malignant. *Canadian Medical Association Journal, 4*, 61–68.

Lipowski, Z. J. (1980). *Delirium: Acute brain failure in man*. Springfield, IL: Charles C Thomas.

Lishman, W. A. (1987). *Organic Psychiatry* (2nd Ed.) Oxford: Blackwell Scientific.

Little, A., Levy, R., Chuaqui-Kidd, P., & Hand, D. (1985). A double-blind, placebo controlled trial of high-dose lecithin in Alzheimer's disease. *Journal of Neurology, Neurosurgery, and Psychiatry, 48*, 736–742.

MacInnes, W. D., Gillen, R. W., Golden, C. J., Graber, B., Cole, J. K., Uhl, H. S. M., & Greenhouse, A. H. (1983). Aging and performance on the Luria-Nebraska Neuropsychological Battery. *International Journal of Neuroscience, 19*, 170–190.

MacInnes, W. D., Paull, D., Uhl, H. S. M., & Schima, E. (1987). Longitudinal neuropsychological changes in a "normal" elderly group. *Archives of Clinical Neuropsychology*, 2, 273–282.

Mahurin, R. K., & Pirozzolo, F. J. (1986). Chronometric analysis: Clinical applications in aging and dementia. *Developmental Neuropsychology*, 2, 345–362.

Martin, M. J., & Black, J. L. (1987). Neuropsychiatric aspects of degenerative diseases. In R. E. Hales & S. C. Yudofsky (Eds.), *Textbook of Neuropsychiatry* (pp. 257–286). Washington, DC: American Psychiatric Press.

Marvel, G. A., Goden, C. J., Hammeke, T., Purish, A., & Osmon, D. (1979). Relationship of age and education to performance on a standardized version of Luria's neuropsychological tests in different patient populations. *International Journal of Neuroscience, 9*, 63–70.

McCaffrey, R. J., Steckler, R. A., Gansler, D. A., Roman, L. O., & Holub, B. N. (1987). An experimental evaluation of the efficacy of suloctidil in the treatment of primary degenerative dementia. *Archives of Clinical Neuropsychology*, 2, 155–161.

Merritt, H. H. (1973). *A Textbook of Neurology*, (5th ed.). Philadelphia: Lea & Febiger.

Miller, P. S., Richardson, J. S., Jyu, C. A., Lemay, J. S., Hiscock, M., & Keegan, D. L. (1988). Association of low serum anticholinergic levels and cognitive impairment in elderly presurgical patients. *American Journal of Psychiatry, 145*, 342–345.

Muramoto, O., Sugishita, M., & Ando, K. (1984). Cholinergic system and constructional praxis: A further study of physostigmine in Alzheimer's disease. *Journal of Neurology, Neurosurgery, and Psychiatry, 47*, 485–491.

Neary, D., Snowden, J. S., Northen, B., & Goulding, P. (1988). Dementia of frontal lobe type. *Journal of Neurology, Neurosurgery, and Psychiatry, 51*, 353–361.

Prockop, L. D. (1984). Hydrocephalus. In L. P. Rowland (Ed.) *Merritt's Textbook of*

Neurology (7th ed.) (pp. 433–441). Philadelphia: Lea & Febiger.

Reed, H. B. C., & Reitan, R. M. (1963). Changes in phychological test performance associated with the normal aging process. *Journal of Gerontology, 18*, 271–274.

Reitan, R. M. (1967). Psychologic changes associated with aging and cerebral damage. *Mayo Clinic Proceedings, 42*, 653–673.

Salmon, D. P., Shimamura, A. P., Butters, N., & Smith, S. (1988). Lexical and semantic priming in patients with Alzheimer's disease. *Journal of Clinical and Experimental Neuropsychology, 10*, 477–494.

Schwartz, M. F. (1987). Focal cognitive deficits in dementia of the Alzheimer's type. *Neuropsychology, 1*, 27–35.

Skenazy, J. A., & Bigler, E. R. (1984). Neuropsychological findings in diabetes mellitus. *Journal of Clinical Psychology, 40*, 246–258.

Smith, T. W., Anwer, U., DeGirolami, U., & Drachman, D. A. (1987). Vacuolar changes in Alzheimer's disease. *Archives of Neurology, 44*, 1225–1231.

Spittle, B. J., Fliegnar, J., & Faed, J. A. (1977). Post-infectious encephalopathy simulating functional psychosis. *New England Medical Journal, 85*, 180–181.

Spitzform, M. (1982). Normative data in the elderly on the Luria-Nebraska Battery. *Clinical Neuropsychology, 4*, 103–105.

Strider, M. A. (1982). Neuropsychological concomitants of diabetes mellitus. *Dissertation Abstracts International, 43*, 888B.

Summers, W. K., Majovski, L. V., Marsh, G. M., Tachiki, K., & Kling, A. (1986). Oral tetrahydroaminiacridine in long-term treatment of senile dementia, Alzheimer's type. *The New England Journal of Medicine, 315*, 1241–1245.

Thompson, L. L., Heaton, R. K., Matthews, C. G., & Grant, I. (1987). Comparison of preferred and non-preferred hand performance on four neuropsychological motor tasks. *The Clinical Neuropsychologist, 1*, 324–334.

Vorstrup, S., Christensen, J., Gjerris, F., Sorensen, P. S., & Thomsen, A. M. (1987). Cerebral bloodflow in patients with normal pressure hydrocephalus before and after shunting. *Journal of Neurosurgery, 66*, 379–387.

Wells, C. E. (1979). Pseudodementia. *American Journal of Psychiatry, 136*, 895–900.

Willis, L., Yeo, R. A., Thomas, P., & Garry, P. J. (1988). Differential declines in cognitive function with aging: The possible role of health status. *Developmental Neuropsychology, 4*, 23–28.

Wise, M. G. (1987). Dementia. In R. E. Hales & S. C. Yudofsky (Eds.), *Textbook of Neuropsychiatry*. Washington, DC: American Psychiatric Press.

Chapter 6

The Interface Between Neuropsychology and Behavior Therapy

Kathryn Lawson-Kerr, Stanley S. Smith, and DuAnn Beck

THE NEED FOR AN INTERFACE

The field of neuropsychology is evolving at a tremendous pace. With the development of better neurodiagnostic techniques, neuropsychologists are being asked to provide less in the way of lesion localization, and provide more input regarding long term treatment/rehabilitation services that may be needed. Referral questions have also changed radically over the years. As a result, assessment strategies have had to change in order to answer these questions. Case formulations are more sophisticated and are more likely to be directed toward rehabilitation issues.

Neuropsychologists are fielding questions that demand broad-based, detailed assessment strategies geared towards practical treatment alternatives. Questions that seem relataively straight forward, such as assessment of memory problems, may require extensive evaluation because of the larger issues involved. Referral questions often touch on a variety of areas that may not seem readily apparent from the start (see Table 6.1). One can no longer provide a simple psychometric assessment of the presence of absence of deficits with addressing the implications of such a disturbance.

Table 6.1 Areas Relevant to Neuropsychological Assessment

Major areas	Specific Areas
Ability to manage personal affairs:	Money management Daily self care Child rearing-Care of others
Employment Issues:	Ability to work Need to change occupations Job retraining
Psychological Issues:	Marital problems Poor judgment-Impulsivity Personality changes
	Social skills problems Current stressors Availability of social supports
Legal Issues (Criminal and Civil Issues):	Responsibility for engaging in criminal acts Competence (with regard to money management estate planning, wills)
Medical Considerations:	Chronic pain problems Acquired physical handicaps Medication side-effects

To make matters more complex, psychologists are coming into increasing contact with patients who have a variety of medical problems. With the advent of the behavioral medicine movement, psychologists are m ore likely to provide services to patients with heart disease, diabetes, cancer, drug abuse, and other medical problems that may not have been evaluated by a neurologist. The central nervous system (CNS) does not exist in isolation, however; all kinds of medical problems that seem far removed from the field of neurology can produce various psychological disorders that psychologists must assess and/or treat (Hales & Yudofsky, 1987; Hall, 1980; Tarter, Van Thiel, & Edwards, 1988). Consequently, psychologists are being pushed to become aware of a broad spectrum of physical disorders that may be associated with neuropsychological deficits.

As the field of behavioral medicine grows, psychologists are identifying more patients who need neuropsychological services. However, few psychologists are aware of the spectrum of medical conditions that can produce organic brain syndromes/disorders, or the base rates for these medical problems within their own service delivery population. Interestingly, little has been written regarding the incidence and prevalence of neurological or neuropsychological disorders among patients with illnesses typically treated by non-neurologists. As a result, psychologists are becoming increasingly aware that patients with medical problems may n eed to be assessed by neurologists or neuropsychologists, but they may not have a true feeling for the number of patients requiring such services. Table 6.2 delineates some of the most prevalent medical disorders that may produce CNS dysfunction.

It has been estimated, for example, that 15–46% of all patients seen in a cancer treatment center require neurological evaluation (Posner, 1979; Gilbert & Grossman, 1986). The National Cancer Institute (American Cancer Society, 1988) estimates that approximately 985,000 people will be diagnosed as having cancer this year. Of this group 152,000 will have lung cancer and 135,900 will have breast cancer. These two forms of cancer are most likely to metastasize to the brain (Escourolle & Poirer, 1973), and approximately 15–25% of all brain tumors are due to metastases (Rubinstein, 1972).

Alcoholism, one of the most common diagnostic entities among state hospital patients (Redlich & Kellert, 1978), may affect as many as 5–10% of the population at large (Horton, 1982). Although these individuals may show no outward neurologic problems, research suggests that as many as 50% of all alcoholics may show evidence of neuropsychological deficits 3–4 weeks after their last drink (Grant, Reed, & Adams, 1987).

Diabetics are 1.7 times more likely to be at risk for cerebrovascular disease than nondiabetics (Palumbo, Elveback, & Whisnant, 1978), and 6–8% of all deaths in this population are due to cerebrovascular disease (Alex, Baron, Goldenberg, & Blumenthal, 1962; Palumbo, Elveback, Chu, Connolly, & Kurland, 1976). Mental status changes in this population are often due to metabolic aberrations (e.g., hypoglycemic episodes), or actual destruction of brain tissue (e.g., infarction).

Patients with hypoxemic chronic obstructive pulmonary disease are also more likely to show evidence of neuropsychological impairment. A recent

Table 6.2 Disorders That May Cause Central Nervous System Dysfunction

General Medical Disorders	Central Nervous System Disorders
Metabolic disorders	Vascular events
Endocrine disorders	Stroke
Nutritional deficiencies	Hemorrhage
Systemic disorders	Tumors
Infectious processes	Trauma
Drug use/abuse	Infection
Toxins	Degenerative disorders
Congenital disorders/birth defects	Demyelinating disorders

study indicated that 42% of the patient sample evaluated were found to have moderate to severe cognitive deficits as compared to 14% of a matched control sample (Grant, Heaton, McSweeny, Adams, & Timms, 1982). As one can surmise, many patients with non-neurologic medical problems are at risk for the development of serious neurological dysfunction and concurrent neuropsychological deficits.

We are also faced with an aging population that will be more at risk for the development of neuropsychological deficits. Thirty-eight percent of the population of the United States will be over the age of 65 by the year 2030 (Horton, 1982, p. 100). In addition, medicine and biotechnology have become so sophisticated that psychologists are seeing more "survivors" of conditions that would have been fatal 5–10 years ago.

For many reasons, but in part due to this shift and increased demand for provision of neuropsychological services, clinicians have become more interested in assessment and treatment methodologies that have empirical clinical utility. Within the field of psychology, behavior therapy has offered one of the most attractive models for the assessment and remediation of behavioral deficits and excesses that are often related to CNS dysfunction. Behavioral case formulations differ radically from traditional assessment/treatment models in many ways. Behavior therapy focuses on the assessment of specific strengths and weaknesses rather than exploration of a presumed ill-defined underlying intrapsychic disturbance. This approach is geared towards the assessment of specific, well delineated problems that can be operationally defined. It is an approach that does not assume behavior is constant; it is situationally specific although influenced by previous learning experiences. In this manner it differs significantly from trait theory, the foundation of traditional assessment. Behavior therapy does not rely on "traits" as the ultimate explanation of behavior, although it does focus on an individual's learning history. As it rests on the principle that many maladaptive behaviors are learned, it follows that learning principles can be used to modify maladaptive behavior. This approach advocates the identification of well defined treatment goals. In addition, behavior therapists adapt their method of treatment to the client's problem. Treatment programs are continuously monitored to determine their efficacy, and altered if they prove to be of little utility. Empirical evaluation and modification is essential if treatment techniques are ineffective (Rimm & Masters, 1979).

Behavioral neuropsychology (Horton & Wedding, 1984; Wedding, Horton, & Webster, Eds. 1986) has appeared as an entity within the last two decades. The development of such a subspecialty has had tremendous theoretical as well as practical implications. Behavioral neuropsychology has been the logical outgrowth of the interface between clinical psychologists, behavioral neurologists, and behavior therapists. As Horton (1978) states:

> Behavioral neuropsychology may be defined as the application of behavior therapy techniques to problems of ofganically impaired individuals while applying a neuropsychologically based assessment and treatment perspective. That is, the careful delineation of data from neuropsychological assessment strategies would enhance the generation of tentative hypotheses in relation to the antecedent variables (either external or internal) for observed conditions of psychopathology. This neuropsychological perspective will significantly aid the behavior therapist's ability to make accurate discriminations as to the origin of the client's maladaptive behavior. Further the development of a thoughtful treatment plan and its skillful application could be facilitated by a specific task analysis of behavior deficits implicating impairment of higher cortical functioning. (p. 20)

This model has had tremendous appeal for a number of reasons: it is a tangible, operationally defined approach towards assessment; it has face validity to those being assessed, their family members, and other professionals; treatment techniques follow a logical pattern and are based on a careful analysis of behavioral strengths and weaknesses; and treatment techniques, by definition, are also assessed to demonstrate their utility. The latter point is not one to be taken lightly. The cost of remediating neuropsychological deficits in terms of time and money is staggering. Third party payers (i.e., insurance companies) are becoming increasingly concerned about the efficacy of rehabilitation techniques.

Neuropsychological assessment procedures provide limited, albeit useful, information. Although there has been much in the way of empirical support for the use of neuropsychological tests, psychologists stilll have a long way to go in terms of making specific predictions regarding the impact of the patient's identified deficits on their activities of daily living. It is not unusual, for example, for patients to display a wide variety of neuropsychological impairments on an assessment battery, and yet function adaptively within their environment. Other individuals may display only subtle deficits on testing, yet be unable to care for themselves or function without continual supervision. Neuropsychologists need to improve the ecological validity of their assessment and treatment techniques. Behavioral approaches to assessment and treatment can help them achieve this goal.

The need for behavioral neuropsychology becomes clearer in context. Patients with congenital or acquired neurologic problems present with a spectrum of psychological and behavioral disturbances that interfere with their activities of daily living and adjustment within their environment. They may also have a range of interpersonal difficulties which contribute to a lack of social support. The case of John S. is fairly typical:

> Mr. John S., a 32-year-old married logger, was involved in a car accident four months ago while working in northern Mississippi. He fractured his leg,

> arm, and ribs, and had a moderately serious head injury (i.e., unconscious for ten hours). Although his physical problems have gotten better, he has been extremely irritable, depressed, and withdrawn. His relationship with his family has become strained. They say his personality has changed; he is more demanding and dependent on them. They have noticed that he doesn't sleep well and he has pain problems. His attention is impaired and he doesn't remember things. They worry about his ability to drive because he seems to have little awareness of oncoming traffic. Although John is cognizant of some of his problems, he doesn't seem to think his difficulties are as serious as his family does. He tried to return to his job, but his pain problems interfered with heavy labor. His employer laid him off. He has not been able to find another job, as he has never done any other kind of work, and he has a tenth grade education. Since his accident, he has had trouble with reading and writing, but hasn't mentioned it to anyone. He is embarrassed because his wife has gone to work in order to support the family. She has also been managing their finances, as he seems unable to manage a checkbook or keep track of the bills. His friends are confused because he looks physically fit, yet he hasn't returned to work. They have noticed that his conversations are repetitive and seem devoid of substance. They also wonder why his personality has changed. They have begun to withdraw some of their support, as he seems very self-centered. (Lawson-Kerr & Smith, 1988)

This case is characterized by a wide range of problems that become apparent in the initial stages of answering a simple referral question such as: "Please assess Mr. S's neuropsychological deficits." This case is typical of those referred for neuropsychological assessment and rehabilitation, and will serve as a basis to illustrate the need for an interface between behavioral approaches and neuropsychology.

INITIAL STAGES OF CASE FORMULATION

Assessment

Behavioral assessment techniques can be easily utilized within the context of neuropsychological assessment. First, behaviors that are problematic must be defined and identified. Second, antecedent conditions and consequences (both internal and external) that influence the rate, degree, and range of problematic behaviors must be delineated. Third, behaviorists recognize that assessment techniques have their limitations. For example, one needs to take into account flaws inherent in self-report measures, as patients and their family members are not always accurate historians. Direct observation of behavior in the natural setting lends validity to an assessment process, and bridges the gap between psychometric and ecologically valid inferences. Neuropsychological assessment techniques can be easily couched within this framework, although much needs to be done to extend the validity of inferences often based on these assessments. Neuropsychological assessments serve primarily to delineate one more facet of the patient's overall functioning, a facet that interacts with all other levels of functioning (see Figure 6.1).

Neuropsychological consultations are solicited because of an assumption that an individual may have cerebral dysfunction that may be contributing to the expression of maladaptive behavior. In an initial intake session, basic information must be gathered to lay the groundwork on which other assumptions stand. Simple, yet crucial questions must be answered first. For example, who requested the evaluation: the patient, a family member, an employer, or a health care professional? In each instance, the information that can be obtained from each source, and the questions that need to be addressed, may be vastly different because of situationally specific factors.

The patient's gender, age, education, and occupational background set the stage for the development of various clinical hypotheses as well. Certainly, a referral received from a teacher concerning a 12-year-old student with an average school record, whose grades deteriorated after a head-injury, may raise an entirely different set of clinical questions than a 55-year-old, head-injured executive, who has been recently fired and was referred for evaluation by his physician. In most instances, the initial information to be collected must

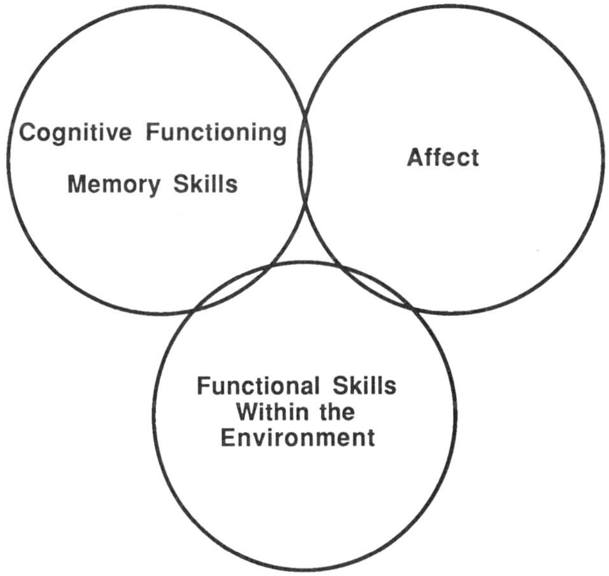

Figure 6.1. Facets of functioning.

be broadbased in scope, and progressively narrowed down in order to focus on specific problems. This philosophy is no different than that proposed by Cone and Hawkins (1977) when carrying out a behavioral assessment.

Areas to be covered during formal assessment include the patient's:

1. Developmental history (with particular attention to attainment of developmental milestones).
2. Social history (including factors such as exposure to models of illness behavior).
3. Academic history (focusing on achievement scores, grades, absences from school, history of delinquency/discipline problems).
4. Medical history (including all current and past medical problems that can cause CNS dysfunction, length of illness, drug use/abuse, and medical problems that have been present in parents or siblings).
5. Psychiatry history (treatment for psychological problems of any kind).
6. Work history (listing all jobs held, history of frequent job changes or terminations).
7. A history of current or past legal problems (engaged in past, current, or future law suits, criminal charges pending or brought in the past).

A history also needs to be taken regarding the patient's self-report of deficits and how this report may or may not match the perception of others who have had contact with the patient. Disagreements regarding the patient's strengths and deficits may be due to a wide variety of reasons. For example, family members may have had little contact with the patient after they became ill. Patients and family members can also exaggerate or downplay the severity of an acquired deficit. Patients may also be at risk for not being able to evaluate the seriousness of their deficits. If discrepancies exist in the histories obtained, the origin for the differences needs to be examined. Failure to do so may result in patients and families disagreeing over how problems are addressed in treatment.

Specific medical problems are associated with characteristic behavioral deficits. The clinician should be knowledgeable enough to read a medical record and develop some immediate hypotheses regarding the types of difficulties the patient may display in carrying out daily activities. For example, it is not uncommon for individuals with a right posterior cerebrovascular accident to have significant problems seeing anything in their left visual field. Such patients are also at risk for having a neglect syndrome. An examiner who is aware of this should immediately ask questions relevant to the concurrent behavioral deficits that might be present (such as poor driving skills).

The information obtained can be organized into two sections: a problem list (refer to Table 6.3), and a flow chart (see Figure 6.2). Table 6.3 summarizes John S.'s problem list and helps organize information while taking a history.

Table 6.3 John S.'s Problem List and Condensed History

Problems Identified on Interview:	Condensed Significant History:
1. Medical problems (secondary to MVA)	Attained developmental milestones at appropriate age
S/p left leg, left arm, rib fractures	Always right handed
Moderately serious head injury (LOC 10 hrs.)	
Pain problems	Average student in elementary school and high school (C's)
Visual field defect (doesn't see traffic)*	
2. Psychological Problems	Was not in special education classes
Personality changes*	Was not suspended while in school
Mood disturbance (depression)	
Increased levels of stress/frustration	Legal problems: 2DUI convictions in the past
Disrupted family situation changes in the division of responsibilities increased stress on family relationships*	
Decreased social contact	May have abused alcohol in the past (note: Drinking Under Influence convictions)
Uncertainty regarding current capabilities	Steady work history
Insomnia	
3. Possible Neuropsychological Problems	No significant or major marital problems prior to recent injury
Attention, memory, and possible* problem solving difficulties	
May have poor judgment in terms of evaluating his capabilities	No significant medical problems prior to injury
May have lack of insight regarding* the impact of his behavior on others	No models for sick role behavior in his family
May have problems with mathematics*	
4. Vocational Problems	Stressors prior to injury: Death of father (2 months before his accident)
Unemployment (with financial problems a possibility)	Additional current stressors: involved in two car accidents as driver*
Inability to return to former job at this time, and may possess limited "other job skills"	
Limited educational background	
Transportation problems possible (given the description of current driving skills)	

*Indicates problems emphasized by Mrs. John S.; not Mr. John S

Flow charts are particularly useful, as the clinician can roughly diagram the course of clinical symptoms over time. This can often suggest the etiology of the physical disorder if the history obtained can be trusted, as different neurologic disorders are characterized by changes in behavior that may follow a specific behavioral pattern over time. They can also be helpful from a prognostic standpoint. Patients and family members should be interviewed separately, utilizing a flow chart format, in order to determine whether there is a congruence between their reports. For example, curve A on Figure 6.2 is typical of the kind of course often seen in patients who have experienced an acute event, such as John S. Pattern B is more typical of patients who have had a progressive downhill course such as Alzheimer's disease. Pattern C is more commonly seen in individuals who have had multiple strokes and exhibit stepwise deterioration. Flow charts can also be used to indicate when specific events occurred over time, and the patient's perception of how these events had an impact on their level of functioning. As psychological stressors interfere with a patient's level of functioning, records reflecting whether events were psychological or physical in nature may also help determine the relative contribution of these problems to changes in levels of performance.

Based on information obtained during an interview with the patient (and other relevant individuals), and a review of the patient's records (medical, academic, occupational, and legal), some hypotheses about the presence/absence and degree of behavioral deficits/strengths can be made. Standardized neuropsychological tests can then be used to examine the types of strengths and deficits that may be observed in various areas, such as: intellectual skills, orientation, verbal and nonverbal memory, attention, language, visual-spatial skills, sensory-perceptual processes, and motor performance. Neuropsycholo-

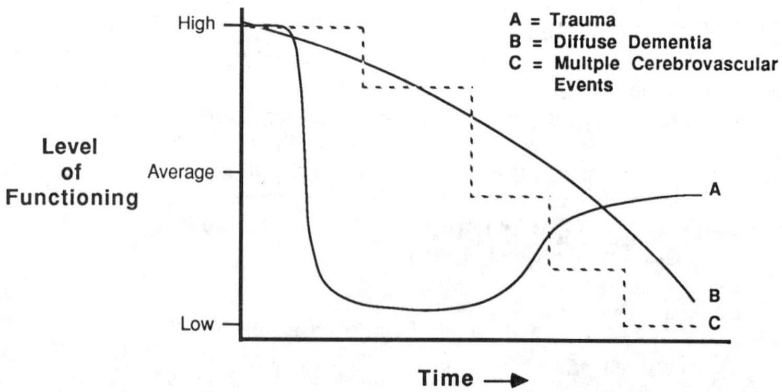

Figure 6.2. Flow chart mapping functioning over time.

gists often add other assessment instruments to a battery of neuropsychological tests, such as achievement tests and personality assessment instruments, in order to broaden their data base by looking at other facets of functioning.

Neuropsychologists are often called upon to determine the relation between deficits identified on testing and an individual's ability to return to their former occupation, manage their affairs, or other issues that relate to activities of daily living. This can present a number of difficult problems, as there are no clear guidelines for such judgments, particularly if the deficits identified are subtle. Behavioral approaches have helped in this regard by taking assessments one step further. For example, if a patient is identified as having acalculia during a neuropsychological assessment, a behaviorally oriented clinician might conduct an additional series of ecologically relevant tailor-made tests, such as: checkbook balancing, an assessment of change-making skills, and an evaluation of the patient's ability to use a calculator. In each case, the clinician can examine the relation between identified strengths and weaknesses on neuropsychological tests, and the corresponding skill dependent activities that the patient needs to do on a day to day basis. Specific deficient skills can be targeted and broken down into their component parts for further skills analysis. Assessment strategies can then be used to assess whether the patient cannot conceptualize the steps needed to analyze or complete a task, or whether they may have a sequencing deficit, etc. Identification of skill strengths can also be of value in determining which compensatory skills might be used to override deficient areas.

A detailed assessment that is based on a multimethod assessment base (e.g., chart reviews, interviews, psychometric assessment, and ecological assessment) is a time consuming process, but well worthwhile prior to a labor intensive treatment program. Clinicians are strongly encouraged to discuss case formulations with their patients, relevant family members, and other members of the treatment team before starting treatment, as treatment goals need to be agreed upon by all. Often, compromises must be struck in order to engage cooperation from relevant parties.

IMPLICATIONS FOR TREATMENT

Behavioral approaches to the treatment of the neurologically impaired individual offer many potential advantages. These include:

1. The ability to target problematic behaviors.
2. The ability to shape and reinforce appropriate behaviors.
3. The use of significant others as possible treatment technicians.
4. The availability of a wide variety of treatment interventions.
5. The ability to monitor the progress of treatment.

6. The flexibility to modify the strategy as necessary to maximize treatment efficacy.

Although by no means exhaustive, it is hoped that the material presented will offer the clinician suggestions and guidelines for selecting appropriate target behaviors and behavioral interventions for use in the treatment of the neurologically impaired individual. Specifics regarding the use of techniques suggested for use with target behaviors can be found elsewhere (Rimm & Master, 1979). It should also be noted that neurologically impaired individuals are likely to present with a constellation of behaviors that are in need of intervention. Hypotheses regarding an individual's ability to benefit from an intervention and other factors which determine whether a treatment will be effective (e.g., clinician experience, degree of impairment, family support, etc.) are beyond the scope of this discussion.

According to Prigatano (1986a), the goals of interventions with the neurologically impaired individual should:

1. Provide a model or models that help the patient understand what has happened to him or her.
2. Help the patient deal with the meaning of the brain injury in his or her life.
3. Help the patient achieve a sense of self-acceptance and forgiveness for himself or herself and others who have caused the accident.
4. Help the patient make realistic commitments to work and interpersonal relations.
5. Teach the patient how to behave in different social situations (to improve competence).
6. Provide specific behavioral strategies for compensating for neuropsychological deficits.
7. Foster a sense of realistic hope. (p. 71)

Within this context, a behavioral therapist uses behavior as a means of constructing mental life and modifies the behavior of the neurologically impaired individual to optimize functions (Diller & Gordon, 1981).

The determination of problematic (i.e., target) behaviors and treatment interventions used within a behavioral context rests soundly on the thoroughness of the assessment that has been conducted through careful psychometric testing and observation of the neurologically impaired individual in the natural environment. The selection of target behaviors and the development of a treatment strategy, therefore should follow logically from the information obtained during the assessment process. It might be easiest to conceptualize the behavioral treatment of the neurologically impaired individual as a multistep task. First, the assessment provides information regarding strengths and weaknesses of both the behavioral problems of the individual and the supporting environment (which includes family members, other caregivers, etc.). Second, appropriate target behaviors are selected based on the assessment. Third, target behaviors are categorized according to class (e.g., behavioral deficits, etc.). Fourth, an intervention is selected on the basis of effectiveness for a class of target behaviors. Fifth, the target behavior is monitored throughout treatment and both the intervention and target behavior are modified when necessary as new information becomes available. This is graphically represented in Figure 6.3.

As other chapters provide an excellent source of information regarding specific populations and monitoring strategies (see Chapters 5 and 8), this section will focus on general issues involving the selection of target behaviors, categorizing of target behaviors, and behavioral interventions for use with the neurologically impaired individual.

TARGET BEHAVIORS

It is important to describe the types of cognitive, affective, and behavioral sequelae often observed in the neurologically impaired individual and which are often the target of behavioral interventions. These sequelae can broadly be described as disturbances of mood, interpersonal behavior and activity, and cognition. These categories are not intended to be either exhaustive or mutually exclusive, but they do provide a framework from which appropriate target behaviors may be selected. Disturbances in mood may be manifested by emotional or personality changes. Disturbances in interpersonal behavior and activity often present as impulsivity, restlessness, impatience, and social dependency. Disturbances in cognition often result in reduced self-perception or awareness of changes in ability, problems with memory and new learning, and planning difficulties, to name a few.

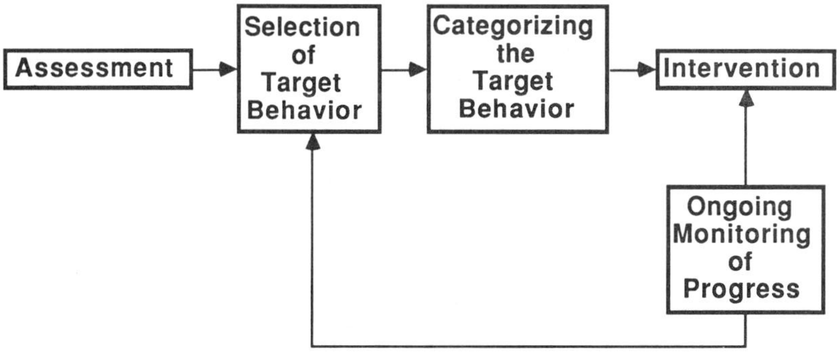

Figure 6.3. Stages of case management.

In order for a behavioral intervention to be effective, however, potential target behaviors need to be functionally defined, rather than limited to the content areas described above. For example, problems of social dependency may present by the individual not making choices about activities, not participating in planning them, yet enjoying the social contacts if initiated by someone else. Or the aggressive head-injured individual may be physically agressive against only certain individuals under certain circumstances. The important point to be made is that the more specifically the target behavior can be defined under precise conditions, the greater the likelihood an appropriate intervention will be used, and the more likely the problem behavior will be changed.

CATEGORIZING TARGET BEHAVIORS/BEHAVIORAL INTERVENTIONS

Kanfer and Grimm (1974) state that problem behaviors can be categorized by one of more of the following:

1. deficiencies in information or required behaviors
2. behavioral excesses
3. inappropriate environmental stimulus control
4. inappropriate self-generated stimulus control
5. problematic reinforcement contingencies (p. 10)

These categories of problematic behaviors are readily applicable to the neurologically impaired individual. Problematic behaviors most often associated with the neurologically impaired individual are behavioral excesses and deficits. As Kanfer and Grimm suggest, however, many behaviors can be classified as both an excess or deficit. For example, the impulsive behavior of a neurologically impaired individual might be described as excessive (from the family's perspective) or a deficit (from the patient's perspective) in self-control. Kanfer and Grimm's model provides a useful format in which to illustrate the matching of target behaviors, specifically deficits and excesses, and behavioral interventions with neurologically impaired individuals. No attempt is made to provide a detailed discussion of specific behavioral interventions or to discuss the appropriateness of an intervention with a particular group of neurologically impaired individuals. For an excellent review of specific treatment methods with a wide variety of patient populations see Horton and Miller (1985). For purposes of clarity and comparison the information is conveniently presented by behavioral excess or deficit in tabular form in Tables 6.4 and 6.5.

Table 6.4 Examples of the Application of Behavioral Interventions in the Treatment of Behavioral Excesses in Neurologically Impaired Individuals

Behavioral Excess	Possible Behavioral Interventions to Consider
Conditioned anxiety	Modeling, systematic desensitization, flooding, relaxation training, biofeedback
Impulsivity	Self-monitoring, modeling
Restlessness	Self-monitoring, modeling
Aggression	Timeout, modeling, overcorrection, DRO, extinction, DRI
Preservation	Shaping
Emotional lability	Modeling

Table 6.5 Examples of the Application of Behavioral Interventions in the Treatment of Behavioral Deficits in Neurologically Impaired Individuals

Behavioral Deficits	Possible Behavioral Interventions to Consider
Planning	Shaping, self-monitoring
Social Dependency	Social skills training, behavioral rehearsal, role-playing, modeling, shaping
New Learning/Memory	Behavioral rehearsal
Aggression (due to decreased self-control)	Positive reinforcement of appropriate behaviors, self-monitoring, stress inoculation training
Poor self-awareness/denial of problems	Provide information, self-monitoring
Depression	Social skills training, shaping, modeling, DRO
Withdrawal	Communications training, shaping, social skills training

The suggestions in Tables 6.4 and 6.5 for behavioral interventions with a variety of neurobehavioral sequelae of brain injury are simplistic in their presentation. The effects of inappropriate stimulus control, whether self-generated of environmental in nature, and problematic environmental contingencies are also likely to have profound impact on the effectiveness of any behavioral intervention.

A greater understanding of the use of the above interventions may be provided by discussing how behavioral interventions could impact one broad class of target behaviors, namely emotional sequelae of acquired brain impairment. Emotional sequelae of acquired brain impairment can obviously have a profound impact on treatment of observed cognitive deficits. Emotional changes as a result of trauma can be seen as directly related to the trauma itself and also as secondary to the injury (Brooks & McKinlay, 1983). In the first case, many neurologically impaired individuals experience behavioral/emotional sequelae in the form of increased irritability or social withdrawal that is directly related to the site of injury (Levin, Benton, & Grossman, 1983). In addition, the deficits that result from the injury may be perceived by the individual as so severe and such a change from premorbid levels that psychological difficulties arise as the individual attempts to cope with the changes in functioning that have occurred. Both of these can be considered emotional sequelae to an injury and may affect treatment design and outcome.

Emotional or affective behavior, from a physiological perspective, is associated with level of arousal. Changes in level of arousal and one's ability to modulate levels based on environmental stimuli are often compromised as a result of a head injury. The neurologically impaired patient may display inappropriate affect, outbursts of temper, and increased irritability. In addition, decreased initiative is a common emotional concomitant of brain injury. The emotional sequelae that are directly related to the injury can be conceptualized as primary emotional factors. As mentioned above, psychological factors secondary to the injury can develop as the recovery process occurs. These psychological factors include feelings of confusion and inadequacy, loss of self-worth, fear of the future, uncertainty about recovery, and social withdrawal. In addition, organic syndromes of a delusionary or halucinatory nature can develop as the result of brain injury (Strub & Black, 1981).

A number of treatment strategies are used with patients evidencing varying emotional concomitants to their injuries (Prigatano, 1986b). The withdrawn patient typically does not interact with others in the environment. Requiring the withdrawn neurologically impaired patient to engage in some activity in order to receive reinforcement is a possible treatment strategy. Putting non-responsive behavior on extinction while at the same time verbally reinforcing performance of desirable behaviors, such as speech or social interaction with others, may increase the social behavior of these individuals. There may also be some difficulty finding effective reinforcers in the environment for socially withdrawn individuals using a simple behavior modification program. Withdrawal may be a function of decreased responsiveness to environmental stimuli as a direct consequence of the brain insult, in which case behavioral interventions may need to be simplified. As recovery from the brain injury continues, programming to change the behavior(s) can become more complex.

The paranoid patient is often combative and suspicious of others. Excessive attending to paranoid behavior should be avoided and interventions should be implemented in a consistent manner. In addition, it appears that minimal changes in the individual's environment should facilitate improvement in any observed paranoid behavior. The agitated patient has difficulty in controlling arousal levels and often is excessively stimulated by environmental stimuli, resulting in agitated behavior. The main emphasis in initially dealing with agitated or irritable behavior is to identify the environmental factors which may precipitate and maintain this behavior. Most typically, the amount of stimulation provided by the environment is decreased in order to decrease the level of agitation.

As mentioned earlier, depression is often a concomitant of brain injury. As the recovery process continues the neurologically impaired invididual may become increasingly aware of changes in functioning from premorbid levels. Depression should be considered a part of the recovery process, and means to lessen the depression include reinforcement of activity, individual and family psychotherapy, and possible pharmacotherapy in order to promote appropriate feelings of concern over level of functioning and to provide a supportive environment during the period of recovery.

These suggestions for amelioration of the emotional sequelae are fairly simplistic solutions to a very complicated process of recovery. It is necessary to initially assess whether the observed emotional sequelae are the result of primary or secondary factors related to the injury. The primary sequelae may be more amenable to change using behavior modification principles alone. However, if assessment reveals that the emotional sequelae are reactive in nature, a multidisciplinary treatment approach may be necessary to help pinpoint treatment targets. An assessment of the level of support provided by the patient's family is also essential for maximum recovery following brain injury. If the support provided by the family is inadequate, any intervention implemented by the behavior therapist is likely to fail. This is still a rather simplistic description of the issues and interventions involved in the remediation of a problematic group of behaviors for many neurologically impaired individuals. It does provide a framework in which interventions with this population can occur. Let's investigate how the above treatment consideerations might be applied to our hypothetical head-injured individual, John S.

CASE EXAMPLE

An assessment of John S. indicated that he had numerous problems that could be loosely described under the following categories: medical, psychological, neuropsychological, and vocational problems (see Table 6.3). Information obtained from his medical records, interviews with John S. and his family, and from medication monitoring (pill count), indicated that John was using his pain medication inappropriately. He was solely responsible for remembering to take his medications, which he frequently forgot. On several occasions, he took more than one dose within a short period of time. Neuropsychological testing suggested the presence of moderate verbal and nonverbal memory problems. In fact, John could not tell his neuropsychologist how he was supposed to take his medications, and he had difficulty reading the labels on the bottles. These problems led to frequent medication changes, as he often complained to his physician that "these drugs just aren't giving me any relief." His family was not aware that this pattern of problems existed.

In addition, John often denied that he had any visual problems whatsoever, despite the fact that he often overlooked anything in his left visual field. He stated on interview that he saw no reason for his family's concern about his driving skills or his ability to use a gun while hunting. He admitted that he had been involved in a car accident after his discharge from the hospital, but denied that the accident was his fault. On further questioning, it became apparent that he had crossed the center line and hit an oncoming car in the opposite lane while driving with his wife. He reluctantly admitted that this was the case.

Information obtained on interview from his wife indicated that she had observed a distinct change in her husband's personality. He was verbally abusive to her, particularly if she was trying to be helpful and correct mistakes of his. He used foul language in front of their friends, and he would avoid social situations unless other family members were present. He would frequently get up and leave social gatherings without explanation and demand that they go home immediately. His wife felt that he would become physically aggressive toward her if she did not comply with his demands, although he had not yet reached this point. She also noticed that in addition to being irritable, he would not sleep well at night, preferring to sleep during the day. Both John and his wife reported that few things entertained him any more. He continued to go duck hunting on occasion, but usually went by himself, and he often came home in a bad mood. His wife worried about his owning a gun.

A neuropsychological evaluation was carried out six months after his injury. He was initially very congenial, although his attitude changed rapidly when he was confronted with frustrating tasks. He rarely recognized his mistakes and his performance was often characterized by impulsiveness. If errors were pointed out to him, he became sullen, and his behavior bordered on being verbally abusive toward the examiner. Testing revealed a pattern of strengths and deficits. His army records indicated that his premorbid functioning had been within the high average range of intellectual functioning at one time. Post injury, he was found to be functioning in the borderline range of intelligence (Full Scale IQ = 79 ± 2, as assessed by the Wechsler Adult Intelligence Scale-Revised), and he demonstrated significant impairments on visual-spatial tasks (such as block design), as he tended to ignore the left side of space. He also had mild to moderately impaired performance on tasks that were dependent on verbal and nonverbal memory skills. John had difficulty retaining test instructions, often forgetting what the examiner said. He would frequently repeat himself on the rare occasions when he initiated conversation.

Examination of language functioning revealed relatively intact oral comprehension for short sentences (but not for extended conversation), slightly impaired verbal expressive skills (e.g., characterized by word finding difficulties and circumlocutions), problems with writing (e.g., characterized by spelling errors and grammatic mistakes), and difficulty reading, as he would not scan far enough to the left. He was not aware of his visual field problem, and he did not spontaneously correct his scanning errors, despite the fact that text didn't make sense when it was incorrectly scanned.

He also had an inordinate amount of difficulty with math. He frequently misinterpreted the operation to be carried out, forgetting to "carry" numbers when doing addition, subtraction, multiplication, or division. He could not use a calculator with precision. He could identify coins and bills, but often could not tell how much money he had, as he would spread it out on a table to count it, and would count only what he could see. Also, he was unable to add up sums in his head, and he was rarely accurate in assessing whether he had received the correct change after a purchase. In addition to a dense left homonymous visual field defect, John was unable to identify numbers drawn in his left palm, or identify objects in his left hand if he had to rely on his sense of touch. During test breaks, he was noted to walk on the right side of the hallway only, and often bumped into furniture and door frames to his left.

When the examiner attempted to "test limits" by administering tasks with guidelines provided to increase success, he did not seem to benefit unless the instructions provided were explicit and there were a minimum number of distractions in the environment.

John stated that he wanted to resume his former job as a logger. He felt that his pain problems and insomnia were the only barrier between employment and unemployment, and he felt very frustrated that his medications provided little relief. He couldn't imagine himself engaging in any other form of employment, stating, "I've never done anything else for a living; why should I change now?" He resented his wife's implication that he was no longer a safe driver, and denied that this might have an impact on his future employment.

A flow chart can be outlined, delineating how Mr. S.'s problems evolved over time (see Figure 6.4).

At this level in the assessment process one can begin to form hypotheses about some of the problems that need to be addressed in treatment, and the

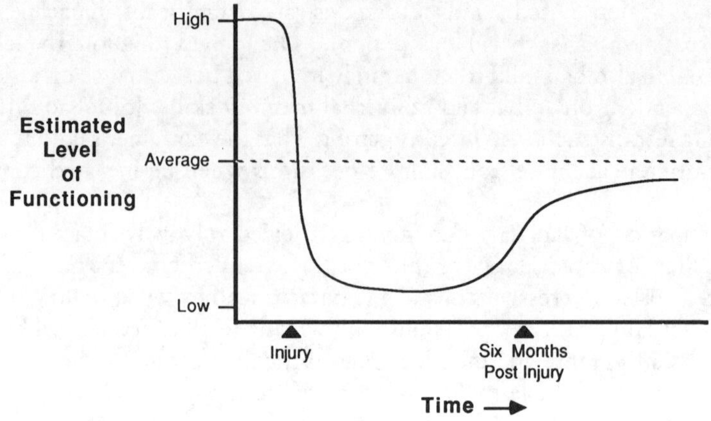

Figure 6.4. John S.'s flow chart.

impact of John S.'s neuropsychological deficits and strengths on his continued social and occupational functioning. From the preceding discussion of problems identified by John S., his family, and through the formal assessment it is necessary to prioritize the problems which will be targeted for intervention.

In general, the need to prioritize the treatment list is based on several important considerations. First, one must recognize that all behavior problems may not be amenable to change through behavioral interventions. For example, it may be impossible for the neurologically impaired individual to return to his/her previous employment secondary to physical or neurologic injury. Second, many behaviors which are targeted for intervention may become less problematic if an initial target behavior is chosen that will impact other problem areas. For example, successfully reducing aggressive behavior may have a positive effect on social interactions, and reduce the necessity of targeting social interactions at a later time. Third, it is important to recognize that neurologically impaired individuals and their families may determine that a certain problem area should be targeted for intervention before the professional does, and they may be unwilling or hesitant to treat other target behaviors first. Fourth, it is important to target behaviors that can be readily changed in order to give the patient and family experience with a successful intervention. Fifth, the expertise of the change agent, whether behavior therapist, vocational rehabilitation counselor, family member, or patient, and potential environmental constraints, must be taken into account when determining both target behavior and intervention strategy. If the primary change agent is the family and it is unlikely that they will be able to receive adequate training in the use of an intervention (for whatever reason), the probability that the intervention will be a failure increases.

In determining a prioritized list of target behaviors and interventions for John S., it is important to consider the factors described above which are likely to impact the success of any behavioral intervention. Table 6.6 provides a list of the four general areas of problematic behaviors identified during the assessment of John S. In this hypothetical case, a specific list of problematic (target) behaviors was developed and prioritized taking into account the previous considerations. For the purpose of our hypothetical case, the general areas to be targeted are prioritized, but only insofar as they apply to the initial specific target behavior within each area.

In the case of John S., four general areas of problematic behaviors were generated from the assessment information: psychological, neuropsychological, medical, and vocational. In each of these general areas, one behavior was selected as an initial target behavior primarily due to the severity of the behavior as a problem relative to the others in the category. In the case of John S., aggressive behavior, and more specifically, verbal abuse directed at his spouse, was targeted for initial intervention (see Table 6.6). A number of assumptions were made in prioritizing this behavior before others on the list. First, we assumed that John's verbal aggression was a source of considerable stress for all family members. Second, decreasing verbal aggression will likely positively impact other identified target behaviors, both within the general area of aggression and also within other areas (e.g., demanding car keys to avoid social interactions, initiating and engaging in conversations, screaming when memory problems are presented, and coping with other potentially frustrating situations, such as difficulty finding words to use during conversations). Finally, aggression is a common neurobehavioral sequelae to traumatic brain injury and is often the target of behavioral interventions (Lishman, 1978).

Some understanding of the nature of aggression in the neurologically impaired individual may be useful. Wood (1987) describes two major forms of aggression commonly associated with traumatic brain injury:

1. Impulsive and unprovoked aggression of a type which probably occurs as a result of some kind of electrical abnormality within the brain . . . and has been described as 'episodic dyscontrol.'
2. Poor emotional control. The two forms of this type of aggression are emotional lability, where prevailing mood shifts rapidly, with little provocation, but without the mood being sustained. The second is a loss of control over emotional expression, but with little or no meaningful affectional changes accompanying the behavior. (pp.18–19)

Table 6.6 Prioritized Treatment Targets: An Abbreviated List

Target Behaviors (General)	Target Behaviors (Specific)
1. Psychological Problems	1. Verbal abuse directed at spouse—foul language used when performance errors are pointed out by wife 2. Sleeps during day—may need further assessment to tease this out; could be medication related, RAS damage, depression 3. Does not engage in formerly pleasurable activities, lack of desire, and lack of financial resources
2. Neuropsychological Problems	1. Evidence of visual neglect—poor performance on visual-spatial reasoning tasks 2. Memory/attentional deficits—forgets what he has been told by wife and others, forgets meds 3. Inability to recognize errors or modify performance without specific feedback 4. Acquired intellectual decline as evidenced by dyscalculia, word finding difficulty, and impaired abstract verbal reasoning
3. Medical Problems	1. Inadequate coping with pain (excessive/inappropriate medication use)—forgets when he has taken medication and how much 2. Inadequate compensation for visual field defect—driving problems and shoots game to the right
4. Vocational	1. Unwilling to consider other job alternatives 2. Limited job skills 3. Unable to return to former job because of physical, psychological, and neuropsychological problems

Table 6.7 John S.'s Aggressive Behavior: Treatment Options

Behaviors Targeted	Frequency per day	Situation	Possible Intervention Techniques
Verbal abuse towards wife	6	Control of checkbook	Distraction Patient/Family Education Self-monitoring Use of alternative money management techniques-Allowance Stress inoculation training
Demands car keys in order to drive away	1	Forced social interaction with others	Shaping exposure to increasing levels of interaction Modeling (social skills training) Behavioral rehearsal
Screams "you're lying to me"	4	Can't recall what has been discussed	Educate family and patient about the effect of memory problems on social skills deficits Get spouse to provide appropriate prompts

It is also important within a behavioral perspective to recognize that learning plays a major role in the maintenance of behavior. This is no less true of the maintenance of behavior in the neurologically impaired individual. Typical of the aggressive behavior exhibited in this population is a combination of poor emotional control and powerful environmental contingencies. That is, the neurologically impaired individual not only has difficulty inhibiting aggressive impulses secondary to the brain injury, but the environment in which the aggression occurs may also tend to maintain the behavior. For example, if a neurologically impaired individual responds to environmental demands (e.g., family requests) with verbal or physical agression (i.e., poor emotional control) and the family responds by decreasing demands on the individual (i.e., negatively reinforces the aggressive behavior), the aggressive behavior is likely to be maintained and strengthened. It is important, therefore, in developing a treatment program for the neurologically impaired individual, to carefully assess the situation (i.e., antecedents and consequences) in which the behavior occurs, as well as operationally define the aggressive behavior itself.

Classifying the aggressive behavior as both a behavioral excess and deficit suggests multiple behavioral intervention strategies, all of which, it is hoped, will result in a reduction in aggressive behavior and an increase in appropriate nonaggressive behaviors. As the scope of this chapter is to provide general guidelines for using behavioral interventions with a neurologically impaired population, specific strategies will only briefly be discussed. (The reader is directed to review Tables 6.4 and 6.5 for a list of possible interventions.) To provide one example, a decreased ability to inhibit aggressive responses in response to environmental demands has been successfully treated with stress inoculation procedures (Lira, Carne, & Masri, 1983); increased self-control in the environment is taught to the neurologically impaired individual, resulting in increased nonaggressive responses (as viewed from a behavioral deficit perspective) and decreased aggressive behaviors (as viewed from a behavioral excess perspective).

In the hypothetical case of John S., behavioral treatment of aggression (e.g., verbal abuse directed at his spouse), if viewed from both a behavioral excess and deficit perspective, may include any one of the procedures listed in Tables 6.4 and 6.5. Stress inoculation training may be an appropriate intervention strategy for John S. Only a careful analysis of the issues already discussed can determine the specific intervention strategy to use in the individual case. In John S.'s case, rationale for the development of aggressive behaviors in neurologically impaired individuals would be provided to John S. and his family. Alternative behaviors would then be discussed, followed by training in specific behavioral coping strategies (e.g., relaxation training, distraction, etc.). Then John might be exposed to a hierarchy of anger-provoking analogue situations (developed by John and his wife) as he implements the behavioral coping strategies he has learned. He would then be given corrective feedback regarding the effectiveness of his responses, and reinforced for his attempts. It is hoped that this strategy should increase John's self-control over anger-provoking situations, at which time other problematic behavior should be reassessed and targeted for intervention.

REFERRALS

Although aggression was listed as a primary treatment target, it is important to stress that behavioral neuropsychologists work most effectively within a health care team when there are multiple problems that must be assessed and/or treated. Referrals are an integral part of any assessment/treatment program within this framework (see Figure 6.5).

Other professionals and family members add a unique perspective to case assessment and management, and all can evaluate specific aspects of behavior

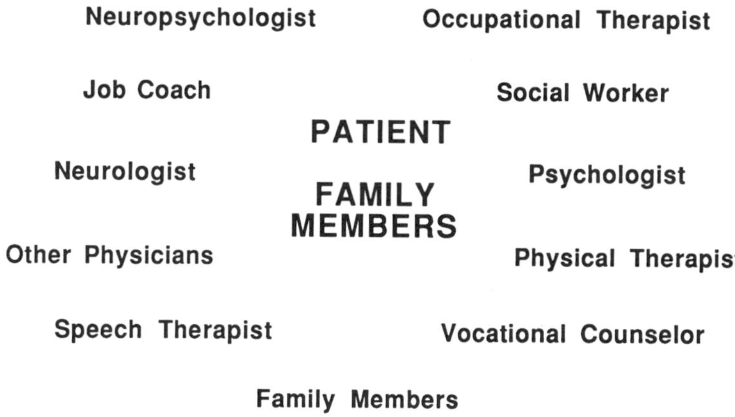

Figure 6.5. Consultants involved in case management.

that become the focus of treatment. Once the team members, patient, and family members reach an agreement on the legitimacy of a case formulation and of the treatment approaches that can be used, then the team acts in concert to address the problems at each step in the treatment plan. In John S.'s case, information obtained from physicians is necessary to delineate his current physical status, anticipated recovery, the effects of various medications (and medication interactions), and alternative pain management techniques (e.g., TENS unit, nerve blocks, etc.). At the very least, his neuropsychologist could consult with his physician and point out that John's memory problems interfere with appropriate medication compliance. Physical therapists can increase his mobility, physical strength, agility, and endurance. Speech and communication therapists can set up programs to improve communication skills, attention, and problem solving abilities. Occupational therapists can assess his range of self-care skills (e.g., personal care, money management, cooking skills, etc.) within his environment. On an immediate basis, his driving skills warrant further assessment, and a referral to an occupational therapist could be initiated before formal psychometrics have been scheduled. Social workers and attorneys can immediately intervene by helping patients and their family members better organize their resources, and suggest alternative solutions to financial problems. At a later date, vocational counselors can further family members provide support, and can become involved at multiple levels in a treatment team. They may also become the focus of treatment, and/or direct service providers when appropriate.

A behaviorally oriented neuropsychological assessment can provide a framework in which other team members can assess the feasibility of their anticipated treatment objectives. In John S.'s case, the neuropsychologist can alert other team members to the types of anticipated deficits that may interfere with his ability to progress in treatment, how to compensate for these problems, or adjust to altered levels of performance. In turn, behavioral neuropsychologists need to continually question the patient's current progress within the treatment program. Client, therapist, and intervention variables interact across time to produce change in various ways. For example, a neuropsychologist could stress to his therapists that John will need a quiet environment during therapy sessions, and short, concrete instructions in order to succeed at various tasks. Performance feedback would have to be very explicit, and brief.

Frequent team meetings can be used to monitor changes in targeted behaviors across settings, and alter treatment if it is ineffective. Team members must stay in constant communication in order to monitor progress and suggest other techniques that may be more effective if progress stagnates. Assessment never stops; it continues within each treatment phase as well.

CONCLUSIONS AND CAVEATS

Neuropsychologists have much to learn from behaviorists, as behavioral assessment and treatment techniques provide a rich framework that offers flexibility, ecological validity, and face validity to all those involved. Behavioral neuropsychology is a very concrete, tangible approach that can be used across a wide variety of patients with CNS dysfunction.

John S. is typical of many brain injured clients, and served as a reference point for readers to illustrate the interface between behavioral approaches and neuropsychology. Patients like John S. help to remind us that case formulations can be difficult and time consuming. Psychologists must realize that patients with neurologic problems are unique. One cannot apply behavioral assessment and treatment techniques without an understanding of neurologic disorders, as they evolve and progress at different rates, and have an impact on functioning that is quite different from other medical disorders. Neuropsychologists must come to understand that the days of defining esoteric strengths and weaknesses on psychometric instruments in order to "localize the lesion" are long gone. They must demonstrate their ability to make accurate prognostic statements about a patient's ability to function within specific environments. They must also be able to design realistic and effective treatment programs that utilize techniques that can be empirically evaluated. Behavioral approaches can provide this bridge.

Critics have suggested that behavioral neuropsychology may not be cost effective as this approach is so time consuming. Although it is labor intensive in the beginning, one must recognize that the patients that present for services are usually quite complex from any perspective. A therapist does not do a patient justice by applying quick solutions to complex problems. Few therapeutic orientations stress the need for methodical assessment frameworks like behavioral neuropsychology, and even fewer evaluate post treatment outcome. As the aging population grows, survival rates after injury increase, and medical technology improves, we are faced with a rapidly expanding population in need of effective rehabilitation. Patients, family members, and third-party payers will not be satisified by ineffective treatment programs, nor should they tolerate them.

Although this field is growing rapidly, it still has a broad spectrum of objectives to be achieved. Few training programs are available at a graduate level for clinical psychologists who wish to learn about behavioral neuropsychology, and few neuropsychologists are exposed to behaviorally oriented programs during their graduate training. More needs to be done to recruit innovative, creative individuals, who are well versed in the use of single case design research. Most of all, behavioral neuropsychologists need to continue efforts to document the effectiveness of their treatment programs by grounding their clinical work with empirically based research studies. These changes are occurring slowly, but are not keeping up with demand for quality services. There is also a great need for more health care training programs that stress case management from a team perspective.

Although behavioral approaches will help us achieve objectives we wish to pursue, they are not a panacea for everything. Neuropsychologists must always realize that other treatment approaches are also of value, and that therapeutic rigidity leads to case management mistakes. In addition, they must temper their judgment with compassion. Above all, they must realize that patients, family members, and even therapists need vacations from assessment/treatment. A therapist's absence can be therapeutic as well.

ACKNOWLEDGMENTS

We would like to thank Glenn Knowlton for his assistance in preparing figures for this manuscript. We would also like to thank our editor, Arthur MacNeil Horton, Jr. for his input, and David Baughn for his assistance in reviewing the manuscript.

REFERENCES

Alex, M., Baron, E.K., Goldenberg, S., & Blumenthal, H. T. (1962). An autopsy study of cerebrovascular accident in diabetes mellitus. *Circulation, 25*, 663–673.

American Cancer Society. (1988). *Cancer Facts and Figures-1988*. New York: Author.

Brooks, D.N., & McKinlay, W. (1983). Personality and behavioral change after severe blunt head injury-A relative's view. *Journal of Neurology, Neurosurgery, and Psychiatry, 46*, 336–344.

Cone, J.D., & Hawkins, R. P. (1977). Current status and future directions in behavior assessment. In J. D. Cone and R. P. Hawkins (Eds.), *Behavioral assessment: New directions in clinical psychology* (pp. 381–392). New York: Brunner/Mazel.

Diller, L., & Gordon, W. A. (1981). Rehabilitation and clinical neuropsychology. In S. B. Filskov & T. J. Boll (Eds.), *Handbook of clinical neuropsychology* (pp. 641–682). New York: Wiley.

Escourolle, R., & Poirier, J. (1973). *Manual of basic neuropathology*. (L. J. Rubinstein, Trans.). Philadelphia: W. B. Saunders.

Gilbert, M. R., & Grossman, S. A. (1986). Incidence and nature of neurologic problems in patients with solid tumors. *The American Journal of Medicine, 81* (6), 951–954.

Grant, I., Heaton, R. K., McSweeny, A. J., Adams, K. M., & Timms, R. M. (1982). Neuropsychologic findings in hypoxemic chronic obstructive pulmonary disease. *Archives of Internal Medicine, 142*, 1470–1476.

Grant, I., Reed, R., & Adams, K. M. (1987). Diagnosis of intermediate-duration and subacute organic mental disorders in abstinent alcoholics. *Journal of Clinical Psychiatry, 48* (8), 312–323.

Hales, R. E., & Vudofsky, S. C. (Eds.). (1987). *Textbook of neuropsychiatry*. Washington, DC: The American Psychiatric Press.

Hall, R. C. W. (Ed.). (1980) *Psychiatric presentations of medical illness. Somatopsychic disorders.* Jamaica, NY: Spectrum Publications.

Horton, A. M., Jr., (1978). Behavioral neuropsychology: A tentative definition. *Behavioral Neuropsychology Newsletter, 1*, 1–2.

Horton, A. M., Jr. (1982) Behavioral neuropsychology: A brief rationale. *The Behavior Therapist, 5* (3), 100–102.

Horton, A. M., Jr., & Wedding, D. (1984). *Clinical and behavioral neuropsychology*. New York: Praeger.

Horton, A. M., & Miller, W. G. (1985). Neuropsychology and behavior therapy. *Progress in Behavior Modification, 19*, 1–55.

Kanfer, F. H., & Grimm, L. G. (1974). Behavioral analysis. *Behavior Modification,1* (1), p. 10.

Lawson-Kerr, K., & Smith, S. S. (1988) *Making headway into awareness.* (Available from the Mississippi Head Injury Association in cooperation with the Mississippi Vocational Rehabilitation Division, P. O. Box 55912, Jackson, MS 39216)

Levin, H. S., Benton, A. L., & Grossman, R. G. (1983). *Neurobehavioral consequences of closed head injury*. New York: Oxford University Press.

Lira, F. T., Carne, W., & Masri, W. (1983). Treatment of anger and impulsivity in a brain damaged patient: A case study applying stress inoculation. *International Journal of Clinical Neuropsychology, 5*, 159–160.

Lishman, W. A. (1978). *Organic psychiatry*. Blackwell: Oxford University Press.

Palumbo, P. J., Elveback, L. R., Chu, G. P., Connolly, D. C., & Kurland, L. T., (1976). Diabetes mellitus: Incidence, prevalence, survivorship and causes of death in Rochester, MN, 1945–1970. *Diabetes, 25*, 566–573.

Palumbo, P. J., Elveback, L. R., & Whisnant, J. P. (1978). Neurologic complications of diabetes mellitus: Transient ischemic attacks, stroke and peripheral neuropathy. In B. S. Schoenberg (Ed.), *Advances in Neurology* (pp. 593–599). New York: Raven Press.

Posner, J. B. (1979). Neuro-oncology: An overview. In B. W. Ongerboer de Visser, D. A. Bosch, & W. M. H. van Woerkom-Eykenboom (Eds.), *Neuro-oncology: Clinical and experimental aspects* (pp. 1–11). Boston: Martinus Nijhoff.

Prigatano, G. P. (1986a). Psychotherapy after brain injury. In G. P. Prigatano (Ed.), *Neuropsychological rehabilitation after brain injury* (pp. 67–95). Baltimore: Johns Hopkins University Press.

Prigatano, G. P. (1986b). Personality and psycholocial consequences of brain injury. In G. P. Prigatano (Ed.), *Neuropsychological rehabilitation after brain injury* (pp. 29–50). Baltimore: Johns Hopkins University Press.

Redlich, R., & Kellert, S. R. (1978). Trends in American mental health. *American Journal of Psychiatry, 135*, 1–12.

Rimm, D. C., & Masters, J. O. (1979). *Behavior therapy: Techniques and empirical findings (2nd Ed.)*. New York: Academic Press.

Rubinstein, L. J. (1972). Tumors of the central nervous system. *Atlas of tumor pathology*, (2nd series, Fasc 6). Washington, DC: Armed Forces Institute of Pathology.

Strub, R. L., & Black, F. W. (1981). *Organic brain syndromes: An introduction to neurobehavioral disorders*. Philadelphia: F. A. Davis.

Tarter, R. E., Van Thiel, D. H., & Edwards, K. L. (Eds.). (1988) *Medical neuropsychology. The impact of disease on behavior*. New York: Plenum Press.

Wedding, D., Horton, A. M., Jr., & Webster, J. (Eds.). (1986). *The neuropsychology handbook. Behavioral and clinical perspectives*. New York: Springer Publishing Co.

Wood, R. L. (1987). *Brain injury rehabilitation: A neurobehavioral approach*. Rockville, MD: Aspen.

Chapter 7

Cognitive Interventions Across the Life-Span

Linda M. Brown,
Wm. Drew Gouvier, and
Fredda Blanchard-Fields

The focus of this chapter involves the use of cognitive interventions across the lifespan. Specific techniques for use with children, adults, and the elderly will be provided. Cognitive interventions used to enhance developmental processes or remediate behavioral problems in children will include problem solving and self-instructional training. The next section will include techniques targeting attention, memory, language, and perceptual disorders that occur in adults following traumatic brain injury. And last, cognitive interventions attempting to remediate orientation, memory, and intellectual deficits in elderly populations will be discussed. Given the extent of information on cognitive interventions currently in use, the following review of the literature is by no means exhaustive; rather, it is simply a representation of what is currently found in the research and literature. The prominent techniques and areas of research are presented with more detail than others which are simply presented by way of reference. Wherever possible, references are cited which provide a more detailed and thorough discussion of particular topic areas for the interested reader. The use of cognitive interventions has increased over the past several years and it is frequently used in conjunction with behavioral techniques, often referred to as cognitive-behavioral therapy. Behavioral techniques are discussed in an alternate chapter and only cognitive interventions will be discussed here.

CHILDREN

According to Braswell and Kendall (1988), the use of cognitive interventions with children has been influenced by both the development of cognitive interventions with adults and issues in developmental psychology such as self-control, memory, and attribution theories. These authors state that "the task of the cognitive-behavioral therapy is to train the child in the use of verbal mediation strategies for developing more reflective problem-solving behavior and self-control." (Braswell & Kendall, 1988, pp. 167–168). Cognitive techniques with children can be traced back to Luria (1961) and Vygotsky (1962) who proposed a stage theory explaining the development of self-control of speech in children. Later, Meichenbaum (1977) used this theory to develop his self-instructional training procedures (Braswell & Kendall, 1988). Currently three major areas of cognitive interventions with children have emerged. They include cognitive modeling, problem-solving, and self-instructional training (Szymula, 1988). Each of these procedures will be briefly discussed, followed by a review of research involving applications of these cognitive interventions to several childhood problems.

Cognitive Modeling

Cognitive modeling is a technique for teaching a child how and what to think about in executing a task. It involves verbally providing the child with the appropriate steps to attain a desired behavior along with presenting the overt behavior itself (Szymula, 1988). Meichenbaum (1971) found that modeling involving models who "talk out loud" is more effective than simply modeling behaviors alone. Research involving cognitive modeling approaches will be covered in the review of problem-solving training and self-instructional training in that both approaches utilize cognitive modeling procedures in teaching adaptive behaviors.

Problem-Solving

The following review of problem-solving approaches used with children and with families was in part derived from Braswell and Kendall (1988) and Meyers and Cohen (1984). The interested reader is encouraged to refer to these works for a more complete review of the literature.

Problem-solving approaches currently used with children are based on

D'Zurilla and Goldfried's (1971) model of problem solving, which involves defining the problem, generation of alternatives, evaluation of alternatives, choosing an alternative, and evaluation of the outcome. Spivack, Platt and Shure (1976) added a cognitive flavor to problem-solving approaches with their interpersonal cognitive problem-solving (ICPS) approach. According to Meyers and Cohen (1984), ICPS involves an awareness of human problems, generation of alternative solutions, definition of steps to solve the problem (means-end thinking), and consideration of both consequences of behavior and cause-effect relationships. Spivack and Shure (1974) demonstrated the effectiveness of problem-solving training in an educational setting using 113 preschool children who were trained in problem-solving techniques every day for 12 weeks. The Preschool Interpersonal Problem-Solving Test was used to assess results. These authors found that these children generated more alternative solutions and exhibited improvements in consequential thinking, cause-effect thinking and levels of adjustment as rated by teachers.

However, results of research examining how ICPS deficits affect social adjustment in children are inconclusive (Krasnor & Rubin, 1983). Kendall and Fischler (1984) found only a slight relationship between ICPS skills and adjustment using children aged 6 to 12 and Rickel and Burgio (1982) did not find a relationship between social behavior and cognitive problem-solving skills. Weissberg and Gesten (1982) argue that problem-solving skills and improved adjustment have not been found to generalize across all situations, but rather improvement is found in only specific problem-solving skills.

Problem-solving training has been used with aggressive and delinquent children. Robin and Schneider (1974) developed the "turtle technique" in which children are taught to withdraw like a turtle during which time they are to generate alternative solutions and consider consequences of behavior before acting aggressively and impulsively. A significant decrease in aggressive behavior was found using this "turtle technique" (Robin, Schneider, & Dolnick, 1976). Snyder and White (1979) found significant reductions in aggressive behaviors when cognitive training was provided to five adolescents already involved in a token economy program. Problem-solving techniques including role-play and modeling were used to teach these adolescents adaptive behaviors when faced with aggressive situations. Sarason and Ganzer (1973) also used role playing and modeling with institutionalized delinquents. Particular social situations were presented at which time models exhibited adaptive and maladaptive approaches to solving the problems and handling the situations. The adolescents were then to role-play both techniques, followed by discussion of approaches which produced the most favorable results. Outcome data revealed significantly less recidivism, greater recall of goals of treatment, and an overall more positive rating of institutionalized treatment as compared to the control group. Sarason and Sarason (1981) followed up this research using problem-solving training in a preventive approach with high school students who were likely to exhibit delinquent behaviors. Significant decreases in tardiness, absences, and need for disciplinary actions were found with the subjects receiving the problem-solving training.

Problem-solving techniques have been applied in educational settings. Allen, Chinsky, Larcen, Lochman, and Selinger (1976) had teachers train 150 children in third and fourth grades in problem-solving techniques. Outcome measures included tests of problem-solving skills including means-end thinking and generation of alternatives. Children in the treatment group demonstrated significant improvement in defining the steps to solve a problem and in generation of alternatives when compared to the control group. However, these improvements were not found four months after training had been discontinued.

Given the significant impact family members have on children, additional research in problem-solving training has focused on involving significant others in the problem-solving process. The Family Contract Game was developed by Blechman, Olson, and Hellman (1976) in training both children and family members in appropriate problem-solving and conflict management. However, results of this research have shown that, although improvements in problem-solving are exhibited during treatment, generalization to domestic settings remain limited (Braswell & Kendall, 1988). In attempts to address this issue, some researchers have found that treatment results can generalize to home settings by providing the parents with separate problem-solving and behavior management techniques to encourage behavior change in children also receiving training in problem solving (Coyne, Meyers, & Clark, 1985).

Self-Instructional Training

Self-instructional training (SIT) involves providing the child with "self-directed statements of an internal dialogue that an individual uses to guide him- or herself through a problem-solving process" (Braswell & Kendall, 1988, p. 182). SIT was developed by Meichenbaum and Goodman (1971) who taught impulsive children to control overt behaviors through the use of self-verbalizations. Cohen and Meyers (1984) outlined Meichenbaum's (1977) five step fading procedure to be followed in a SIT program. The first step involves a model verbally demonstrating self-instruction statements, followed by a behavioral display of these statements. In the second step, the model verbally provides self-instruction statements while the child rehearses these statements and performs the behaviors included in these statements. The third step involves the model prompting the child with the first word of each self-instruction statement and appropriate behaviors. In the fourth, the model whispers the prompt followed by the child whispering the entire statement and demonstrating the motor behaviors. Last, the model silently thinks the statement and instructs the child to do the same, as he or she displays the motor behaviors of the statement.

Meichenbaum (1977) predicted that such training would be likely to show good generalization of treatment results to home and academic environments. However, results from subsequent research have failed to produce these results (Meichenbaum & Asarnow, 1979). Schleser, Meyers, and Cohen (1981) have argued that traditional SIT programs do not facilitate generalization and active participation by the child. Using first and second graders, these authors found that children provided with specific self-instructions demonstrated significantly more improvement on a specific post-test training task (Matching Familiar Figures test) compared to other groups. However, only subjects who received general self-instructional training improved significantly on the perspective-taking generalization task indicating that generalization of training is less likely to follow from specific than general self-instruction training. They define general self-instructional training to include "general content strategies statements, which provided a broad-based problem-solving plan—a plan that children could apply to numerous tasks" (Cohen & Meyers, 19984, p. 102). In addition, Schleser, Meyers, and Cohen (1981) also found that active participation resulted in higher performance than didactic groups (passive listening to self-instructional training without rehearsal).

In other research, Schleser, Cohen, Meyers, and Rodick (1984) used a general self-instructional training procedure entitled "directed discovery." In this procedure, a programmed Socratic dialogue was used in which the experimenter led the subjects to "discover" the self-instructional statements by asking questions relevant to the task. They found that subjects in the "directed discovery" group achieved significant improvements on the generalization task compared to subjects in the no training control group, didactic instruction control group, and fading self-instructions group.

Clinical applications of SIT and related research topics are quite extensive (Szymula, 1988). The scope of this chapter does not allow a thorough review of the current SIT literature; therefore, only a representative sample of clinical applications will be discussed including SIT with learning disabilities, academic underachievement, aggression, and attentional problems.

Braswell and Kendall (1988) state that the use of SIT with learning disabled children has increased over the last few years primarily due to changing ideas regarding learning disabilities. Although it was once believed that LD children possessed specific deficits related to academic content areas (e.g., reading, arithmetic) or neuropsychological domains, it is now hypothesized that these children lack an ability to purposely plan and self-regulate behaviors (Braswell & Kendall, 1988). However, the increased use of cognitive interventions with

LD children does not necessarily indicate effectiveness. In their review of the literature, Gouvier, Webster, and Blanton (1986) found results of studies using cognitive interventions with LD children to be inconclusive. These authors cite reviews by Myers and Hammill (1976), Koppitz (1971), and Treiber and Lahey (1983) who found that interventions designed to address "underlying deficits" such as perceptual-motor, visual discrimination, and auditory sequential deficits were not effective in enhancing overall academic success. However, cognitive interventions targeting specific academic problems have produced more favorable results. Leon and Pepe (1983) compared SIT and direct instruction in the training of math skills to learning disabled children. They found that SIT produced greater improvement than direct instruction. Harris and Graham (1985) reported favorable results in the writing skills of two learning disabled children with the use of SIT.

SIT has also been used with children who are academic underachievers. These children are not considered learning disabled; however, they demonstrate deficiencies in reading, spelling, and math skills which are inconsistent with their average range of intellectual functions (Thackaway, Meyers, Schleser, & Cohen, 1985). Robin, Armel, and O'Leary (1975) compared SIT, direct training, and no treatment in improving handwriting performance of kindergarten students. Although both treatment groups resulted in greater performance than no treatment, subjects receiving SIT performed significantly better than the direct training subjects on target letters. However, these results were not found with a generalized task of untrained letters. No significant differences were noted among groups on this task. In addition, the subjects' self-instructions were not significantly related to increased performance. Szymula (1988) concludes that the improvement found in the SIT group may not be due to the self-instructions, and Wong (1985) has suggested that differences in level of skill before training may affect outcome of treatment and skills training. In their review of the literature, Meyers and Cohen (1984) discuss applications of SIT to other academic areas including mathematics and reading comprehension.

Attentional problems including hyperactivity and impulsivity have also been the focus of SIT. Meichenbaum and Goodman (1971) pioneered the use of SIT with attentional problems in a study of 15 hyperactive or impulsive second graders. These children were trained in SIT, self-monitoring, and self-reinforcement, using Meichenbaum's five step fading procedure. Significant improvements in the SIT group, as compared to control groups, were noted on outcome measures including Matching Familiar Figures Test, Porteus Maze, Picture Arrangement of the WISC-R, and a prorated WISC-R Performance IQ. In other research, Kendall and associates discovered that including behavioral contingencies (response cost) with SIT significantly improved the behavior of impulsive children (Kendall & Finch, 1976; Kendall

& Finch, 1978; Kendall & Wilcox, 1980; and Kendall & Zupan, 1981). However, evidence for maintenance and generalization of SIT treatment of impulsive/hyperactive chidren is inconclusive and weak (Szymula, 1988; Braswell & Kendall, 1988).

Lastly, SIT has been used with children demonstrating aggressive behavior. Camp, Blom, Herbert and van Doorninck (1977) developed a program entitled "Think Aloud" which trained aggressive children in SIT and problem-solving training. They postulated that aggressive children possess a deficit in social skills performance despite knowledge of appropriate social skills (Meyers & Cohen, 1984). Significant improvement was found on cognitive tasks and prosocial behavior, but not teacher ratings of aggressive behavior and problem solving. Other studies have indicated that maintenance and generalization of treatment results across situations remain problematic (Kennedy, 1982).

ADULTS

Americans experiencing traumatic cerebral injury including cerebrovascular accidents and head injuries result in significant financial loss and change in life style (Gouvier, Webster & Blanton, 1986). The number of individuals affected by strokes during the 1970s was estimated to be nearly one million patients per year including those institutionalized and disabled (NCHS, 1977; Mills & Thompson, 1978) with estimated costs of over $7 billion annually (Weinfeld, 1981). Incident of head injuries was estimated to be nearly half a million per year during the 1970s with costs of $4 billion annually for rehabilitation (Anderson & McLaurin, 1980). Gouvier et al. (1986) argue that rehabilitation programs must address cognitive and personality issues, along with medical concerns, for effective intervention following cerebral trauma.

Diller and Gordon (1981) differentiate cognitive remediation/retraining from rehabilitation. These authors define remediation/retraining as providing patients with problem-solving and behavioral skills training in tasks they cannot currently perform but for which they were effective prior to cerebral insult. On the other hand, these authors refer to rehabilitation as a multidisciplinary process involving physical, speech, and occupational therapies, medicine, and cognitive training. The focus of this section will include cognitive interventions used with brain damaged individuals for attention, memory, language and perceptual disorders.

Attention

Sophisticated interventions for attention and concentration have recently been developed in the form of computer programs. The Orientation Remedial

Module (ORM) (Ben-Yishay & Diller, 1981) consists of five tasks designed to increase arousal, attention, concentration, and persistence in purposeful tasks (Horton & Miller, 1984). For a discussion of other NYUIRM modules, see Horton and Miller (1984). A major limitation to these modules is that, in conceptualizing remediation, no unifying theoretical framework exists (Satz & Fletcher, 1981). Other computer programs include the Foundation Skills programs (Bracy, 1982) which focus on auditory and visual reaction time, and programs by Gianutsos & Klitzner (1981) involving visual processing (Speeded Reading of Word Lists), perceptual skills (Searching for Shapes), and memory tasks (Free Recall, Memory Span, Triplet Recall, Sequence Recall). While many of these packaged sets of computer programs for cognitive rehabilitation are now entering their fifth or sixth generation, empirical research documenting their effectiveness still lags far behind.

Self-instructional training has been used with head injured individuals in improving attention and memory difficulties due to attentional deficits (Webster & Scott, 1983). These authors used SIT based on Meichenbaum's five step fading model. The patient was initially taught self-instructions which he would rehearse before exposure to training materials. After presentation of the material, the patient was instructed to verbally repeat discrete sections. The following steps involved having the subject whisper the material, then subvocally repeat the material with eventually decreasing amounts of time between each presented unit. The patient was able to recall significantly more bits of information, from the Story Memory Examination after SIT, has compared to pretest results and scored within the normal range of immediate recall. An 18-month follow-up of this patient revealed a significant decrease in errors on verbal memory questions from the Luria-Nebraska Neuropsychological Test Battery (Golden, Hammeke, & Purisch, 1980) and immediate recall in the normal range on the paragraph recall task described by Talland (1965).

Memory

Memory problems are not only common after brain damage, but they may continue for years after the injury (Schacter & Crovitz, 1977). External memory aids including notebooks, schedules, wristwatches, and home computers have been used to enhance memory (Gouvier et al., 1986). Visual imagery techniques have been widely used in the remediation of memory disorders. Peg-word systems in which peg-words are paired with other words to form visual images to facilitate recall have been adapted from use with normals to use with brain damaged patients (Cermack, 1975; Patten, 1972). Visual imagery has also been used in the recall of paired-associates and to enhance face-name associations (Lewisohn, Danaher, & Kikel, 1977). However, the use of visual imagery in memory retraining has been criticized due to the lack of generalization and maintenance demonstrated in empirical studies (Wilson, 1982; Crovitz, Harvey, & Horn, 1979). Schacter and Glisky (1986) argue that sophisticated processing is required for the success of these mnemonics and that this processing is greatly affected in brain damaged individuals (Butters & Cermack, 1980).

Other memory strategies include semantic elaboration and the use of encoding and retrieval cues (Gouvier et al., 1986). With semantic elaboration, subjects are taught to verbally form relationships among words. Some research has indicated that subjects providing their own personal relationships facilitates recall more effectively than experimenter-provided meanings (Webster, Hammer, & Moss, 1980). Robinson (1970) developed the PQRST system which improves recall of written material. This system involves *previewing* the written information, generating *questions* about the information, *reading* in order to answer the generated questions, *stating* the answers to the questions, and *testing* for recall by again providing the correct answers to the questions. Glasgow, Zeiss, Barrera, and Lewinsohn (1977) used the PQRST method in enhancing retention of newspaper articles. These authors added an additional step to the procedure which involved *verifying* answers to the questions by consulting the written passage. Encoding strategies have been used to retain information. Crovitz (1979) used a procedure he called "The Airplane List" in which words are associated to form a story with the use of vivid images. Retrieval cues are then provided to envoke the strange images used to recall the unrelated words.

Language

While treatment of language disorders (aphasia) is generally regarded as the domain of speech therapists, input from cognitive rehabilitation specialists can sometimes enhance the effectiveness of traditional speech therapy (Gouvier et al., 1986). Melodic Intonation Therapy which uses rhythm and melody in speech and has been shown to improve verbal communications in aphasics who were no longer improving in traditional speech therapy (Sparks, Helm, & Albert, 1974). Miller (1984) provides a rationale for this therapy in that using the intact right hemisphere through the use of singing can support levels of verbal behavior which could not be managed by the defective left hemisphere. The subject begins by singing along with the experimenter, followed by singing alone with gradual fading of melody altogether (Miller, 1984).

Non-verbal communication systems including artificial language and sign language (Glass, Gazzaniga, & Premack, 1973) and visual communication systems (Gardner, Zurif, Berry & Baker, 1976) have been used with aphasics with moderate success. Interested readers are referred to Miller (1984) for details regarding specific types of sign language. Involvement of family members and relatives is emphasized in aphasia therapy. In a study at NYU (1974), spouses were trained to use behavioral techniques and the functional speech of their partners increased moderately but significantly. Other studies have also shown modest success over time with aphasia programs involving relatives (Bornstein, Linell, & Wahrborg, 1987; Lesser, Bryan, Anderson, & Rose, 1986).

Perceptual Disorders

Retraining of perceptual deficits is often the major focus in the rehabilitation of brain damaged individuals due to the impact on the independent functioning of the patient. Persons with right hemisphere cerebral trauma are more likely to experience perceptual difficulties involving neglect of visual stimuli in the left hemispace (Gouvier, 1987). Diller and Weinberg (1977) employed a visual scanning technique to train patients to scan their environment from left to right utilizing the functioning right-sided visual skills to compensate for the left-sided visual impairments. Lightboards have been used to train patients to visually search, scan, and track stimuli presented in their entire visual field (NYU, 1974). Other researchers have found that improved visual scanning skills enhanced with the use of lightboards and other techniques can generalize to wheelchair navigation and that results are maintained over time (Webster, Jones, Blanton, Gross, Beissel, & Wofford, 1984; Gouvier, Cottam, Webster, Beissel, & Wofford, 1984). For the interested reader, Gouvier, Webster, and Warner (1986) provide a thorough review of remediation techniques for patients with visuoperceptual deficits.

ELDERLY

The use of cognitive interventions with the elderly has increased in popularity over the last several years as evidenced by burgeoning research in this field (Gouvier et al., 1986). In her excellent review of geriatric neuropsychology, Albert (1981) argues that several problems exist in the accurate assessment and treatment of cognitive impairments in the elderly. These problems include lack of age-appropriate norms and differentiating cognitive impairments due to age-related changes as opposed to those caused by toxic-metabolic or psychiatric (e.g., depression) illnesses. The following review will focus on cognitive training used with common geriatric impairments including orientation, memory, and intellectual functioning.

Orientation

Attentional impairments are often the initial focus of assessment and rehabilitation due to the importance of sustaining attention for learning tasks and responding appropriately to environmental stimuli (Albert, 1981). Lewis (1982) offers a thorough description of a Reality Orientation (RO) program which was originally developed by James C. Folsom (1968). She describes three key features to any RO program which include 24–hour RO, environmental RO, and classroom RO. Twenty-four hour RO typically occurs in a hospital setting in which staff, volunteers, and visitors are instructed in RO activities. Communication is to occur at all times when the patient is awake, (providing information such as person, place, time, activities, and expectations). Environmental RO is often used, in addition to 24 RO, in which reminders are used to orient the patient such as RO boards, color-coded doors and hallways, personal identifying symbols and labels, holiday decorations, etc. Classroom RO involves orientation tasks provided to groups of four to six patients in a classroom setting. Basic and advanced level classes are offered in which practice of person, place, time, current events, etc. occurs. In their review of the literature, Gatz, Popkin, Pino, and VandenBos (1985) found results of RO programs to be inconclusive. Although improvement was demonstrated by those patients participating in RO programs compared to control groups, orientation was not maintained at follow-up (Zepelin, Wolfe, & Kleinplatz, 1981).

Memory

Memory impairments which are commonly found in geriatric populations have been the focus of the majority of aging research over the past 20 years (Poon, 1985). Poon, Fozard, and Treat (1978) argue that diagnosis, assessment, and remediation of memory deficits in the elderly remain problematic. This is due to the lack of adequate assessment measure of specific memory problems and emotional response to memory loss, as well as a taxonomy of memory complaints. These authors recommend an individualized approach to assessment and treatment of memory disorders due to differences in etiology and memory complaints of individuals. They also recommend group and individual therapy targeting specific problems of each individual and a supportive environment to achieve the best results of any memory remediation program.

Treat, Poon, Fozard, and Popkin (1978) also discuss techniques for improving the effectiveness of a cognitive skills training program for memory. They offer four suggestions. First, mnemonic skills must be used to improve encoding and organizational skills in the elderly. Several mnemonic techniques are discussed in detail including imagery, method of loci, and self-instructional training. The interested reader is referred to Treat et al. (1978) for a more thorough description of these techniques. Second, motivational aspects of memory retraining, including various reinforcers, should be utilized to promote attention, practice, and maintenance of memory skills. Third, a retraining program should be tailored to an individual's needs with full consideration of individual differences such as intellectual functioning, education, and personality variables. In another study, Costa and Fozard (1978) found that recognition memory was significantly correlated with personality variables, including openness and anxiety which provides further evidence of the importance of incorporating individual differences in any memory program. Finally, consultations with medical professionals should be considered, if necessary, to identify and manage any medical complications which might affect the effectiveness of any memory program.

Camp and his colleagues have studied memory retraining and maintenance of such effects over time (Auschutz, Camp, Markley, and Kramer, 1987). They trained 10 elderly subjects in the use of the method of loci, which involves using the mental imagery of walking through a familiar pathway "placing" the words along the route (Poon, 1984). Nine of the 10 subjects were tested at a follow-up of three years after initial training. Recognition of the three-year-old word list and loci was relatively better than that of free recall of the same items. Free recall of a new word list was found to be similar to results achieved before mnemonic training three years earlier. The authors conclude that the subjects did not use the mnemonic techniques in their daily living activities and that compliance issues must be addressed to increase the effectiveness of memory retraining programs. It is difficult to envision how the subjects were expected to incorporate the method of loci into their daily activities, however. A crucial shortcoming of nearly all mnemonic strategies is that they are most effective for enhancing the sort of memory that people seem to use the least, such as rote recall for lists of related or unrelated words.

Camp (in press) used the spaced-retrieval technique in the training of face-name associations in Alzheimer patients. Spaced-retrieval training involves progressively increasing the time intervals between presentation of the same visual stimuli (pictures) to facilitate long-term retention of face-name associations. If the subject was unable to recall the name when presented with the picture, the correct answer was provided and the time interval was shortened to the longest previous successful interval. Camp and his colleagues used conversation and participation in games such as checkers during intervals to prevent rehearsal. Their initial results appear favorable; however, Camp discusses areas of limitations including interference effects, maintenance, generalization, and the relatively limited amount of information which can be learned using the spaced-retrieval technique.

In a series of studies, Zarit and his colleagues found that attitudes and expectations among the elderly concerning deficits associated with increasing age can result in subjective memory complaints independent of actual performance. Zarit, Cole, and Guider (1981) found that subjective complaints of memory significantly decreased in both the memory retraining group in which memory techniques were used (i.e., imagery, categorization, etc.) and the current events group in which no memory training was provided. However, only subjects receiving the memory training performed significantly better on tests of recall compared to the subjects receiving no memory training. In another study, Zarit, Gallagher, and Kramer (1981) found that both subjects receiving memory training and subjects participating in "growth" sessions including such topics as social skills training, problem-solving, relaxation, and cognitive reappraisal exhibited a decrease in subjective memory complaints and improvement in memory performance. However, decreases in memory complaints were not related to improved memory performances, but rather to decreases in depressive symptoms highlighting the effects of mood in the elderly on subjective memory complaints. The authors postulate that improved memory performance in the "growth" group may be attributed to increased motivation among these subjects. As a result, they emphasize the importance of incorporating attentional and motivational factors in any memory training program.

In his review of the literature, Poon (1985) states that although it appears that memory training can enhance performance in the elderly, results are far from conclusive. He argues that memory training will not result in increased memory performance in all elderly subjects and many memory improvements are not maintained after training. Poon (1985) cites studies which show that many subjects do not use memory techniques in daily living which indicates the importance of addressing motivation and generalization in memory programs.

Intellectual Functioning

Cognitive interventions have been applied to improving intellectual functioning in the elderly. Cattell (1971) describes two distinct types of intelligence, crystallized and fluid intelligence. Crystallized intelligence involves knowledge based on experience, whereas fluid intelligence involves abstract reasoning and information processing (Carlson, 1984). Fluid abilities are generally found to decrease with age compared to crystallized intellectual abilities (Willis, 1985). Willis (in press) provides a thorough review of the literature regarding cognitive interventions and intellectual functioning in the aged. She and her colleagues have conducted several studies addressing cognitive training of fluid intelligence in geriatric populations with the Adult Development and Enrichment Program (Baltes & Willis, 1982).

Plemons, Willis, and Baltes (1978) compared subjects receiving training on figural relations to those receiving no training. The training program consisted of eight one-hour sessions including modeling, practice, review, and group discussion of relational rules and practice items. The experimental subjects' performances were found to be significantly greater on the Figural Relations Diagnostic Test compared to control subjects at one-week, one-month, and six-month follow-ups, and on the Cattell-Horn measures of Figural Relations one week after training. In addition, significant retest results were found in both the experimental and control subjects possibly indicating the occurrence of increased test-taking abilities. In a subsequent study, Willis, Blieszner, and Baltes (1981) found significant performances after training and these effects were maintained at a 10-month follow-up. Additional training sessions at follow-up enhanced performance of figural relations but at a lower level than what was found after initial training. The interested reader is referred to Willis (in press) for a review of the literature regarding cognitive training in the aged with inductive reasoning, problem solving, Piagetian tasks, spatial orientation, and perceptual speed.

SUMMARY AND CONCLUSIONS

This chapter focuses on cognitive interventions viewed from a life-span perspective. Specific techniques found in the literature and clinical practice which are currently in use with children, adults, and the elderly were discussed. Cognitive interventions with children have primarily involved problem-solving and self-instructional training which have been applied to such domains as aggression, impulsivity, learning disabilities, and academic underachievement. Although the immediate effectiveness of these techniques appear favorable, generalization of results across behaviors and settings is limited, as well as maintenance of treatment effects over time.

Braswell and Kendall (1988) offer the following suggestions to enhance generalization and maintenance of cognitive interventions with children. They recommend a thorough analysis of individual differences before initiation of treatment including developmental level (cognitive, physical), cognitive skills, and locus of control (internal vs. external). In addition, they suggest that training involve persons and environments comprising the targets of generalization. For example, parents, teachers, peers and siblings within home and academic environments should assume active roles in the treatment program. Cognitive training should also include teaching children application of techniques to problems similar to those targeted in training but not directly addressed. Szymula (1988) discusses problems in methodology and assessment found in the current research of cognitive interventions with children.

He suggests a need for operational definitions of terms in defining groups for study, describing specific treatment techniques and procedures, use of better control groups, and a multimethod approach to assessment considering both social and developmental variables of subjects.

Cognitive interventions used with adults have generally targeted attention/concentration, memory, language, and perceptual disorders following acquired brain injury. Several computer programs have recently been developed to enhance attention and concentration which appear promising. However, systematic research documenting the effectiveness of these programs is currently not available, indicating a dire need for such research. In their review of the literature, Gouvier, Webster, and Blanton (1986) report favorable results with the use of noncomputerized techniques for improving memory, language, and perceptual abilities, but they also discuss limitations of these procedures as well. With memory retraining, particularly imagery training, there is a lack of generalization and maintenance of effects from the laboratory to the patient's environments. They suggest that controlled research is needed to delineate individual deficits which may interfere with treatment effectiveness and to determine the techniques which are most effective with particular deficits.

In language retraining, Gouvier (1987) suggests involving significant others in the training program in order to enhance the overall quality of life for the patient. He also indicates a need for research which involves identification and management of interpersonal factors which may reduce the effectiveness of cognitive retraining programs. In contrast to other cognitive interventions, generalization and maintenance of treatment effects have been found with perceptual retraining, particularly with the use of visual scanning techniques (Gouvier, Webster, & Blanton, 1986).

Gouvier (1987) provides the following suggestions to enhance the effectiveness of cognitive interventions with adults. Preceding any cognitive program, a detailed assessment and formulation is required, along with education of the patient and significant others in all techniques to be used. Once the cognitive program has begun, techniques should be regularly practiced with changes made according to the patient's needs over time. As patients progress in retraining, more emphasis should be placed on self-management techniques and involvement of more diverse environments and "ecologically relevant behaviors" to promote generalization of treatment results.

Lastly, cognitive interventions with the elderly has recently gained popularity. However, in comparison with other age groups, research in this area remains limited. Targets of cognitive interventions include attention/orientation, memory, and intellectual functioning. A review of the Reality Orientation program (Folsom, 1968) was discussed, but results regarding the effectiveness of this program remain inconclusive due to lack of maintenance of effects over time. Although memory has been researched more than other cognitive deficits in the elderly, several important limitations concerning these findings currently exist including lack of operational definitions of memory complaints and appropriate assessment techniques (Poon, Fozard, & Treat, 1978). Suggestions to enhance memory training in geriatric populations by Treat, Poon, Fozard, and Popkin (1978) were discussed earlier.

Other researchers have indicated a need to address motivational factors in memory programs in that these factors have been shown to reduce the effectiveness of such techniques. Anschutz, Camp, Markley, and Kramer (1987) discuss failure of subjects to comply with instructions regarding the use of memory techniques in daily living. In his review of the literature, Poon (1985) also attributes lack of generalization and maintenance of treatment effects to noncompliance of subjects with memory techniques.

Research has shown enhancement of fluid intelligence with cognitive training in the elderly with maintenance of treatment effects over time. Willis (in press) suggests a need for addressing individual differences in cognitive training programs with the adoption of an individual approach to treatment rather than a normative approach to achieve maximum effectiveness. In studying individual differences in the elderly, Willis and Schaie (1988) recommended a thorough assessment of the patient's developmental history in order to tailor a treatment program to the specific needs and abilities of the patient. Camp (in press) also argues for the need of an individualized approach to cognitive impairments in the aged and recommends involving significant others in the treatment program to enhance effectiveness of treatment techniques.

CONCLUSION

At the present time, a life-span perspective appears warranted with the use of cognitive interventions. Treatment techniques cannot be uniformly applied to subjects regardless of age, due in part to the differences in developmental level and abilities. Although the targets of cognitive interventions may be similar across age groups (i.e., attention/concentration, memory, intellectual functioning, etc.), an individualized approach to cognitive retraining must be taken to achieve maximum benefits from any program. That is, cognitive training programs must be sensitive to developmental changes in cognitive and physical functions as people age, and tailor specific cognitive interventions accordingly.

REFERENCES

Albert, M. S. (1981). Geriatric neuropsychology. *Journal of Consulting and Clinical Psychology, 49*, 835–850.

Allen, G., Chinsky, J., Larson, S., Lochman, J., & Selinger, H. (1976). *Community psychology and the schools: A behaviorally oriented multilevel parentive approach.* Hillsdale, NJ: Earlbaum.

Anderson, D., & McLaurin, R. (1980). Report on the national head and spinal cord injury survey. *Journal of Neurosurgery, 53,* (Suppl.), 1–43.

Anschutz, L., Camp, C. L., Markley, R. P., & Kramer, J. J. (1987). Remembering mneumonics: A three-year follow-up on the effects of mneumonics training in elderly adults. *Experimental Aging Research, 13,* 141–143.

Baltes, P. B., & Willis, S. L. (1982). Enhancement (plasticity) of intellectual functioning in old age: Penn State's adult development and enrichment project (ADEPT). In F. I. M. Craik & S. T. Trehub (Eds.), *Aging and cognitive processes* (pp. 353–389). New York: Plenum Press.

Ben-Yishay, Y., & Diller, L. (1981). Rehabilitation of cognitive and perceptual deficits in people with traumatic brain damage. *International Journal of Rehabilitation Research, 4,* 208–210.

Blechman, E., Olson, D., & Hellman, I. (1976). Stimulus control over family problem-solving behavior: The family contract game. *Behavior Therapy, 7,* 686–692.

Bornstein, R. A., Linell, S., & Wahrborg, R. (1987). An innovative therapeutic program for aphasia patients and their relatives. *Scandinavian Journal of Rehabilitation Medicine, 19,* 51–56.

Braswell, L., & Kendall, P. C. (1988). Cognitive-behavioral methods with children. In K. S. Dobson (Ed.), *Handbook of cognitive-behavioral therapies* (pp. 167–213). New York: Guilford Press.

Butters, N., & Cermak, L. S. (1980). *Alcoholic Korsakoff's syndrome.* New York: Academic Press.

Camp, B., Blom, G., Hebert, F., & vanDoorninck, W. (1977). "Think aloud": A program for developing self-control in young aggressive boys. *Journal of Abnormal Child Psychology, 5,* 157–169.

Camp, C. J. (1989). Facilitation of new learning in Alzheimer's diesease. In G. Gilmore, P. Whitehouse, & M. Wykle (Eds.), *Memory, aging and dementia. Theory, assessment and treatment.* New York: Springer Publishing Company.

Carlson, N. R. (1984). *Psychology. The Science of Behavior.* Boston: Allyn & Bacon.

Cattell, R. B. (1971). *Abilities: Structure, growth and action.* New York: Houghton-Mifflin.

Cermak, L. (1975). Imagery as an aid to retrieval for Korsakoff patients. *Cortex, 11,* 163–169.

Cohen, R., & Meyers, A. W. (1984). The generalization of self-instructions. In B. Gholson & T. L. Rosenthal (Eds.), *Applications of cognitive-developmental theory* (pp. 95–112). New York: Academic Press.

Costa, P. T., & Fozard, J. L. (1978). Remembering the person: Relations of individual difference variables to memory. *Experimental Aging Research, 4,* 291–304.

Coyne, T., Meyers, A., & Clark, L. (1985, November). *Behavioral treatment for obese children: Does parental problem solving solve the problem?* Paper presented at the meeting of the Association for Advancement of Behavior Therapy, Houston.

Crovitz, H. (1979). Memory retraining in brain-damaged patients: The airplane list.*Cortex, 15,* 131–134.

Crovitz, H., Harvey, M., & Horn, R. (1979). Problems in the acquisition of imagery mneumonis: Three brain damaged cases. *Cortex, 15,* 225–234.

Diller, L., & Gordon, W. A. (1981). Interventions for cognitive deficits in brain-injured adults. *Journal of Consulting and Clinical Psychology, 49,* 822–834.

Diller, L., & Weinberg, J. (1977). Hemi-inattention in rehabilitation: The evolution of a rational remediation program. In E. Weinstein & R. Friedland (Eds.), *Advances in neurology* (pp. 63–82). New York: Raven Press.

D'Zurilla, T. J., & Goldfried, M. R. (1971). Problem-solving and behavioral modification. *Journal of Abnormal Psychology, 78*, 107–126.

Folsom, J. C. (1968). Reality orientation for the elderly mental patient. *Journal of Geriatric Psychiatry, 1*, 291–307.

Gardner, H., Zurif, E., Berry, T., & Baker, E. (1976). Visual communication in aphasia. *Neuropsychologia, 14*, 275–292.

Gatz, M., Popkin, S. J., Pino, C. D., & VandenBos, G. R. (1985). Psychological interventions with older adults. In J. E. Birren & K. W. Schaie (Eds.), *Handbook of the psychology of aging* (pp. 775–785). New York: Van Nostrand Reinhold Company.

Gianutsos, R., & Klitzner, C. (1981). *Handbook: Computer programs for cognitive rehabilitation.* Bayport, New York: Life Sciences Associates.

Glasgow, R., Zeiss, R., Barrera, M., & Lewinsohn, P. (1977). Case studies on remediating memory deficits in brain-damaged individuals. *Journal of Clinical Psychology, 33*, 1049–1054.

Glass, A., Gazzaniga, M., & Premack, D. (1973). Artificial language training in global aphasics. *Neuropsychologia, 11*, 95–104.

Golden, C. J., Hammeke, T. A., & Purisch, A. D. (1980). *The Luria-Nebraska neuropsychological battery*. Los Angeles: Western Psychological Services.

Gouvier, W. D. (1987). Assessment and treatment of cognitive deficits in brain-damaged individuals. *Behavior Modification, 11*, 312–328.

Gouvier, W., Cottam, G., Webster, J., Beissel, G., & Wofford, J. (1984). Behavioral interventions with stroke patients for improving wheelchair navigation. *International Journal of Clinical Neuropsychology, 6*, 186–190.

Gouvier, W. D., Webster, J. S., & Blanton, P. D. (1986). Cognitive retraining with brain-damaged patients. In D. Wedding, A. M. Horton & J. Webster (Eds.), *The neuropsychology handbook: Behavioral and clinical perspectives* (pp. 278–324). New York: Springer Publishing Company.

Gouvier, W., Webster, J., & Warner, M. (1986). Treatment of acquired visuoperceptual and hemiattentional disorders. *Annals of Behavioral Medicine, 8*, 15–20.

Harris, K. R., & Graham, S. (1985). Improving learning disabled students' composition skills: Self-control strategy training. *Learning Disabilities Quarterly, 8*, 27–36.

Horton, A. M., & Miller, W. G. (1984). Brain damage and rehabilitation. In C. J. Golden (Ed.), *Current topics in rehabilitation psychology* (pp. 77–105). Orlando: Grune & Stratton.

Kendall, P. C., & Finch, A. J., Jr. (1976). A cognitive-behavioral treatment for impulsivity: A case study. *Journal of Consulting and Clinical Psychology, 44*, 852–857.

Kendall, P. C., & Finch, A. J., Jr. (1978). A cognitive-behavioral treatment for impulsivity: A group comparison design. *Journal of Consulting and Clinical Psychology, 46*, 110–118.

Kendall, P. C., & Fischler, G. L. (1984). Behavioral and adjustment correlates of problem-solving: Validational analyses of interpersonal cognitive problem-solving measures. *Child Development, 55*, 879–892.

Kendall, P. C., & Wilcox, L. E. (1980). A cognitive-behavioral treatment for impulsivity: Concrete versus conceptual training in non-self-controlled problem children. *Journal of Consulting and Clinical Psychology, 48*, 80–91.

Kendall, P. C., & Zupan, B. A. (1981). Individual versus group application of cog-

nitive behavioral strategies for developing self-control in children. *Behavior Therapy, 12*, 344–359.
Koppitz, E. (1971). *Children with learning disabilities—A five year follow-up.* New York: Grune & Stratton.
Krasnor, L. R., & Rubin, K. H. (1983). Preschool social development problem-solving: Attempts and outcomes in naturalistic interaction. *Child Development, 54*, 1545–1558.
Leon, J. A., & Pepe, H. J. (1983). Self-instructional training: Cognitive behavior modification for remediating arithmetic deficits. *Exceptional Children, 50*, 54–60.
Lesser, R., Bryan, K., Anderson, J., & Rose, H. (1986). Involving relatives in aphasia therapy: An application of language enrichment therapy. *International Journal of Rehabilitation Research, 9*, 259–267.
Lewinsohn, P., Danaher, B., & Kikel, S. (1977). Visual imagery as a mneumonic aid for brain-injured persons. *Journal of Consulting and Clinical Psychology, 45*, 717–723.
Lewis, C. A. (1982). Facilitating a better reality: A treatment approach for the confused and disoriented. In A. M. Horton (Ed.), *Mental health interventions for the aging* (pp. 85–111). New York: Praeger.
Luria, A. R. (1961). *The role of speech in the regulation of normal and abnormal behaviors.* New York: Liveright.
Meichenbaum, D. (1971). Examination of model characteristics in reducing avoidance behavior. *Journal of Personality and Social Psychology, 17*, 298–307.
Meichenbaum, D. (1977). *Cognitive behavior modification: An integrative approach.* New York: Plenum Press.
Meichenbaum, D., & Asarnow, J. (1979). Cognitive-behavior modification and metacognitive development: Implications for the classroom. In P. C. Kendall & S. D. Hollon (Eds.), *Cognitive behavioral interventions: Theory, research and procedures* (pp. 11–35). New York: Academic Press.
Meichenbaum, D., & Goodman, J. (1971). Training impulsive children to talk to themselves. *Journal of Abnormal Psychology, 77*, 115–126.
Meyers, A. W., & Cohen, R. (1984). Cognitive behavioral interventions in education. In P. C. Kendall (Ed.), *Advances in cognitive-behavioral research and therapy* (pp. 131–166). New York: Academic Press.
Miller, E. (1984). *Recovery and management of neuropsychological impairments.* New York: Wiley.
Mills, E., & Thompson, M. (1978). Economic costs of stroke in Massachusetts. *New England Journal of Medicine, 299*, 415–418.
Myers, P., & Hammill, D. (1976). *Methods for learning disorders.* New York: Wiley.
National Center for Health Statistics. (1977, December). *Profile of chronic illness in nursing homes U. S.* August 1968-April 1974. Vital and Health Statistics, Series 13, No. 29, Hyattsville, MD. USDHEW, December.
New York University, Institute of Rehabilitation Medicine. (1974). *Studies in cognition and rehabilitation in hemi-plegia.* (Rehabilitation Monograph No. 50). New York: NYUIRM.
Patten, B. (1972). The ancient art of memory. *Archives of Neurology, 26*, 25–31.
Plemons, J., Willis, S., & Baltes, P. B. (1978). Modifiability of fluid intelligence in aging: A short-term longitudinal training approach. *Journal of Gerontology, 33*, 224–231.
Poon, L. W. (1984). Memory training for older adults. In J. P. Abrahams & V. Crooks (Eds.), *Geriatric mental health* (pp. 135–15). Orlando: Grune & Stratton.

Poon, L. W. (1985). Differences in human memory with aging: Nature, causes and clinical implications. In J. E. Birren & K. W. Schaie (Eds.), *Handbook of the psychology of aging* (pp. 427–462). New York: Van Nostrand Reinhold.

Poon, L. W., Fozard, J. L., & Treat, N. J. (1978). From clinical and research findings on memory to intervention programs. *Experimental Aging Research, 4*, 235–253.

Rickel, A. V., & Burgio, J. C. (1982). Assessing social competencies in lower-income preschool children. *American Journal of Community Psychology, 10*, 635–645.

Robin, A. L., Armel, S., & O'Leary, K. D. (1975). The effects of self-instruction on writing deficiencies. *Behavior Therapy, 6*, 178–187.

Robin, A. L., & Schneider, M. (1974). *The turtle-technique: An approach to self-control in the classroom.* Unpublished manuscript. Stony Brook: State University of New York.

Robin, A. L., Schneider, M., & Dolnick, M. (1976). The turtle technique: An extended case study of self-control in the classroom. *Psychology in the Schools, 13*, 449–453.

Robinson, E. (1970). *Effective study.* New York: Harper & Row.

Sarason, I. G., & Ganzer, V. J. (1973). Modeling and group discussion in the rehabilitation of juvenile delinquents. *Journal of Counseling Psychology, 20*, 442–449.

Sarason, I. G., & Sarason, B. R. (1981). Teaching cognitive and social skills to high school students. *Journal of Consulting and Clinical Psychology, 49*, 908–918.

Satz, P. & Fletcher, J. M. (1981). Emergent trends in neuropsychology: An overview. *Journal of Consulting and Clinical Psychology, 49*, 851–865.

Schacter, D. L., & Crovitz, H. F. (1977). Memory function after closed head injury: A review of the quantitative research. *Cortex, 13*, 150–176.

Schacter, D. L., & Glisky, E. L. (1986). Memory remediation: Restoration, alleviation, and acquisition of domain-specific knowledge. In B. P. Uzell & Y. Gross (Eds.), *Clinical neuropsychology of intervention.* Boston: Martinus Nijhoff.

Schleser, R., Cohen, R., Meyers, A. W., & Rodick, J. D. (1984). The effets of cognitive level and training procedures on the generalization of self-instructions. *Cognitive Therapy and Research, 8*, 187–200.

Schleser, R., Meyers, A., & Cohen, R. (1981). Generalization of self-instructions: Effects of general versus specific content, active rehearsal, and cognitive level. *Child Development, 52*, 335–340.

Snyder, J., & White, M. (1979). The use of cognitive self-instruction in the treatment of behaviorally disturbed adolescents. *Behavior Therapy, 10*, 227–235.

Sparks, R., Helm, N., & Albert, M. (1974). Aphasia rehabilitation resulting from Melodic Intonation Therapy. *Cortex, 10*, 303–316.

Spivack, G., Platt, J. J. & Shure, M. B. (1976). *The problem-solving approach to adjustment.* San Francisco: Jossey-Bass.

Szymula, G. J. (1988). *The effects of parent administered self-instructions on home and classroom behavior of non-self-controlled children.* Unpublished doctoral disseertation. Chicago: Illinois Institute of Technology.

Talland, G. A. (1965). *Deranged memory.* New York: Academic Press.

Thackaway, D., Meyers, A., Schlesser, R., & Cohen, R. (1985). Achieving generalization with general versus specific self-instructions: Effects on academically delinquent children. *Cognitive Therapy and Research, 9*, 297–308.

Treat, N. J., Poon, L. W., Fozard, J. L., & Popkin, S. J. (1978). Toward applying cognitive skill training to memory problems. *Experimental Aging Research, 4*, 305–319.

Treiber, F., & Lahey, B. (1983). Toward a behavioral model of academic remediation with learning disabled children. *Journal of Learning Disabilities, 16*, 111–116.

Vygotsky, L. (1962). *Thought and language.* New York: Wiley.
Webster, J., Hammer, D., & Moss, R. (1980, August). Functional analysis of brain disorder: A model for assessment and rehabilitation. Symposium presentation at the 14th annual convention of the Association for the Advancement of Behavior Therapy, New York.
Webster, J., Jones, S., Blanton, P., Gross, R., Beissel, G., & Wofford, J. (1984). Visual scanning training with stroke patients. *Behavior Therapy, 15*, 129–143.
Webster, J., & Scott, R. (1983). The effects of self-instructional training on attentional deficits following head injury. *Clinical Neuropsychology, 5*, 69–74.
Weinfeld, F. D. (1981). National survey of stroke. *Stroke, 12*, (Suppl. #1), i-1-91.
Weissberg, R. P., & Gesten, E. (1982). Considerations for developing effective school-based social problem-solving (SPS) programs. *School Psychology Review, 11*, 56–63.
Willis, S. L. (1985) Toward an educational psychology of the older adult learner: Intellectual and cognitive bases. In J. E. Birren & K. W. Schaie (Eds.), *Handbook of the psychology of aging* (pp. 818–847). New York: Van Nostrand Reinhold Company.
Willis, S. L. (1989). Improvements with cognitive training: Which old dogs learn what tricks? In L. Poon, D. Rubin, & B. Wilson (Eds.), *Everyday cognition in adult and late life* (pp. 545–569). New York: Cambridge University Press.
Willis, S. L., Blieszner, R., & Baltes, P. B. (1981). Intellectual training research in aging: Modification of performance on the fluid ability of figural relations. *Journal of Educational Psychology, 73*, 41–50.
Willis, S. L., & Schaie, K. W. (1988). Gender differences in spatial ability in old age: Longitudinal and intervention findings. *Sex Roles, 18,* 189–203.
Wilson, B. (1982). Success and failure in memory training following cerebral vascular accident. *Cortex, 18, 581–594.*
Wong, B. Y. L. (1985). Issues in cognitive-behavioral interventions in academic skill areas. Journal of Abnormal Child Psychology, 13, 425–442.
Zarit, S. H., Cole, K. D., & Guider, R. L. (1981). Memory training strategies and subjective complaints of memory in the aged. *The Gerontologist, 21*, 158–164.
Zarit, S. H., Gallagher, D., & Kramer, N. (1981). Memory training in the community aged: Effects on depression, memory complaint, and memory performance. *Educational Gerontology, 6*, 11–27.
Zepelin, H., Wolfe, C. S., & Kleinplatz, F. (1981). Evaluation of a year-long reality orientation program. *Journal of Gerontology, 36,* 70–77.

Chapter 8

Applications of Single Subject Design to Cognitive Rehabilitation

Michael D. Franzen and Grant L. Iverson

INTRODUCTION

Although the stereotype of the clinical neuropsychologist is as a professional who works with middle aged adults, clinical neuropsychologists work with individuals from across the entire age spectrum. The traditional role of the clinical neuropsychologist has been to provide consultative services in the form of diagnostic evaluations. However, more modern conceptions of the role include the clinical neuropsychologist as primary caregiver or as a member of an interdisciplinary treatment team for brain-impaired individuals. Part of this change reflects an increased interest in treating brain-impaired individuals. This increased interest has been brought about by three sets of conditions: an explosion in the information base of clinical neurosciences, an increase in the number of people surviving traumatic injuries, and an increase in our society in the number of older people who are at greater risk for brain impairment (Franzen & Sullivan, 1987).

Yet another reason for this expanded role of clinical neuropsychology is the influx of behaviorally oriented professionals into the field. Behavioral interventions have been successfully applied to numerous populations including the mentally retarded and the developmentally delayed. Encouraged by these successes, behavioral neuropsychologists are attempting to favorably impact the level of cognitive skill and functional adaptation of the individual with an acquired brain impairment. This seems to be a natural extension of prior successes. The next decade will undoubtedly see an explosion of services to the mild-moderately traumatically brain injured patient. Even more encouraging is the application of behavioral techniques to patients with severe neurological deficits, as demonstrated by the work of Goldstein and Oakley (1985). These researchers have provided preliminary evidence for successful association learning in patients with extremely poor prognoses.

The services offered by a clinical neuropsychologist may include developing and implementing rehabilitation programs, offering psychotherapeutic services to the impaired individual or relatives of the individual, as well as the more traditional services of assessment and diagnosis. Not all clinical neuropsychologists have become involved in the provision of treatment services. In fact, treatments aimed at the remediation of cognitive deficits secondary to acquired impairment have recently become a focus of behaviorally oriented clinical neuropsychologists. Additionally, cognitive rehabilitation is still in the early stages of its development. Despite the success of some rehabilitation programs such as the one at NYU under Diller and Ben-Yishay (Diller & Gordon, 1981) or the one directed by Prigatano (Prigatano, Fordyce, Zeiner, Roueche, Pepper, & Wood, 1986), there are many issues in the field of cognitive rehabilitation yet to be investigated. As in the nascence of many other clinical interventions, much of the clinical work is conducted by clinical investigators.

The types of problems for which intervention is sought will vary across the life-span. Very young subjects may require treatment in order to remediate cognitive deficits that are inherited or otherwise acquired congenitally. The focus here might be on enrichment of early learning experiences. Somewhat older children may require intervention for academic problems secondary to acquired brain impairments such as might be occasioned by closed head injuries. Adults may require interventions for cognitive deficits caused by either closed head injuries or cerebral vascular accidents. Finally, older adults may require interventions in order to minimize the effects of progressive neurological disorders. There can be no single treatment that is effective with each type of problem. Nor is there likely to be a single type of research method that is optimal in evaluating the effectiveness of the interventions. The best research paradigm may be one, such as single subject design, that is flexible and responsive to the various individual concerns.

Both the researcher and the clinician in the area of cognitive rehabilitation face many challenges in the development of treatment methods for cognitive impairments. Many of these challenges are related to the detection and documentation of change. A second major area of challenge is related to the difficulty of ascribing the change to the effects of the treatment. Still another area of challenge is the wide variety of problems that can be the result of head injuries.

This chapter will discuss the implications of heterogeneity of problems, the difficulty of separating the confound between treatment effects and spontaneous recovery, and the problems of assessment and documentation. It will be argued that applications of certain methodologies, borrowed from single subject methodology and revised to meet the particular situational demands of cognitive rehabilitation, are applicable to these problems. The use of the case study has a long history in neuropsychology, however, most of these applications have involved intensive study of a single case without any attempt to demonstrate change due to an intervention (Clark, 1986; Marshall & Newcombe, 1984). Other authors have suggested the use of operant methods in neuropsychological rehabilitation without considering design and methodology issues (Seron, 1987). We will investigate the relevant issues as related to experimental design. Clinical examples of intervention, assessment, and treatment methods will be presented, and a sample process model will be discussed. Finally, there will be a discussion of how these methods would need to be modified for differences in the age of the patient.

Multidisciplinary Requirements in Treating the Brain-Impaired Individual

It is no exaggeration to say that the individual with an acquired brain impairment faces a monumental set of changes in his/her daily life. Even for the individual with a minor head injury, there may be limitations in occupational position, family role, and recreational activities. For the individual with a moderate or severe acquired brain impairment, these changes also may require treatment from a variety of health care professionals. Medical treatment from orthopedic specialists, neurosurgeons, neurologists, psychiatrists, or physiatrists may be necessary. The brain-impaired individual may also be in need of psychotherapeutic intervention from a neuropsychologist. This intervention may be to aid in the acceptance of, and adjustment to, newly acquired limitations. Additionally, the resultant decrease in the available repertoire of reinforcers may be associated with affective changes. The brain-impaired individual who discovers that he or she is no longer able to independently meet his/her wants or is no longer able to engage in pleasurable activities may react with depressive affective changes.

Rehabilitation of Brain Impairments In addition to psychotherapeutic interventions, the neuropsychologist may be called upon to design a program to directly retrain impaired cognitive skills. Alternately, the neuropsychologist may design an intervention to improve the functional capacity of certain cognitive skills. For example, a memory-impaired individual may benefit from an intervention aimed at teaching the use of mnemonics. Additionally, the implementation of a behavioral program to control maladaptive behaviors may be necessary (Franzen & Lovell, 1987). The behavioral clinical neuropsychologist may also design a cognitive rehabilitation program to be implemented by another professional, such as an occupational therapist. The application of single subject designs is appropriate in each of these alternatives.

In designing a program to retrain cognitive skills, the neuropsychologist must carefully consider the relative merits of various treatment strategies. Although treatment packages with specific protocols present advantages for many different types of psychological problems, such as social skills deficits, it is unlikely that such programs would be viable for the treatment of cognitive deficits secondary to acquired brain impairment. A primary difficulty is that although there is some consistency in the localization of psychological skills, exact localization is somewhat variable across individuals due to interactions between the individual and the environment during the learning history. Therefore, grouping patients by location of injury may result in heterogeneous groups of problems. Grouping patients by type of problem is also unsatisfactory because there are multiple etiological reasons why an individual may show similar cognitive deficits. For example, word finding difficulties may be the result of a stroke or of a progressive dementia. The mechanisms responsible for the two similar clinical presentations may be quite different, and a successful treatment for one may not be successful for the other. Alternately, treatment for an acquired deficit in reading skills secondary to a penetrating wound of the head in a 30-year-old adult would be very different from treatment of the same type of deficit in a 10-year-old child who shows deficit in ability to learn reading.

There may also be differences due to sex or age (and associated developmental stage) of the patient, either in the behavioral and cognitive sequelae of brain impairment or in the recovery from those sequelae (Miller, 1984). The specific learning history and level of premorbid functioning of the individual may also result in different sequelae or recovery associated with similar injuries in different individuals. All of these factors are evidenced for the need to develop idiographic cognitive rehabilitation programs where single subject design is implemented.

The Role of Spontaneous Recovery Regardless of whether the neuropsychologist is performing strictly clinical work or is conducting clinical research, there must be some attempt to demonstrate that any improvement shown by the patient is due to the intervention and not to some other variable (Brooks, Deelman, van Zomeren, van Dongen, van Harskamp, & Aughton, 1984). In brain injuries, one potential confounding variable is the phenemenon known as spontaneous recovery (Miller, 1984). The term "spontaneous recovery" is a misnomer because is implies that recovery from brain impairment is occurring in the absence of any changes in other brain/behavior variables. Although the exact mechanisms behind spontaneous recovery are unknown, there are reasonable theories that explain recovery in the absence of intervention. These theories can be divided into physiological models and experiential models.

Physiological models of recovery of function rely on a homeostatic or self-restorative conceptualization of body functions. Many body parts have restorative or repair functions that are initiated by injury. The most extensive repair and regeneration is performed by skin cells. Other examples include the knitting of broken bones and the response of the immune system to infection. However, the nervous system has a lesser capacity to repair itself than do other bodily systems. Cellular regeneration is extremely rare in the central nervous system of mammals. However, there are mechanisms by which injury to the central nervous system is followed by changes that facilitate at least partial recovery of functional capacity. These changes include post-synaptic hypersensitivity (Marshall, 1984), diachisis (von Monakow, 1914), inhibition and dinhibition (Luria, Nayden, Tsetkova, & Vinarskaya, 1969), and collateral sprouting of axons (Bjorklund, Baumgarten, Lachemayer, & Rosengren, 1975).

Other physiological models are concerned with reorganization of remaining intact brain tissue rather than with the repair of damaged tissue. These include utilization of intact regions homologous to the injured sites (Bach & Rita, 1981) and the development of alternate functional systems (Luria, 1981). This reorganization is thought to occur "spontaneously" as the result of interaction with the environment, and the goal of treatment is to facilitate the reorganization process in a systematic fashion. All of the above models are concerned with the recovery of function as a means; that is, the recovery of the physiological substrate underlying the behavior or the adaptation of a physiological system to compensate for the loss.

Experiential models have also been proposed to explain spontaneous recovery. These models are concerned with the recovery of function as an end, that is, the recovery of behavioral endpoints. Some of these models ascribe positive changes to the influence of nonsystematic, environmental variables. Under these models, it is assumed that increases in functional capacity are innately reinforcing. The individual practices the impaired skill, or attempts different methods of reaching the same behavioral endpoint, and is reinforced by success in achieving the goal. Other experiential models state that improvement may be obtained by the influence of nonsystematic modeling of alternate methods of achieving the behavioral goal. Regardless which model correctly explains the phenomenon, spontaneous recovery can be seen as a confounding variable in attempt to demonstrate improvement due to intervention.

Applicability of Single Subject Designs

Many of the problems related to implementation of group treatment protocols can be ameliorated through the use of single subject designs. One of the advantages of single subject designs is their inherent capacity for tailoring an intervention to the specific problems of an individual patient. Single subject designs involve constant monitoring and recording of treatment related data in order to facilitate the determination of whether a given treatment approach is successful in remediating the problem. Furthermore, this constant monitoring of data allows a researcher to manipulate the independent variables within the experiment if the data are showing limited efficacy. The single subject design discussed here is different from the case study approach that has been frequently used in neuropsychology. The case study approach is derived from the medical neurological tradition (Shallice, 1979). This approach utilizes an intensive study of the clinical presentation of a single individual. Unlike the single case design approach, there is no manipulation of variables in the case study approach.

Gianutsos and Gianutsos (1987) have delineated a number of other advantages for using single subject designs in rehabilitation settings. First, small-n designs allow for an analysis of the course of treatment effect. For example, did the change in the target behavior occur gradually or suddenly following the intervention. Second, the researcher can investigate changes in the consistency of the target behavior, such as whether the subject responded in a consistent manner across days. Third, the researcher is able to determine the magnitude of change in specific individuals. On the other hand, group designs tend to mask individual differences. A treatment effect in a group design may be the result of a few individuals showing large improvements, while the majority of subjects may remain unchanged. A fourth advantage of the single subject design pertains to the ethical issue of withholding treatment from a group of patients. Withholding treatment is not necessary in a single subject design.

In addition to the above advantages, another potential benefit in using single subject designs is the ability to differentiate the effects of spontaneous recovery from the effects of the intervention. If level of skill is measured on several occasions, both during the application of the intervention and during the absense of an intervention, differentially greater improvement, temporally associated with the application of the intervention, can be reasonably ascribed to the intervention. Additionally, if level of skill is measured in multiple skill areas and improvement is greater for the treated skills, one could have greater confidence that the treatment was responsible for the gains.

Types of Single Subject Designs

Simple Designs The simplest design is that of baseline-treatment or A-B design. This design is more applicable to group designs than to single subject designs because it does not control for confounding influences that may be responsible for the behavior change. Group designs control for this possibility by including a comparison group that has not received the treatment.

The next most simple design is that of treatment-withdrawal or A-B-A design. First, the baseline is obtained, then the treatment is initiated, following which the treatment is withdrawn. Control over the relevant variables is demonstrated and casual inferences may be suggested with the treatment phase shows improvement over the baseline phase and if the withdrawal phase shows a decline in improvement. Single subjects designs have been utilized to demonstrate environmental control over behavior that is malleable, largely volitional, and reversible. However, the baseline-treatment and the withdrawal designs may have limited utility in cognitive rehabilitation. For example, the basic research utilizing single subject designs involves implementing changes in the rate with which animals emit simple motor behaviors such as bar presses. Therefore, designs such as withdrawal or reversal are possible.

In the withdrawal design, one assumes that the intervention does not have a permanent effect, which one hopes is not the case in cognitive rehabilitation. If an alternate functional system is taught or if a homologous region takes over the lost behavioral function, removing the treatment intervention should not result in a decline in the target behavior. Another consideration involves the realm of ethics. It would not be ethical to remove a treatment that appears to have been successful. Similarly, replication (A-B-A-B) designs may not be appropriate in cognitive rehabilitation except in the treatment of social or affective behavior. There, the environmental control of behavior is more directly applicable than is the case with cognitive impairment resulting from organic damage.

Multiple Baseline Designs A design that holds promise for application in the rehabilitation of cognitive skill behaviors is the multiple baseline design, described in Baer, Wolf, and Risley (1968). There are two general forms of the multiple baseline design for treating an individual: multiple baselines across behaviors (neuropsychological skill areas) and multiple baselines across settings. A third variation is the multiple baseline across individuals (Barlow & Hersen, 1984). The basic premise is to measure behaviors in different, topographically unrelated areas and to apply treatment interventions to the behaviors individually. If the intervention is responsible for the behavior change, the change will occur after application of the intervention to the target behavior. The untreated behaviors will remain relatively unchanged until the intervention is implemented. The treatment phase of behavior A serves as the baseline phase of behavior B. The interpretation of results from the application of this design is based on the low probability of successive changes in behavior coincidental with the application of the treatment (Hayes, 1985). Another benefit of the multiple baseline design is the ability to control person variables (Harris & Jenson, 1985).

Gianutsos and Gianutsos (1979) present an example of the use of the multiple baseline across subjects design in evaluating a treatment for memory impairment. The authors sequentially introduced the training program to four subjects with brain damage and resultant memory deficits. They found improvement in memory skills coincident with the introduction of the treatment and concluded that the treatment was effective separate from training and practice effects.

Let us consider a simplified example of the multiple baseline across behaviors design as applied to cognitive rehabilitation. This case involves an individual who has deficits in visual memory skills, word finding (naming) skills, and in arithmetic calculations. In the multiple baseline design, baseline data is obtained concurrently on all three skill areas. In the first treatment phase, an intervention is applied to increase the level of performance in the visual memory skills. Data are collected on performance in the other two areas. When the improvement appears to stabilize, treatment of the visual memory skills ceases and is directed at the word finding difficulties. When improvement is demonstrated in that area, treatment is ceased and is instead applied to the arithmetic skills. Although the treatment is aimed at the three skill areas differentially during the three treatment phases, data are collected on each of the skill areas throughout the implementation of the design.

The application of the multiple baseline design to cognitive rehabilitation has both advantages and disadvantages. The advantages are related to the therapist's ability to demonstrate improvement in a certain skill which is temporally related to the application of the intervention while other untreated skills do not show the same amount of improvement. A drawback is that use of the multiple baseline design seems to assume that spontaneous recovery is uniform for different skill areas, an assumption that is unlikely to be true. However, use of the multiple baseline does not require that improvement occur only during the intervention phase. It does require that the greatest improvement occur during the relevant treatment phase, and that there be a discontinuity of slope of improvement consistent with the application of the intervention.

A second major drawback to the application of the multiple baseline design to cognitive rehabilitation is that the order of behaviors to be treated cannot be randomly assigned. Randomization of treatment is not essential to use of the multiple baseline design, but it does increase our confidence in the inference that improvement is due to the treatment. Randomization cannot be accomplished in the rehabilitation of neuropsychological impairments where skills are nested hierarchically. Here, the term "hierarchical" refers to the fact that neuropsychological skills are interrelated and interdependent. This is not the meaning as implied by Kanfer (1985) who used the term to signify behavior classes that are organized in a simple casual sequence, such as is the case with psychodynamic models of pathology. Here, we mean only that observable behavior is the product of combinations of molecular neuropsychological skills with varying levels of generality.

For example, the maximum gains in treatment of memory deficits would occur after attentional problems were treated, and deficits in verbal abstraction skill are more efficiently treated following treatment of deficits in receptive language. It is likely that related behaviors will show improvement before the specific intervention, but this improvement should be minor in comparison to the improvement associated with the implementation of the intervention.

The assumption of multiple baseline designs that behaviors are independent, is an even more important consideration. We have already seen that many neuropsychological skill areas are interrelated and interdependent. This interdependence is more robust in the case of intact individuals. Focal injuries, such as strokes or tumors can cause a breakdown in this interdependence with some skills remaining spared and others being impaired. This breakdown of interdependence also occurs in cases of closed head injury, but to a lesser extent than is the case with focal injuries. In essence, the independence of behaviors is demonstrated by the differential response of skills to consecutively applied treatments. As is the case with the problems raised by the lack of randomization, the temporal relation between application of the treatment and subsequent improvement in the relevant skill area can help demonstrate the efficacy of the treatment.

A drawback of not just the multiple baseline design, but also of all single subject designs, is the difficulty in generalizing significant findings beyond the subject (Hersen & Barlow, 1984). Because the single subject design does not sample randomly from the universe of possible subjects, the obtained results may pertain only to that subject. Generalization would be more likely if there were direct and systematic replications using heterogeneous samples (Sidman, 1960). Yet another drawback derives from the fact that subject-related variables such as age, gender, level of education, and type of injury are not systematically manipulated as part of the experimental design, and the role of these variables in the recovery of the subject cannot be determined.

The Determination of Change

Most psychologists are familiar with the statistical methods used to determine the significance of quantitative change following an intervention. The statistical methods require that data be obtained from a group of subjects. In its simplest form, group means are examined and the difference between the group means are compared to the amount of variance within the groups in order to determine the "significance" of the change. These statistical methods are not directly applicable to single-subject designs. However, there are other methods available.

The simplest and most commonly used method is visual inspection. The data are plotted across time and then inspected for both level and trend. Examination of the data for changes in level is roughly analogous to a comparison of group means. However, in this case, the mean is taken of multiple data points from observations of the same individual. If the mean of the data points during the treatment phase is higher than the mean of data points during the treatment phase is higher than the mean of data points during the preceding baseline period, the treatment might be said to have had an effect. Unfortunately, the use of this method may produce results confounded with spontaneous recovery. If the individual shows improvement across time irrespective of treatment, each subsequent phase will have a higher mean value. Inspection for trend is commonly used to determine whether the data are stable before implementing a change of treatment phases; however, it can also be used to determine whether the slope of the data is discontinuous at the point of the implementation of the intervention. This second use of inspection for trend has applications in cognitive rehabilitation where spontaneous recovery may result in moderately improving trends in the absence of an intervention. Demonstrating a more rapid rate of improvement following the application of the intervention may be used to document the effect of the treatment.

Another means of examining the data for evidence of change involves determining the range of values found in each treatment phase. This method may be appropriate where there is a great deal of variability in the data. In order to use this strategy, a horizontal line in drawn at the highest value of each phase and at the lowest value of each phase. The extent to which the treatment phase has an upper range of values higher than that of the baseline may indicate the extent to which the treatment was effective.

Each of these methods has the undesirable characteristic of being subjective. There may be a large amount of disagreement regarding the presence of a treatment effect among people evaluating the data. Some aspects of this unfortunate consequence can be minimized by having established a priority of rules regarding the presence of an effect. For example, an effect may be defined as a deviation of more than 15 degrees in slope, or as a range at least 20% higher in the treatment phase. However, there are also statistical means of determining whether or not a change has occurred. Barlow & Hersen (1984) discuss other alternatives, such as combining nonadjacent treatment phases in order to reduce the effects of autocorrelation and then computing F-tests or t-tests and time series analysis. Time series analysis may have limited applications because of the requirement of extremely large sets of data points.

There have been several methods suggested for the analysis of changes in data trends. Two such methods are the semi-average method and least squares method (Parsonson & Baer, 1978). Other methods include the median slope method and split-middle method (Wolery & Harris, 1982). If there are at least four baselines in the design, the Rn statistic can be used (Revusky 1967). The Rn statistic is sensitive only to changes in level, but a recent expansion of the statistic has made it sensitive to changes in trend as well (Wolery & Billingsley, 1982).

Marascuilo & Busk (1988) have suggested a set of statistical methods for combining the data obtained from the application of the multiple baseline across subjects design. The proposed methods require that at least three subjects be involved. Furthermore, because the computation of Fisher's exact probabilities is used, the order of subjects should be random.

A PROPOSED PROCESS MODEL FOR COGNITIVE REHABILITATION

The initial assessment should be broad based and comprehensive. Information regarding premorbid level of functioning in a variety of areas is invaluable to the neuropsychologist. The accumulation of medical, academic, vocational, psychiatric, and social history information facilitates the interpretation of neuropsychological test data. This information can be obtained through record reviews and interviews with the patient and significant others. The initial assessment should include screening for sensory impairment (Gouvier, 1987). This will help preclude the possibility of interpreting distorted sensory information functions as cognitive skill deficits.

A broad based initial assessment would optimally involve the use of a battery of tests. The use of a battery rather than of a flexible or problem-oriented approach will allow a determination of both strengths and weaknesses. Neuropsychology has been traditionally more interested in uncovering deficits than in identifying strengths. This interest is due to the diagnostic use to which clinical neuropsychological data were put. However, using neuropsychological data to plan a rehabilitation approach or to improve functional capacity requires that we understand the resources available to the individual. For example, if we know that a patient with deficits in episodic memory secondary to attentional problems has a strength in rote verbal memory skills, we can train the individual to verbally list conversational material or events that need to be remembered. The use of a comprehensive battery during the initial assessment allows identification of the weaknesses of an individual patient and reduces the likelihood that areas of deficit may be missed.

Another important component of the initial assessment is the determination of social resources. For outpatients, this point is immediately recognizable. The neuropsychologist sees the patient for only a short period each week. Other people in the social environment will need to be employed to administer the retraining exercises between therapy sessions. The amount of social support will help determine the extent to which a patient continues to comply with treatment.

The second level of assessment is a more fine grained evaluation of the actual level of skill in discrete areas. The HRNB and the LNNB are well suited to the determination of strengths and weaknesses. However, both the Halstead-Reitan and the Luria-Nebraska batteries would be inappropriate for this purpose because of the nature of a battery. Two characteristics of the batteries lessen their value in this context. First, batteries tend to have complex tasks that require combinations of discrete skills. In fact, the Luria-Nebraska has this characteristic as a central concept in the underlying theory of the battery. An improvement in the score on the C1 (Motor) Scale could be due to a large improvement in a single subarea of motor functioning or to small improvements in multiple subareas. Another characteristic is that batteries tend not to sample skill areas as completely as single tests. The HRNB does sample some skill areas fairly completely; however, the number of skill areas is limited by practicalities.

The score obtained on the smaller tests of discrete skills can serve as a pretest or modified baseline during the treatment phases of rehabilitation. By readministering the short tests at each phase change, differences in level of skill can be estimated with greater precision than is the case with the scores from a battery. Shorter tests have a greater emphasis on molecular skill components than do the batteries. For example, Benton and his colleagues (Benton, Hamsher, Varney, & Spreen, 1983) have developed a set of short tests that individually assess aspects of visual function such as line orientation, visual form discrimination, visual memory, and visual-spatial construction. The existence of appropriate norms is an important consideration in the choice of a short test. Additionally, there should be standardized administration and scoring instructions available. The short tests should also be sensitive to a fairly wide range of skill levels. Finally, because the short tests will be used to document change, the temporal stability of the short tests should be known.

Post Assessment Education

An educational component is critical to successful rehabilitation efforts. Patients and families should be instructed as to the nature of the head injury, the specific brain areas affected, and the implication of the damage for the everyday functioning of the patient. The dissemination of this information should be done in a simple and straight-forward manner employing visual aids and multiple concrete examples (Gouvier, 1987). The psychologist's role as a teacher is necessary to facilitate recognition by the patient of his or her newly acquired deficits. The recognition, acceptance, and support of the family and significant others provides a social milieu for efficacious treatment.

Selection of Target Behaviors

Generally speaking, neuropsychological assessment is a form of analogue assessment. The goal of neuropsychological rehabilitation is to increase behavioral adaptation. Therefore, the clinical neuropsychologist designing a rehabilitation program for cognitive deficits should avoid intervening in a task area that too closely resembles the behavior directly tapped by the test and which has less applicability in the functional adaptation of the patient. The important concept here is generalizability. Treating a behavior that closely resembles the tested task may improve performance on that test, but may have minimal impact on the application of that skill to behavior in the open environment. On the other hand, treating only a single environmental behavior may have little impact on test performance or little generalizability to other environmental behaviors.

As an example, let us consider treating a patient with attention problems following a closed head injury. The attention deficits are documented via the use of standardized tests such as the Paced Auditory Serial Addition Test (PASAT). The behaviors directly tapped by this test (serial addition of auditorily presented digits) are rarely used in the patient's open environment. However, individuals who have difficulty with this test are likely to have problems with other behaviors that require attention, such as concentration on a work-related task or following a conversation. The neuropsychologist may design a program that involves graded practice with changing criterion in tasks that are related to the environmental behaviors, but which require the skill tapped by the test. An example of this principle would be to train the patient to write down the gist of sentences presented auditorily; first without, and then with background noise. The patient could also be reinforced for increasingly longer periods of time spent on task. In this way, attention may be impacted and the change documented by improvement on post-test using the PASAT. By intervening using tasks topographically related to environmental behaviors, it is hoped that generalization will be facilitated. The facilitation of generalization is extremely important in treating the brain-impaired because, even when learning occurs, this learning may be very specific to the conditions under which the learning took place. For example, Goldstein, Ryan, Turner, Kanagy, Barry, and Kelly (1985) found that while there was demonstrable improvement in performance of a memory task in three densely amnestic patients, there was little generalization of the learning strategy itself.

There are many different ways that target behaviors, once chosen, can be measured. Behaviors related to neuropsychological skills are usually conceptualized along an accuracy continuum. For the purposes of recording the effects of the intervention, they can also be conceptualized as either behavioral excesses or behavioral deficits. In this way, the purpose of treatment is to either increase or decrease the frequency of the target behavior, or to increase or decrease the duration of the target event. Another stratgy is to reinforce increases or decreases in the latency of the behavior. These strategies allow quantification of what otherwise might be qualitative data, resulting in the capacity to document incremental changes in skill level.

After selecting the target behavior, a sampling strategy must be chosen. Several sampling strategies are available. One strategy is to use raw frequency data. Raw frequency data is most appropriate when the target behavior is readily quantifiable and reliably measured in terms of occurrence or duration. The rate of occurrence may be another consideration. Very low frequency behaviors may not be appropriate for raw frequency measures, and instead a critical event sampling strategy may be used. Here, the record is made only if the event occurs. For behaviors that have a medium level of frequency of occurrence, interval scoring may be appropriate. Here, the measure of interest is the time between occurrences of the behavior. This strategy is also appropriate when the intervention is intended to impact on frequency of the behavior.

For behaviors that would ordinarily be scored qualitatively, i.e., correct or incorrect, the dependent measure can be the percent of proportion of correct responses. Here again, the procedure allows quantification of what would otherwise be qualitative data. When the data are scored in these terms, the basic design can be a changing criterion design where the patient is reinforced for reaching a certain percentage correct. When that criterion is reached on a regular basis, the criterion can be increased. This procedure, similar to shaping, allows greater frequency of reinforcement than would be possible if the final criterion were adopted at the onset of treatment, thereby keeping motivation high and avoiding unnecessary frustration.

Choice of an Intervention

Both the results of the assessment and the determination of the targt behaviors will have an influence on the choice of the intervention. The assessment will identify problematic areas in need of improvement as well as nonproblematic areas that can be used in obviating the effect of the deficits. For example, if the assessment identifies visual memory as a weakness and verbal memory as a strength, treatment may be directed at training the subject to verbally encode information that ordinarily is presented in a visual modality. The determination of the target behaviors will similarly influence the choice of the intervention. If the target behavior is performance on a complex task of deriving social information from visual input, the intervention may be aimed at improving sequencing skills in pictures that provide a narrative.

Most interventions can be conceptualized as either decreasing behavioral excesses, such as perseverations, or increasing behavioral deficits, such as errors in visual judgment due to insufficiently wide scanning procedures. In the first instance, reinforcement can be made contingent upon a reduction in frequency of the undesired behavior or upon an increase in a behavior incompatible with the behavior in excess. In the second case, reinforcement can be made contingent upon emitting the target behavior.

Although the decision to change treatment phases is made on the basis of stability in the target behavior, the treatment was directly aimed at the target behavior and not at the construct tapped by the short test, use of the short tests can help provide information regarding the generalizability of the treatment effects. (More will be said about generalizability below.) Both the target-relevant and the target-irrelevant short test should be repeated in order to document relatively little change in the target-irrelevant behaviors.

When all of the treatment phases have ended, the larger battery can be readministered in order to document overall change and to assess the degree of generalizability of the results. Because neuropsychological skills are dependent and interrelated, there is likely to be improvement even in nontreated skill areas. Overall improvement may also be due to practice effects and to the gains due to spontaneous recovery. However, because the modified multiple baseline design has been used, the clinician can be relatively sure that at least a portion of the improvement is due to the treatment.

Generalizability

Generalizability is a central goal of almost all clinical activity. The clinician implicitly assumes that the gains made in the therapy session will generalize to the open environment. The clinician also assumes that changes in behavior under certain conditions in the environment will generalize to other, similar conditions. However, it is better to evaluate the extent to which generalization occurs, rather than to assume that generalization has occurred. As mentioned above, the use of short tests can assess the degree to which generalization beyond the target behavior occurs, and the use of the battery assesses the degree of generalization past the short tests. The ultimate goal of treatment is the generalization of gains past the analogue assessment instruments and the subsequent increase in functional adaptation.

Generalization to the environment can be assessed through the use of patient interviews, collateral interviews, or actual observation. Patient interviews are confounded by the degree of patient awareness of change and by the cooperation of the patient in providing accurate information. However, patient interviews are extremely useful in determining whether strategies learned in therapy are being used in the environment. For example, the patient can be asked whether the learned use of verbal encoding of visual information is being applied in other settings in the environment. Collateral interviews can help provide information regarding the utility of the learned strategy in the environment. Actual observation is the sine qua non of obtaining information regarding the generalization of change, but it may not be possible to accomplish with all patients.

It is not enough to merely assess for generalization, the clinician should also attempt to promote it. These attempts are especially important in treating the brain-impaired who may have deficits in their ability to generalize due to acquired limits in abstracting the essential features of a stimulus or a stimulus situation. The promotion of generalization should occur at the beginning of treatment and should continue throughout the treatment process. Stokes and Baer (1977) have proposed a set of procedures to promote generalization. These procedures include: sequential modification in nongeneralized responses, settings, or eliciting stimuli; introduction to natural maintaining contingencies, such as paid reinforcement of accurately performed job activities; training sufficient examplars of the desired behavior; training loosely enough to avoid strict stimulus control; using indiscriminable contingencies, such as intermittent reinforcement schedules; using language to mediate generalization by describing other applications of the learned behaviors; and training to generalize by treating generalization as a response variable. Unfortunately, there are few examples in the literature of empirically evaluated attempts to induce generalization. An example of sequential modification in nongeneralized responses across settings is given by Allen, Bryant, and Bailey (1986). These authors trained parents of mentally retarded subjects to implement a program for modifying adaptive skill behaviors at home. The program had been previously in place at a community treatment center.

COGNITIVE REHABILITATION ACROSS THE LIFE-SPAN

The main focus of this chapter has been methodological, rather than substantive. Other chapters address neuropsychological variables that are relevant to specific age groups. However, a few statements can be made regarding the application of cognitive rehabilitation methods in different age groups.

As described in this chapter, cognitive rehabilitation is an individually designed activity. Some of the person variables related to rehabilitation, such as learning history, time since injury, and premorbid level of skill have already been discussed. There are also variables related to the age of the subject. Every individual is unique, but there are shared aspects, secondary to age. Some theorists have suggested that the younger the age at which the brain impairment is acquired, the more complete the recovery, however, the relationship between age and recovery is more complicated (Miller, 1984). For example, the effects of diffuse brain impairment may be more severe in young children than in older children or adults (Levin, Ewing-Cobbs, & Benton, 1984).

It can be said that age is related to aspects of the treatment goals. For example, in adults with stable employment histories and well-learned behavior patterns, disruptions in new learning are less catastrophic than for children who have not yet acquired a large fund of knowledge. Frequently, a neuropsychologist is asked the question, "Can the person return to his/her job?" It is important to remember that in the case of children, learning is their job. The neuropsychologist treating the brain-impaired child is facilitating cognitive development as well as recovery from the injury (Szekeres, Ylvisaker, & Holland, 1985). The goals of therapy should be appropriate to the developmental age of the child. Furthermore, the goals of cognitive rehabilitation for children differ from those for adults in that it is necessary to minimize the deleterious effects of the injury on the neuropsychological development of the child (Brown & Morgan, 1987). Many school systems are programmatically equipped to handle individual educational plans making schools a potential ally for the neuropsychologist in attempts to implement treatment plans (Ewing-Cobbs, Fletcher, & Levin, 1986). Horton and Puente (1986) have described some of the general considerations in the application of behavioral clinical neuropsychology to children, and the interested reader is directed there.

On the other end of the developmental continuum, older adults are often forgotten in rehabilitation efforts. Whether this lack of program is due to misconceptions about the ability of older people to benefit from training or from a more cynical attitude regarding the deployment of resources, it is a disservice to this segment of our population. The myth of reduced learning potential in older people has been largely dispelled, at least in the technical literature, by the work of Werner Schaie and his associates (Schaie & Willis, 1986). A recent review by Baltes and Lindenberger (1988) indicates that although there are increasing limits on cognitive plasticity as an individual ages, there is the possibility of reversal of age-related declines if training occurs. Older individuals do not learn less well, only differently. Treatment programs are optimally aimed at consolidation of new information with old information and at associative memory rather than rote memory. The single-subject approach is well suited to the cognitive rehabilitation of older people, because this approach requires a minimum of assumptions and is readily adaptable to individual circumstances.

CONCLUSIONS

There are several methodological considerations and challenges in attempting to measure and document the effects of cognitive rehabilitation. Because of the multiplicity of variables influencing both the manifestations of head injuries and recovery from head injury, single subjects designs may be more appropriate than group designs. The multiple baseline design holds much promise in this regard. By treating the different areas of impairment at different times and using the untreated areas as baseline comparisons, relative improvement in the targeted skill area can be demonstrated.

The treatment of the brain-impaired individual needs to address the many different areas of impairment and relative strength. A suggested process model involves a complete initial evaluation using a standardized battery as well as indices of interpersonal functioning, and an assessment of the social network and reinforcers. Once the overall topography of the skills is delineated, a more fine grained assessment of level of skill is conducted using short tests with wide sensitivity and known temporal stability. Skill areas are targeted sequentially, and at each phase the untreated skills are assessed for use as baseline during their respective treatment phases.

Finally, the age and development stage of the individual needs to be taken into account when planning a rehabilitation effort. The rehabilitation of children involves not only the return to premorbid levels of skill but also the facilitation of future development. Older adults should not be excluded from rehabilitation because of inaccurate stereotypes regarding their learning potential. In each case, the treatment should be individualized, an approach that is consistent with single subject methodology.

REFERENCES

Allen, L. D., Bryant, M. C., & Bailey, J. S. (1986). Facilitating generalization: The effectiveness of improved parental report procedures. *Behavior Modification, 10*, 415–434.

Bach y Rita, P. (1981). Brain plasticity as a basis for development of rehabilitation procedures for hemiplegia. *Scandanavian Journal of Rehabilitation Medicine, 13*, 73–83.

Baer, D. M., Wolf, M. M., & Risley, T. R. (1968). Some current dimensions of applied behavior analysis. *Journal of Applied Behavior Analysis, 1*, 91–97.

Baltes, P. B., & Lindenberger, U. (1988). On the range of cognitive plasticity in old age: 15 years of intervention research. *Behavior Therapy, 19*, 283–300.

Barlow, D. H., & Hersen, M. (1984). *Single Case Experimental Designs.* New York: Pergamon.

Bjorklund, A., Baungarten, H. G., Lachemeyer, L., & Rosengren, E. (1975). Recovery of brain noradrenaline after 5, 7-dihydroxytryptamine induced axonal lesions in the rat. *Cell Tissue Research, 161*, 145–155.

Brooks, D. N., Deelman, B. G., van Zomeren, A. H., van Dongen, H., van Harskamp, F., & Aughton, M. E. (1984). Problems in measuring cognitive recovry after acute brain injury. *Journal of Clinical Neuropsychology, 6*, 71–85.

Brown, T. L. & Morgan, S. B. (1987). Cognitive training with brain-injured children: General issues and approaches. In J. M. Williams & C. J. Long (Eds.) (1987). *The Rehabilitation of Cognitive Disabilities* (pp. 217–231). New York: Plenum Press.

Clark, C. M. (1986). Statistical models and their application in clinical neuropsychological research and practice. In S. B. Filskov & T. J. Boll (Eds.), *Handbook of Clinical Neuropsychology, Vol. 2*, (pp. 577–605). New York: John Wiley.

Diller, L., & Gordon, W. A. (1981). Rehabilitation and neuropsychology. In S. B. Filskov & T. J. Boll (Eds.), *Handbook of Clinical Neuropsychology*. New York: John Wiley.

Ewing-Cobbs, L. Fletcher, J. M., & Levin, H. S. (1986). Neurobehavioral sequelae following head injury in children: Educational implications. *The Journal of Head Injury Rehabilitation, 1*, 57–65.

Franzen, M. D., & Lovell, M. R. (1987). Behavioral treatments of aggressive sequelae of brain injury. *Psychiatric Annals, 17*, 389–396.

Franzen, M. D., & Sullivan, C. R. (1987). Cognitive rehabilitation of patients with neuropsychiatric disabilities. In R. E. Hales & S. C. Yudofsky (Eds.), *Textbook of Neuropsychiatry* (pp. 439–449). Washington, DC: American Psychiatric Press.

Gianutsos, R., & Gianutsos, J. (1979). Rehabilitating the verbal recall of brain-injured patients by mnemonic training: An experimental demonstration using single case methodology. *Journal of Clinical Neuropsychology, 1*, 117–135.

Gianutsos, R., & Gianutsos, J. (1987). Single-case experimental approaches to the assessment of interventions in rehabilitation. In B. Caplan (Ed.), *Rehabilitation Psychology Desk Reference*. Aspen Publishers.

Goldstein, G., Ryan, C., Turner, S. M., Kanagy, M., Barry, K., & Kelly, L. (1985). Three methods of memory training for severely amnesic patients. *Behavior Modification, 9*, 357–374.

Goldstein, L. H., & Oakley, D. A. (1985). Expected and actual behavioral capacity after diffuse reduction in cerebral cortex: A review and suggestions for rehabilitative techniques with the mentally handicapped and head-injured. *British Journal of Clinical Psychology, 24*, 13–24.

Gouvier, W. D. (1987). Assessment and treatment of cognitive deficits in brain-damaged individuals. *Behavior Modification, 11*, 312–328.

Harris, F. N., & Jenson, W. R. (1985). AB designs with replication: A reply to Hayes. *Behavioral Assessment, 7*, 133–135.

Hayes, S. C. (1985). Natural baselines across persons: A reply to Harris and Jenson. *Behavioral Assessment, 7*, 129–132.

Hersen, M. & Barlow, D. H. (1984). *Single case experimental designs: Strategies for studying behavior change*. New York: Pergamon.

Horton, A. McN., & Puente, A. E. (1986). Behavioral neuropsychology with children. In J. E. Obrzut & G. W. Hynd (Eds.), *Child neuropsychology, Vol. 2: Clinical practice* (pp. 299–316). Orlando: Academic Press.

Kanfer, F. H. (1985). Target selection for clinical change programs. *Behavioral Assessment, 7*, 7–20.

Levin, H. S., Ewing-Cobbs, L., & Benton, A. L. (1984). Age and recovery from brain damage. In S. W. Scheff (Ed.), *Aging and recovery of function in the central nervous system* (pp. 169–205). New York: Plenum.

Luria, A. R. (1981). *Higher cortical functions in man*. New York: Basic Books.

Luria, A. R., Nayden, V. L., Tsetkova, L. S., & Vinarskaya, E. N. (1969). Restoration of higher cortical function following local brain damage. In P. J. Vinken & G. W. Bruyn (Eds.), *Handbook of clinical neurology, Vol. 3* (pp. 368–433). Amsterdam: North-Holland.

Marascuilo, L. A., & Busk, P. L. (1988). Combining statistics for multiple-baseline AB and replicated ABAB designs across subjects. *Behavioral Assessment, 10*, 1–28.

Marshall, J. F. (1984). Brain function: Neural adaptations and recovery from injury. *Annual Review of Psychology, 35*, 277–308.

Marshall, J. C., & Newcombe, F. (1984). Putative problems and pure progress in neuropsychological single-case studies. *Journal of Clinical Neuropsychology, 6*, 65–70.

Miller, E. (1984). *Recovery and management of neuropsychological impairments.* New York: John Wiley.

Parsonson, B. S., & Baer, D. M. (1978). The analysis and presentation of graphic data. In T. R. Kratochwill (Ed.), *Single subject research: Strategies for evaluating change*(pp. 101–165). New York: Academic Press.

Prigatano, G., Fordyce, D., Zeiner, H., Roueche, T., Pepper, L., & Wood, B. (1986). *Neuropsychological rehabilitation after brain injury.* Baltimore: John Hopkins University Press.

Revusky, S. (1967). Some statistical methods compatible with individual organism methodology. *Journal of the Experimental Analysis of Behavior, 10*, 319–330.

Schaie, K. W., & Willis, S. L. (1986). Can decline in adult intellectual functioning be reversed? *Developmental Psychology,* 22, 223–232.

Seron, X. (1987). Operant procedures and neuropsychological rehabilitation. In M. Meier, A. Benton, & L. Diller (Eds.), *Neuropsychological rehabilitation* (pp. 132–161). New York: The Guilford Press.

Shallice, T. (1979). Case study approach in neuropsychological research. *Journal of Clinical Neuropsychology, 1*, 183–211.

Sidman, M. (1960). *Tactics of scientific research.* New York: Basic Books.

Stokes, T. F., & Baer, D. M. (1977). An implicit technology of generalization. *Journal of Applied Behavior Analysis, 10*, 349–367.

Szekeres, S. F., Ylvisaker, M., & Holland, A. L. (1985). Cognitive rehabilitation therapy: A framework for intervention. In M. Ylvisaker (Ed.), *Head injury rehabilitation: Children and adolescents* (pp. 121–134). San Diego: College-Hill Press.

Von Monakow, C. (1914). *Die lokalisation im grossheim und der abban der funktion durch kortikale herde.* Weisbaden, Germany: J. F. Bergmann.

Wolery, M., & Billingsley, F. F. (1982). An application of Revusky's Rn test to slope and level changes. *Behavioral Assessment, 4*, 93–103.

Wolery, M., & Harris, S. R. (1982). Interpreting results of single-subject research designs. *Physical Therapy,* 62, 445–452.

Index

5 Aug. 93 DR. JOHNSON

J - Johnson
B - Blaine

Colon - Collagenous Colitis
Definitely have disease
Bottom line -
Some coll. bands disappear
The thing about is we don't know much abt -
2 case reports - broughton by non steroidals.
Only treatment is sulfasalazine
3 g. a day could increase that

* Do.
Stay off medicines
Meds could cause enzymes of liver to be off
not do anything at all.
Get off as many meds as possible.
Gluten free
Milk free

Try to make progress
Some each day
1, Collotl
No problem

Cut Bentyl
I

OK Asthma
Azulfisalgin
Theophyline
Inhalers
Albuterol 4 mg.

Put things on hold - job wise
Step back and be a pt.

1 gr. qid - plain Tylenol.

Hematocrit -

4000 Azulfidine

72 hr. stool collection.

- Bleeding from intestines?
= Why =

Azulfidine